LEARNING STATISTICS
A Manual for
Sociology Students

First Edition

By David Swanson
University of California, Riverside

cognella
San Diego, CA

Bassim Hamadeh, Publisher
Michael Simpson, Vice President of Acquisitions
Christopher Foster, Vice President of Marketing
Jessica Knott, Managing Editor
Stephen Milano, Creative Director
Kevin Fahey, Cognella Marketing Program Manager
Marissa Applegate, Acquisitions Editor
Luiz Ferreira, Licensing Associate
Sharon Hermann, Project Editor

15 14 13 12 11 1 2 3 4 5

Printed in the United States of America

ISBN: 978-1-60927-479-5

www.cognella.com 800.200.3908

Acknowledgments

The author is grateful to Paula J. Walashek, not only for her careful reading of drafts and editorial suggestions, but also her willingness to work through the assignments and examples. Whatever faults persist in the book are far fewer than those that would have appeared in the absence of her dedicated work. The author also is grateful to Jeff Tayman and Jerry McKibben for substantive suggestions and to Chuck Gossman, Norm Lindquist, and Ed Stephan for planting ideas about mathematics and statistics many years ago.

As you may suspect from the common family names, the illustrator for this book is one of my sisters. I am very grateful to Kristy A. Swanson for the time she put into helping make inferential statistics come alive with the characters she developed. She had help from her daughter, Kalise A. Wallace, to whom Kristy credits the idea for Statcat.

What you may not suspect is the degree to which this book is the results of three siblings working together, in that Paula J. Walashek is also a sister. She courageously volunteered to revisit statistics when I asked her to review the drafts. This was long after managing to get through her undergraduate course in statistics in pursuit of her Bachelor's degree in Business, and, later facing statistics again, in courses she took to obtain her J.D. degree at the University of Oregon.

I owe a note of thanks to the graduate students who have served as teaching assistants in the statistics courses I have taught at the University of California Riverside. Working with them has been a pleasure and more than a few of their comments and suggestions have found their way into this book.

Finally, I want to thank the editors and staff at Cognella Academic Publishing for their professionalism and dedication to developing materials that are designed to provide quality at low prices for students. I am especially grateful to Marissa (Waggoner) Applegate, Sharon Hermann, Jessica Knott, and Stephen Milano.

Contents

About this Book

Hi, I'm Statman Stu and these are my friends: Stella, Statcat, and Data. We are going to join you on this road trip to learning about statistics. We may even learn some other things as well!

A. Philosophy

This book is designed under the general philosophy and pedagogy described by Swanson and McKibben (1998) for teaching an introductory statistics course to students majoring in fields like sociology, in which "nonexperimental research" is the norm (Dillman, 2000). By this I mean that data are generally collected via samples and methods are used to make inferences about characteristics of interest in the populations from which these samples are respectively selected. As an example of the difference between experimental research and non-experimental research, suppose we want to examine the impact of having a garden on household food expenditures. In an experiment, a set of households in, say, Las Vegas, Nevada, would be randomly assigned to places with gardens and without gardens and then monitored to see how much they spend on food over time, actions that are clearly not feasible. What is feasible is to select a sample of households in Las Vegas and then ask whether or not they have gardens and how much they spend on food. We could have surveyed all households in the city of Las Vegas, but the costs would be very high. Given that there are about 212,000 households, the cost would be about $10.6 million if it required $50 per household to collect and process the information on the questionnaires (a reasonable estimate of the cost, by the way). If we took a random sample of, say, 1,000 households, the cost would be only $50,000. Clearly, trying to survey all households in the city of Las Vegas is about as feasible as it is to "randomly assign" households to places with and without gardens and then watch to see how much they spend on food. Sampling is used to keep costs down since the cost involved with acquiring information from an entire population is generally prohibitive. And where samples are used, so must statistical inference be used, which is what this book is about.

As the preceding discussion suggests, this book is designed for students in a field where non-experimental research is the norm. It also is (1) Embedded in a decision-making context that assumes problems are client-driven; (2) computer-based; and (3) designed with a conceptual umbrella over empirical assignments. The course encompasses the selection, use, and interpretation of statistical tools in conjunction with the effective presentations of results aimed at supporting practical decision making. All of this leads to the fact that this book is based on the idea that you do not really learn statistics by memorizing formulas and taking tests. Instead, it is based on the idea that you learn statistics by *doing* statistics. In line with this perspective, my experience is that learning statistics is much like learning how to drive a car. Thus, this book is designed much like a driving manual. The perspective where one "learns" statistics by memorizing formulas and taking tests is akin to memorizing the fundamentals of driving in order to take a "written" driving examination, but not sufficient for learning how to drive. To learn how to drive, you have to start driving and to learn how to do statistics you have to starting doing statistics.

In line with this perspective, *Learning Statistics: A Manual for Sociology Students* is focused on the essentials you need to be able drive this car. It is designed to get you ready to drive on a side street in traffic, not to drive on a major freeway full of traffic, much less the Indianapolis 500. Among other things, this means that there are statistical tests and procedures I do not cover. Quite frankly, I find most of the introductory statistics textbooks to be filled with a lot of details that detract from the fundamental concepts, especially for students who are in sociology and related fields. As such, this book does not cover most of the statistical tests commonly discussed in introductory statistics textbooks. (If you want to see what you are missing, do an Internet (Google) search on "introductory statistics textbooks," which will yield about 125,000 hits, and check any one of them out.)[1] I want you to leave this book with a road map more or less permanently wired in your head of how inferential statistics works rather than you leaving with a cloud of "statistical tests" buzzing around your head while you are trying to figure out where you are going. The cloud of buzzing statistical tests only serves to distract you from being able to get on the road and doing more statistics.

B. Learning Statistics

So how does one learn statistics? Simply put, one learns it by understanding why it is used, how to use it, and how to describe using it. That basically is what *Learning Statistics* is about. It has the following objectives and learning outcomes:

(1) Understand basic descriptive and inferential tools to answer questions and fulfill informational needs within a decision-making framework; (2) know and select a tool or measure appropriate to the task, to include graphing, table construction, measures of central tendency, and dispersion; (3) understand the conceptual framework underlying classical inferential statistics, to include the role of variation and sample size in conjunction with the Central Limit Theorem and the concept of a Sampling Distribution; (4) understand the use of inferential statistics as a rule-based method of decision making in the face of the uncertainty associated with sample error; (5) select an appropriate inferential tool to solve a problem associated with statistical uncertainty; (6) use statistical estimation and classical statistical tests in conjunction with measures of central tendency and dispersion; and (7) use a ubiquitous software package that can support data analysis and inferential statistics (i.e., Excel).

Learning statistics is really a lot like learning how to drive. You start under controlled conditions (e.g., a deserted parking lot) and learn the basics of starting, steering, and stopping. As you gain experience with these fundamental operations, you can move on to turning, reversing, and parking. After that, you start driving on side streets and learning how to function around other drivers, traffic signals, and the like. At some point you are ready for major highways and freeways. The more you do, the better you become. You learn to "drive ahead," watch for dangerous situations, and try to avoid them to prevent accidents. Some accidents are inevitable. Hopefully, they are minor.

This manual is designed to get you to the point where you can drive on side streets around other drivers. Even getting to this point requires a lot of practice doing statistics. If you don't keep practicing and trying to stretch what you can do, you won't get out of the parking lot.

Malcolm Gladwell wrote a wonderful book titled *Outliers: The Story of Success* that was published in 2008. Chapter 2 deals with the importance of practice to success in every field. In it, Gladwell quotes John Lennon on the huge impact that the many hours of playing time the Beatles had in seedy Hamburg nightclubs on the band's eventual success. By the time the Beatles starting achieving international recognition in 1964, they had played eight hours a night for 270 nights in about 18 months. They were not very good when they first went to Hamburg, but by the time they finished the last of the gigs there, they were very, very good. Gladwell has a similar story about Bill Gates, only he got his practice not in seedy Hamburg nightclubs, but as a high school student taking advantage of having access to "mainframe" computers at the University of Washington late at night when demand was otherwise low.

Oh, and along the way, part of the practice of doing statistics is writing about the results of statistical studies. So, you will also have to write—not just in English but in the jargon of statistics and social science. This means that you will learn something about how applied statisticians and social scientists organize their reports and papers. As part of this process, the following section on liberal education is written like an academic paper, one of the two report-writing styles you can use in this class.

C. Statistical Literacy and a Liberal Education[2]

Since most of you are sociology majors or majors in closely related fields, you are getting what is known as a "liberal education." That is, you are gaining a broad perspective in your education, as opposed to a narrow, "specialist" perspective (as would be the case, in, say, business administration). I hope that you also become "liberally educated." What does this mean? A major goal of liberal education is the development of critical thinking, a set of skills essential for a rational and democratic society (Peter Facione, 1998). It is this same rational and democratic society that forms the key assumptions of the foundation of a liberal education (Anschicks, n.d.). In attempting to develop "critical thinking," many of the courses comprising the liberal education curriculum are either implicitly or explicitly designed to implement a process that has been termed "deep structure learning" by Keith Roberts (2002). Using a framework developed by Patricia King and Karen Kitchener (1994), Roberts views the development of critical thinking as a progression that starts with a stage labeled "pre-reflective thinking," moves to "quasi-reflective thinking," and culminates in the third and final stage, "reflective thinking." King and Kitchener (1994) describe the final stage of the process—reflective thinking—as the ability to reason about unstructured questions that have no absolute answers.

King and Kitchener (1994) organize each of the three major stages in the process according to the manifestation of three issues: (1) Epistemology; (2) an understanding of causality; and (3) evidence and its connection to logical reasoning and conclusions. Outlined in Table 1 are the three major stages and the manifestations of the issues that characterize them. Statistics courses are taught in many fields, and an introductory course in statistics is often a requirement for degrees in physical, biological, and the social sciences.

Table 1. The Three Major Stages of Deep Structure Learning and Their Issues			
STAGE/ISSUE	Epistemology	Causality Understanding	Evidence, Logical Reasoning, and Conclusions
Pre-Reflective	Authority-oriented	Dualistic	Anecdotal, no connections to logical reasoning and conclusions
Quasi-Reflective	Relativism	Context-specific	Idiosyncratic, often unconnected to logical reasoning and conclusions
Reflective	Commitment to an understanding of epistemology	Complex	Probabilistic commitment to a particular interpretation

Statistical literacy can be viewed from the standpoint of six related—but distinctive—conceptualization domains that foster the development of critical thinking: (1) Alternative explanations and solutions to problems; (2) manipulation of symbols; (3) ambiguity and uncertainty; (4) causality as a multivariate process; (5) probabilistic interpretation; and (6) internal and external dialogues needed to communicate analytical results. In terms of the three stages of the deep structure learning process, each of the six domains has a characteristic feature, as shown in Table 2.

TABLE 2. Conceptual Domains and Deep-Structure Learning Stages			
DOMAIN/STAGE	Pre-Reflective	Quasi-Reflective	Reflective
Alternative Explanations	Not sought	Sometimes sought	Actively sought on a routine basis
Manipulation of Symbols	Poorly done	Somewhat well done	Very well done
Ambiguity and Uncertainty	Highly stressful	Somewhat stressful,	Not very stressful
Causality as a Multivariate process	Rarely considered	Sometimes considered	Routinely considered
Probabilistic Interpretation	Rarely used	Sometimes used	Routinely used
Internal and External Dialogues	Rarely used	Sometimes used	Regular and on-going

Milo Schield (1999) argues that statistical literacy is a liberal art—not a mathematical science. He equates critical thinking directly with statistical literacy and differentiates between the two by using the term "critical thinking" when an argument is primarily based on words, and "statistical literacy" when it is primarily based on numbers. In both cases, he points out that while the method of reasoning includes deduction, it is primarily and fundamentally inductive.

In the syllabus for his introductory undergraduate course, Allan Rossman (2002), for example, tells students:

> In contrast to most mathematics courses, we will be using such phrases as "there is strong evidence that ..." and "the data suggest that ..." rather than "the exact answer is ..." and "it is therefore proven that."

To be statistically literate is to be able to reason analytically, an activity that has been identified as the most important intellectual process in liberal education (Atkinson, Swanson, and Reardon, 1998). Seen in this light, the acquisition of statistical literacy represents deep structure learning. What better "learning outcome" is there for students who are participants in a liberal education?

Swanson (2005) and Patten and Swanson (2003) argue that far too few introductory statistics courses have been designed using the principles of deep structure learning (Patten and Swanson, 2003). However, it is worthwhile to point out to those who have not gone near an introductory undergraduate statistics course for some years that the implementation of deep structure principles in these courses has started (Bennett and Briggs, 1998; Patten and Swanson, 2003; Rossman, 2002; Schield, 1999; Swanson and McKibben, 1998; Wolfe, 1993).

Table 2 can be used in the explicit identification and incorporation of these principles. As such, it can serve several purposes. For example, it provides an informal organizational framework for course development and can be used in formally assessing the effectiveness of different pedagogies designed to develop critical thinking. Swanson (2005) and Swanson and McKibben (1999) describe in some detail how this could be accomplished, and describe key benefits such as high levels of student satisfaction and learning retention.[3]

One of the many benefits of developing critical thinking skills is that you will become a much more informed consumer of statistical information. There is a lot of hyperbole and even outright deception in the presentation of statistics for public consumption, examples of which go back a long way into the past (Havil, 2008; Huff, 1954; Mlodinow, 2008; Swanson, 2004; Taleb, 2005, 2007; Ziliak and McCloskey, 2008). Having a basic knowledge of statistics and a well-developed set of critical thinking skills will make you less vulnerable to the hyperbole and deception and more appreciative of good statistical information.

In conclusion, it is worthwhile to note that the consideration of the deep structure learning approach by an introductory statistics instructor is itself a reflective thinking process. That is, as is the case for deep structure learning, the development of an introductory statistics course using this approach is an uncertain, complex process that requires epistemological understanding and probabilistic commitments. What better "learning outcome" is there for faculty who, after all, are lifelong participants in liberal education?

Well, are you ready? Here is what the book (and the course) will cover. Although Chapter 9, "Making Decisions from Samples, Single Variables," is essentially the heart and soul of the book, you have to go through the preceding chapters to prepare yourself for the conceptual picture of inferential statistics it presents. Once you have mastered this conceptual picture, you are ready to move on to the remaining chapters, which serve to fill in the conceptual picture.

Endnotes

1. Here is a list of Web addresses for statistics material that I generally consider quite useful for students.

   1. David Stockburger's open-access, introductory statistics textbook is located at (http://www.psychstat.missouristate.edu/sbk00.htm), last accessed March, 2010.
   2. David Lane's open-access "Hyperstat Online" is located at (http://davidmlane.com/hyperstat/), last accessed March, 2010.
   3. The open-access "Statistics Calculator" is located at (http://www.statpac.com/statistics-calculator/), last accessed March, 2010.
   4. The open-access, statistical formulas available from QualityAdvisor.com are found at (http://www.qualityadvisor.com/sqc/formulas/formulas_menu.php), last accessed March, 2010.
   5. EXCEL STATISTICAL MASTER SERIES (4 MANUALS, $19.95 to download) can be found at (http://Excelmasterseries.com/), last accessed March, 2010.
   6. Research Methods Knowledge Base (http://www.socialresearchmethods.net/kb/index.php).
   7. The Online Statistics Education Interactive Site Developed by David Lane and others can be found at (http://onlinestatbook.com/index.html).

2. This section is adapted from Swanson (2005).
3. This is a point worth considering, because statistics is a required course for students in a broad range of disciplines at both the undergraduate and graduate levels (Gordon, 1995) and, as noted by Sowey (1995), it is in these service courses that the vast majority of statistics students is found. Unfortunately, however, evidence strongly suggests that the students in these courses are not particularly happy to be there (Dillon, 1982; Hogg, 1991; Snee, 1993; Watts, 1991) and, in fact, students often rate them as the worst course or the most useless course they have ever taken

(Romero et al., 1995). These assessments are typically associated with courses not explicitly designed to accommodate the deep structure thinking approach described here (Patten and Swanson, 2003; Swanson and McKibben, 1998). Even more unfortunate, the available evidence is that the students both learn and retain little of the statistics they do encounter in the statistics courses not designed along the deep structure thinking approach (Hogg, 1991; Snee, 1993; Sowey, 1995; Yilmez, 1996).

References

Anschicks, L. (n.d). "Liberal Education." (http://www.cod.edu/people/faculty/anschicks/FacSite/LibEduc.html), last accessed August, 2003.

Atkinson, D., D. Swanson, and M. Reardon (1998). "The State of Liberal Education, Part III: Academic Thinking and Institutional Development." *Liberal Education* 84 (4): 40–47.

Bennett, J., and W. Briggs (1998). *Using and Understanding Mathematics: A Quantitative Reasoning Approach.* Boston: Addison Wesley Higher Education.

Dillman, D. (2000). *Mail and Internet Surveys: The Tailored Design Method, 2nd ed.* New York: John Wiley and Sons.

Dillon, K. (1982). "Statisicophobia." *Teaching of Psychology* 9: 117.

Facione, P. (1998). "Critical Thinking: What It Is and Why It Counts." California Academic Press (http://www.insightassessment.com/pdf_files/what&why/p8.pdf), last accessed August, 2002.

Gladwell, M. (2008). *Outliers: The Story of Success.* New York: Little, Brown, and Company.

Gordon, S. (1995). "A Theoretical Approach to Understanding Learners of Statistics." *Journal of Statistics Education* (online) 3 (3).

Havil, J. (2008). *Impossible? Surprising Solutions to Counterintuitive Conundrums.* Princeton, NJ: Princeton University Press.

Hogg, R. (1991). "Statistical Education: Improvements are Badly Needed." *The American Statistician* 45: 342–43.

Huff, D. (1954). *How to Lie with Statistics.* New York: W.W. Norton and Company.

King, P., and K. Kitchener (1994). *Developing Reflective Thinking: Understanding and Promoting Intellectual Growth and Critical Thinking in Adolescents and Adults.* San Francisco: Jossey-Bass.

Mlodinow, L. (2008). *The Drunkard's Walk: How Randomness Rules our Lives.* New York: Pantheon Books.

Patten, R., and D. Swanson (2003). "Using Cases in the Teaching of Statistics," pp. 31–36 in Hans Emil Klein. (Ed.) *Interactive Innovative Teaching and Training, Including Distance and Continuing Education, Case Method, and Other Techniques.* Boston: World Association for Case Method Research and Application.

Roberts, K. (2002). "Ironies of Effective Teaching: Deep Structure Learning and Constructions of the Classroom." *Teaching Sociology* 30 (January): 1–25.

Romero, R., A. Ferrer, C. Capilla, L. Zunica, S. Balasch, V. Serra, and R. Alcover (1995). "Teaching Statistics to Engineers: An Innovative Pedagogical Experience." *Journal of Statistics Education* (online). 3 (1).

Rossman, A. (2002). "Stat 130—Introduction to Statistical Reasoning—Spring 2002." *Statistics 130 Course Syllabus* (http://statweb.calpoly.edu/rossman/stat130/syllabus.html), last accessed August, 2003.

Schield, M. (1999). "Statistical Literacy: Thinking Critically About Statistics." *Of Significance* 1(1): 15–21.

Snee, R. (1993). "What's Missing in Statistical Education?" *The American Statistician* 47: 149–54.

Sowey, E. (1995). "Teaching Statistics: Making it Memorable." *Journal of Statistics Education* (online) 3 (2).

Swanson, D. (2004.) "Advancing Methodological Knowledge within State and Local Demography: A Case Study." *Population Research and Policy Review* 23 (August): 379–98.

Swanson, D. (2005). "Deep Structure Learning and Statistical Literacy." *Delta Education Journal* 3(1): 41–52.

Swanson, D., and J. McKibben (1998). "On Teaching Statistics to Non-Specialists: A Course Aimed at Increasing both Learning and Retention," pp. 159–65 in L. Pereira-Mendoza et al. (eds.) *Proceedings of the Fifth International Conference on Teaching of Statistics*. Voorburg, The Netherlands: International Statistical Institute.

Taleb, N. (2005). *Fooled by Randomness: The Hidden Role of Chance in Life and in the Markets, 2nd ed. Revised*. New York: Random House Paperbacks.

Taleb, N. (2007). *The Black Swan: The Impact of the Highly Improbable*. New York: Random House.

Watts, D. (1991). "Why Is Introductory Statistics Difficult to Learn? And What Can We Do to Make It Easier?" *The American Statistician* 45: 290–91.

Wolfe, C. (1993). "Quantitative Reasoning Across a Curriculum." *College Teaching* 41: 2–8.

Yilmez, M. (1996). "The Challenge of Teaching Statistics to Non-Specialists." *Journal of Statistics Education* (online) 4 (1).

Ziliak, S., and D. McCloskey (2008). *The Cult of Statistical Significance: How the Standard Error Costs Us Jobs, Justice, and Lives*. Ann Arbor: The University of Michigan Press.

1. What Is Statistics?

Stella, I am excited about our road trip but I wish I knew how to drive so I could help with the driving!

Stu, I have a great idea, why don't you learn how to drive?

A. The Two Meanings of Statistics

The term "statistics" can be traced back to the 17th and 18th centuries, as European countries began collecting demographic and economic data. Since the countries were referred to as "states" (e.g., the state of France), the information they collected became known as "statistics," derived in part from the medieval Latin word "status," which was used to describe a political entity. By the 19th century, the term "statistics" had broadened to include the methods used to assemble, summarize, and analyze information, derived in part from the German word "Statistik," which was used to describe mathematics (Stigler, 1986). In the 20th century, the singular form came to be accepted both in this sense and in another sense. The English statistician R. A. Fisher (1922) used *statistic* to refer to a quantity derived from the observations. It is this sense in which we use the term "statistic" today in describing measures such as the arithmetic mean, median, mode, standard deviation, and so on.

Today, "statistics" has two distinct meanings: descriptive and inferential. Under the first meaning, statistics refers to the use of numbers to describe the world around us. Implied in this meaning is the idea that we have information about all of the elements of interest to us. Suppose we have an election in which there are two candidates running for office, our candidate and candidate "X." The percent of votes cast for our candidate, found when all of the ballots are counted in an election, would fall under the term "descriptive statistics," because it is numeric and it covers all of the counted ballots. In terms of statistical jargon, all of the counted ballots would be called the "population" of interest. Note that we are specifically referring to the votes rather than the people who cast them when we use the term "population" in the statistical sense.

Under the second meaning, "inferential" statistics refers to the use of a process to make decisions about numbers when we do not have access to all of the information. If we did not want to wait until all of the ballots were counted and wanted an idea of the percent of votes received by our candidate, we could ask a portion of voters as they came out of the voting stations which of the two candidates they voted for. As is the case when all of the ballots are counted, the outcome of our survey is still numeric in that we could compute the percent of votes our candidate received among the exiting voters we surveyed, but we do not yet know what percent this candidate will receive when ALL of the ballots are counted. Thus, we have to "infer" from the percent we have among the voters we surveyed (our "sample") what the percent will be when ALL of the ballots are counted. If we selected our voters using certain rules and procedures, we could use inferential statistics to give us an idea of what percent of votes this candidate will receive when ALL of the ballots are counted.

Underlying inferential statistics is its theoretical foundation; the study of this is known as "mathematical statistics." If your recall the analogy I used earlier that this manual is aimed at teaching you how to "drive the car" known as statistics, then you can see that "mathematical statistics" is equivalent to the engineering, design, and manufacturing that goes into "building the car" known as statistics.

You learn to drive by driving.
You learn statistics by doing.

B. Inferential Statistics

This book is an introduction to inferential statistics. In learning about inferential statistics, you also will learn about descriptive statistics. As our example of the percent of votes received by our candidate suggests, the same numbers are used in each case (the percent of votes received by our candidate), but in the first case, we know the percent simply by counting all of the votes and dividing that number into the number received by our candidate. In the second case, we know the percent of votes our candidate received among the people we surveyed (that is, in our sample of voters) , but in order to get an idea of what the percent is among the rest of the votes, we have to use a set a special procedures. These procedures are what make up inferential statistics. They are a powerful tool in that they give us an idea of "what we cannot see," but they have limitations. By the time you have finished "doing statistics" in terms of the introduction to inferential statistics provided by this book, you should have a good idea of what the procedures are, how to apply them, and why they work.

You already know quite a bit about inferential statistics. If you have the entire "population" of interest, you do not need to use inferential statistics, whereas if you are dealing with a sample taken from the population of interest (using appropriate procedures), you need to use inferential statistics to get an idea of what is in the population. In terms of the "population" of counted ballots, we simply count all of the votes for our candidate and divide this number by the total number of votes—end of story. In terms of the "sample," of exiting voters, we need to use the special procedures of inferential statistics to get an idea of what the percent of votes is for our candidate—start of story.

Both the counted ballots from our hypothetical election and the count in our hypothetical "exit sample" of voters are "data" sets. "Data" is the plural form of "datum," which is a single fact or observation. Thus, a set of data is a set of facts or observations. These facts or observations can be numbers, words, or other symbols. As is the case with life in general, one of the uncomfortable but common aspects of data sets is the presence of problems. In statistical and research jargon, these problems are called "errors" (see Dillman, 2000).

C. Errors

There are four types of "error" that occur both in population and sample data sets:

(1) Measurement Error, which is the result of poor wording in a survey or in a form designed to capture data or presenting the questions or data collection entries in such a way that inaccurate or uninterpretable answers are obtained. Does the term "hanging chad" ring a bell in terms of ballots? This would be an example of measurement error in the "population" of votes. In the case of our sample of exiting voters, an example of measurement error would come from a poorly worded question in the survey. For example, if the survey asked if the voter liked our candidate it may be that some voters

in fact liked him or her, but did not vote for our candidate. The question should have been "Did you vote for (our candidate)?"

(2) Non-response Error, which is the result of people who respond to a survey or a data collection form having different responses from people who do not respond. For example, a person may have missed marking the ballot for some of the candidates in the election and an exiting voter may simply not want to answer which candidate he or she voted for.

(3) Coverage Error, which is the result of not allowing all members of the population to have an equal or known nonzero chance of being sampled for participation in the survey or data collection effort. In terms of coverage error in our population of ballots, it may be some voters wanted to vote but were not able to get to the voting stations (no car, for example), and hence were left out of the counted votes; in terms of our sample of exiting voters, maybe our surveyor was stationed near the front door waiting for people to come out and did not know that there was a side door by which voters could exit. Like the voters stuck at home, those using the side door were not "covered."

(4) Coding or Transcription Error, which is the result of a person or electronic procedure coding original answers incorrectly or transcribing original answers incorrectly to another medium. In the case of our population of ballots, it may be that entries were coded for candidate X instead of our candidate because of malfunctioning software. In the case of our sample of exiting voters, the interviewer may have recorded incorrectly the name of the candidate that the exiting voter selected.

All of the preceding types of "error" can occur in data sets, whether a population data set or a sample data set. However, there is a very special type of "error" that statisticians have identified that is unique to samples. Not surprisingly, it is known as …

(5) Sampling Error, which is the result of surveying or obtaining answers from some—but not all—members of the population of interest. This means that, by the luck of the draw, we may have gotten more voters in our exit sample who voted for our candidate than was the case in the "population" of ballots. This may happen even though there was no measurement error, non-response error, coverage error, or coding/transcription errors in our sample. It was simply the "luck" of the draw in terms of the sample we got. Simply put, sampling error refers to the fact that you are likely to get a sample that is different from the population from which it was drawn. Thus, our sample of exiting voters is likely to provide a different percent of votes for our candidate than is found in the entire population of ballots. It is this type of error that inferential statistics deals with, and it does so in some very clever and very useful ways.

The first four types of error—measurement, non-response, coverage, and coding/transcription—are collectively referred to as "non-sampling" error. They are difficult to deal with and not easy to measure (Beimer and Lyberg, 2003; Dillman, 2000; Lessler and Kalsbeek, 1992).

There is another way in which the term "error" is used in statistics. It has to do with two important "summary" measures, the mean, which we will introduce in Chapter 4, and the idea of "dispersion," which we will introduce in Chapter 5. We will discuss the nature of this type of "error" in regard to the mean and the standard deviation, a measure of "dispersion," in Chapter 5.

D. The Trade-Off Between Sampling Error and Cost

So you might ask if we have five types of error in terms of assembling data, one of which only occurs in samples, why not eliminate samples, so that we could focus on the other four types of error? Good question, but the driving force behind using samples is the cost of collecting data and keeping costs down is important when it comes to assembling data. A nice way to look at the trade-off between lower costs and having to deal with sampling error is through the trade-off between sampling error and cost.

If one collects information from the entire population, it is highly accurate in the sense that there is no sampling error, but it comes at a high cost (and also takes a long time to put the information together). By taking a sample (using the correct procedures) we can greatly reduce the costs (and time), but by so doing we are allowing sampling error to enter into our data. However, this is where inferential statistics really comes into its own. Through it we can estimate the sampling error. Let me repeat that: We can estimate the sampling error. Thus, we get an idea of the "precision" of our estimate of the percent of votes among ALL the ballots (the population) if we follow the rules of statistical inference in designing and implementing our sample and making inferences from it to the population. Moreover, we can do this in far less time and for far less money than would have been the case if we had surveyed ALL of the exiting voters in order to predict the election outcome.

E. How Inferential Statistics Works

So how does statistical inference work? There are basically two ways that are used: (1) Estimates (confidence intervals); and (2) hypothesis tests. As you will see later in the book, these two methods represent two sides of same (inferential) coin, but they have distinct uses. The first is simply to gain information about a single fact of interest— based on the information in our sample, we are trying to estimate the percent of votes for our candidate. The second is used to make comparisons—based on the information in our sample, how likely is it that the percent of votes for our candidate will be higher than those for candidate X when all of the ballots are counted?

Both estimation and hypothesis testing are based on the same foundation, which is why I describe them as being two sides of the same (inferential) coin. This foundation is really simple, but like many things that are "simple," it also is elegant. Inference is grounded in uncertainty. That is, we may have the percent of votes for our candidate in our sample, but because it is not the entire set of voters, we are "uncertain" what the actual percent is in the population. That is, we are trying to make decisions in the face of sample error. This uncertainty is elegantly expressed as being a function of the size of the sample and how much "variation" exists in the population (which should be revealed in our sample): Uncertainty = f (sample size and variation). If our sample was the same size as the total population, there is no uncertainty and we know, for example, the percent of votes for our candidate. This gets back to the point that if we have the entire population of interest, we do not need statistical inference.

The other element that contributes to uncertainty (sample error) is variation. What is variation? In terms of an election between two candidates, there would be no variation if one of them received all of the votes. If this was the case, then we could predict the election outcome from one exiting voter. As would be the case if our sample of exiting voters was the same size as all of the voters, there would be no uncertainty in our sample. However, if the election was very close—say 50.2% of the votes were for our candidate and 49.8% were for candidate X—you can see that the sample we draw would have a difficult time telling which candidate is the winner unless the sample was of ALL of the voters.

What this should tell you so far is that uncertainty increases as the sample size gets smaller and as variation increases; it decreases as sample size gets larger and as variation decreases. In the case where either the sample is the same size of the population or there is no variation in the population, then there is no uncertainty in inferring from the sample to the population.

So, in short, the answer to the question, "What is statistics?" is that cost and time constraints encourage the use of scientific sampling, through which a set of rules and procedures we call statistical inference, can be used to support decision making under conditions of statistical uncertainty.

ASSIGNMENT FOR CHAPTER 1

1. Answer the following questions:
    a. What are the origins of the word "statistics?"
    b. What distinguishes inferential statistics from descriptive statistics?
    c. What are the four types of error that potentially affect every set of data, whether it is a sample or a population?
    d. What type of error affects only a data set represented by a sample?
    e. What is statistical uncertainty?
    f. What happens to statistical uncertainty as sample size gets larger and larger?
    g. Why sample?

References

Biemer, P., and L. Lyberg (2003). *Introduction to Survey Quality*. New York: Wiley.

Dillman, D. (2000). *Mail and Internet Surveys: The Tailored Design Method*. New York: John Wiley & Sons.

Fisher, R. A. (1922). "On the Mathematical Foundations of Theoretical Statistics." *Philosophical Transactions of the Royal Society of London, Series A* 222: 309–68.

Lessler, J., and W. Kalsbeek (1992). *Nonsampling Errors in Surveys*. New York: John Wiley & Sons.

Stigler, S. (1986). *The History of Statistics: The Measurement of Uncertainty Before 1900*. Cambridge: Belknap Press of Harvard University Press.

2. Working with Data in Microsoft Excel

I know, I'll learn how to drive!!!

Good idea, Stu!

A. Opening an Excel Workbook

Excel is a spreadsheet developed by the Microsoft Corporation.[1] You need to use Excel in the class for which this book is designed. View this as part of your overall education. Excel and similar products are widely used, and the simple fact you know some of the basics about using Excel may help you land a job. This chapter will get you started, but how proficient you become depends on how much time and effort you put into using Excel. What you will learn here is aimed at becoming functional for the statistics course for which this book is designed. There is much, much more to Excel than this chapter can show you. To help you in this task, some online sites are listed in the appendix found at the end of this chapter.

A Microsoft Excel workbook (also known as a "spreadsheet") is a file that contains one or more worksheets. (A worksheet is like a page in a workbook. It is the primary document that you use in Excel to store and work with data.) A worksheet consists of cells that are organized into columns and rows, which you can use to organize various kinds of related information. If you have not used Excel before, you should now move to a computer and open ("launch") Excel, so you can follow along. Note that my examples are from Excel 2003. If you are using a more recent version of Excel, there will be some differences, but they mainly will be in the "toolbar" area and how you access "tools" from it.

When you launch Excel, you should be looking at a screen that is like the one shown in Exhibit 2.1.

Exhibit 2.1. A Newly Opened Excel Workbook

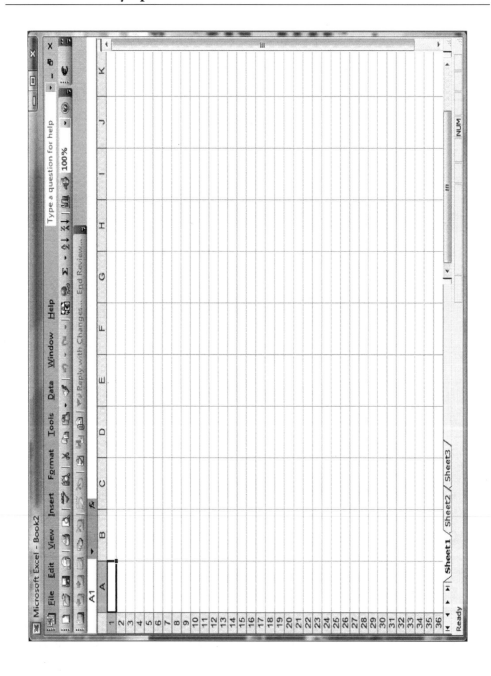

B. Entering Numbers into a Worksheet

Once you have a workbook open, you can enter and save data. Exhibit 2.2 shows the numbers 4 and 5 entered in two "cells" in Excel. The number 4 is in cell A1 and the number 5 is in cell A2.

Exhibit 2.2. Entering the Numbers 4 and 5 in Cells A1 and A2

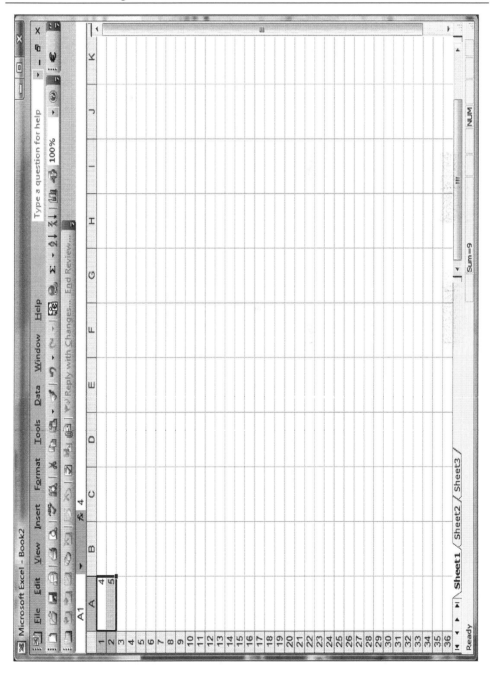

Notice that the sheet shown in Exhibit 2.1 has columns labeled A through K and rows numbered 1 through 36. Cell A1, where we entered the number 4, is at the intersection of column A and row 1. Cell A2, where we entered the number 5, is at the intersection of column A and row 2. There are many more columns and rows in the spreadsheet, but we cannot see them all on the screen. If you move the cursor (scroll) to the right from cell A2 on row 2, you will see new columns come into view as the cursor moves beyond the original area of the worksheet you could see on the screen.

C. Displaying Numbers in a Worksheet

Even though we have entered the numbers 4 and 5 into cells A1 and A2, Excel does not necessarily know that they are numbers, and if they are, how they should be displayed.

You can assist Excel by telling what you have entered and how you want it displayed. For this, you need to tell Excel which cells have the numbers you want displayed in a certain way. This involves two steps. In the first, you need to tell Excel that the numbers are in cells A1 and A2. You do this by putting your cursor on cell A1, and then you point the cursor at the "format"

tab on the toolbar, click to display the dropdown menu, and while holding down the left button on your mouse (or the equivalent on a touch pad), roll the cursor down so that both cells A1 and A2 are highlighted. Now, for the second step, you will tell Excel that

Exhibit 2.3. Formatting Numbers Within Cells

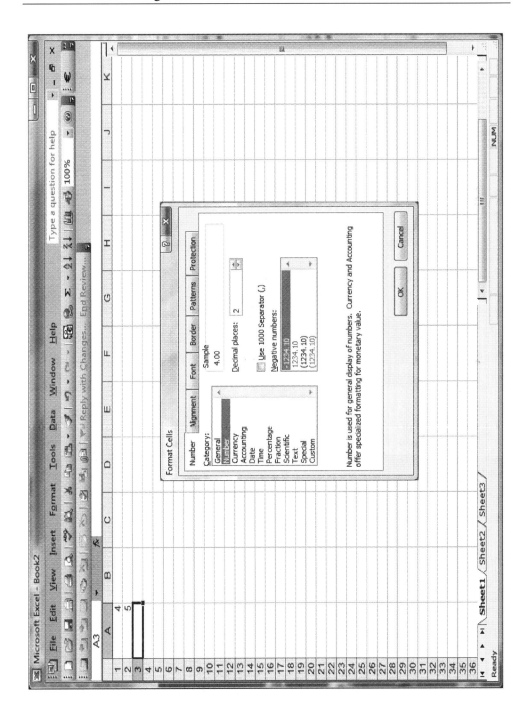

the entries in cells A1 and A2 are, in fact, numbers, and how you want them displayed. To do this, move your cursor to the format tab on the toolbar and click on it (notice that cells A1 and A2 are still highlighted!). When you see the menu drop down from the "Format" tab, click on "Cells." This tells Excel that you are going to start formatting the cells you have highlighted. Once you have clicked on "Cells," you should see a pop-up screen like that shown in Exhibit 2.3. When it appears, click on the "Number" tab.

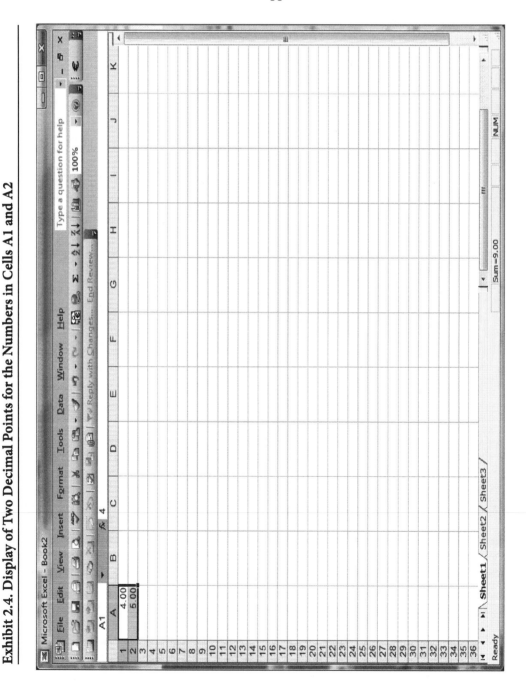

Exhibit 2.4. Display of Two Decimal Points for the Numbers in Cells A1 and A2

Scroll down to "Number" in the pop-up screen and click on it, which will bring up the screen as shown in Exhibit 2.3. This allows you to choose how many "decimal places" you want displayed with numbers. By default, you are already given "2" as the choice. Leave "2" as your choice, move your cursor to the "OK" tab in the pop-up screen, and click on "OK." You should immediately see both of the numbers displayed with two decimal points, as shown in Exhibit 2.4.

D. Entering Formulas into a Worksheet

Now, we turn our attention to getting Excel to doing some work for us. Take a look at Exhibit 2.5, which shows our two numbers, 4.00 and 5.00 in cells A1 and A2 along with a formula in cell A4. Move your cursor to cell A4, and in the first space enter the "=" sign followed by "A1+A2." That is, cell A1 should have =a1+a2 in it as is shown in Exhibit 2.5. Once you have this entered this formula in cell A4, hit the "Enter" key.

You have just informed Excel that you want it to add together the two numbers you have in cells A1 and A2, respectively, and place the sum in cell A4. So, you should have the number "9" displayed in cell A4, as shown in Exhibit 2.6. Notice that it is displayed to two decimal points (9.00).

Exhibit 2.7 gives another example of a formula, but this is one of Excel's many "built-in" functions. In fact, it is one of the statistical functions you will be using. It computes the arithmetic mean (the average) of a set of numbers. Not surprisingly, it is called "AVERAGE." Using this and the other built-in Excel functions is very similar to what you just did when you added the contents of cells A1 and A2 and put the sum in cell A4. That is, you need to put your cursor in the cell where you want the average to be displayed once Excel has calculated it, tell Excel what you want it to do (compute an average), and finally, tell Excel where the numbers are located for which you want an average. As is shown in Exhibit 2.7, put your cursor in cell A3, and enter "=average(A1:A2)."

If you did this correctly, your screen should look like the one shown in Exhibit 2.8, where you can see that cell A3 displays "4.50," which is the average of the contents of cell A1 (4.00) and cell A2 (5.00).

Since you have now seen one of Excel's statistical functions, this is as good a place to list them all for you as any. Here is a list of the commands and what they do. Those shown in BOLDFACE are the ones you need to know. Remember that each of the functions resides in a cell, begins with "=", and has to show where the data are that you want the function performed on. The example you just saw of the arithmetic mean worked because "=average(A1:A2)" was in cell A3, and the two numbers were in cells A1 and A2. If we wanted to put the standard deviation of these same two numbers into cell A4, it would look like "=STDEV(A1:A2)."

Exhibit 2.5. Entering a Formula in Cell A4 That Adds the Contents of Cell A1 and Cell A2

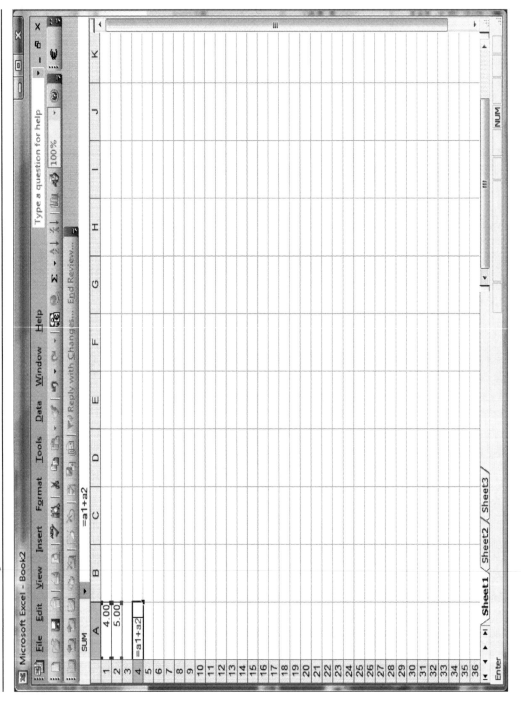

Exhibit 2.6. The Result of the Formula Entered in Cell A4

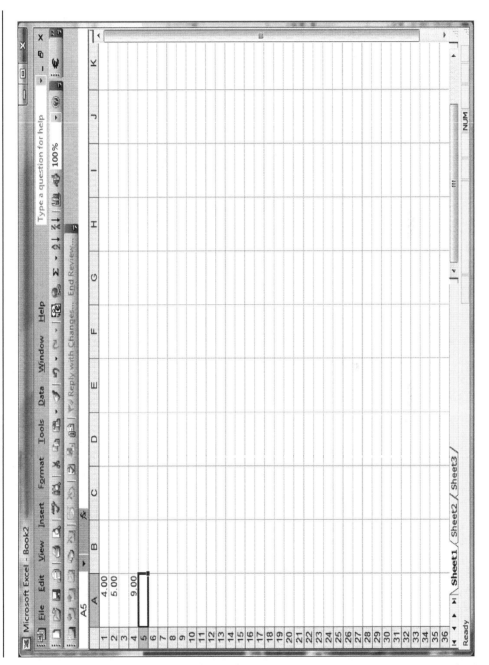

Exhibit 2.7. Computing an Arithmetic Average of the Numbers in Cells A1 and A2 and Placing This Average in Cell A3

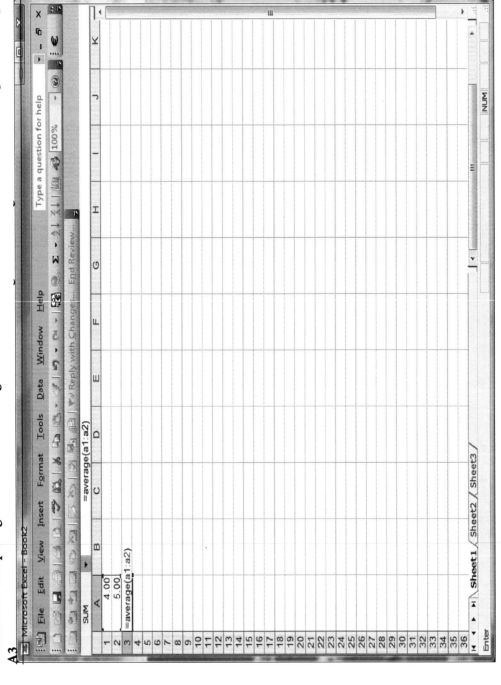

Exhibit 2.8. Displaying the Average (Arithmetic Man) of the Contents of Cells A1 (4.00) and A2 in Cell A3 (4.50)

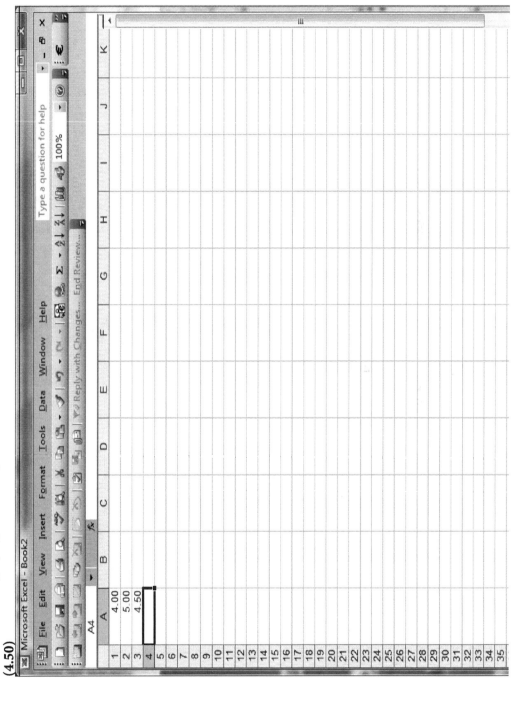

AVEDEV

Returns the average of the absolute deviations of data points from their mean.

AVERAGE

Returns the average of its arguments.

AVERAGEA

Returns the average of its arguments, including numbers, text, and logical values.

BETADIST

Returns the beta cumulative distribution function.

BETAINV

Returns the inverse of the cumulative distribution function for a specified beta distribution.

BINOMDIST

Returns the individual term binomial distribution probability.

CHIINV

Returns the inverse of the one-tailed probability of the chi-squared distribution.

CHITEST

Returns the test for independence.

CONFIDENCE

Returns the confidence interval for a population mean.

CORREL

Returns the correlation coefficient between two data sets.

COUNT

Counts how many numbers are in the list of arguments.

COUNTA

Counts how many values are in the list of arguments.

COUNTBLANK

Counts the number of blank cells within a range.

COUNTIF

Counts the number of non-blank cells within a range that meet the given criteria.

COVAR
Returns covariance, the average of the products of paired deviations.

CRITBINOM
Returns the smallest value for which the cumulative binomial distribution is less than or equal to a criterion value.

DEVSQ
Returns the sum of squares of deviations.

EXPONDIST
Returns the exponential distribution.

FDIST
Returns the F probability distribution.

FINV
Returns the inverse of the F probability distribution.

FISHER
Returns the Fisher transformation.

FISHERINV
Returns the inverse of the Fisher transformation.

FORECAST
Returns a value along a linear trend.

FREQUENCY
Returns a frequency distribution as a vertical array.

FTEST
Returns the result of an F-test.

GAMMADIST
Returns the gamma distribution.

GAMMAINV
Returns the inverse of the gamma cumulative distribution.

GAMMALN
Returns the natural logarithm of the gamma function, $\Gamma(x)$.

GEOMEAN
Returns the geometric mean.

GROWTH
Returns values along an exponential trend.

HARMEAN
Returns the harmonic mean.

HYPGEOMDIST
Returns the hypergeometric distribution.

INTERCEPT
Returns the intercept of the linear regression line.

KURT
Returns the kurtosis of a data set.

LARGE
Returns the kth largest value in a data set.

LINEST
Returns the parameters of a linear trend.

LOGEST
Returns the parameters of an exponential trend.

LOGINV
Returns the inverse of the lognormal distribution.

LOGNORMDIST
Returns the cumulative lognormal distribution.

MAX
Returns the maximum value in a list of arguments.

MAXA
Returns the maximum value in a list of arguments, including numbers, text, and logical values.

MEDIAN
Returns the median of the given numbers.

MIN
Returns the minimum value in a list of arguments.

MINA
Returns the smallest value in a list of arguments, including numbers, text, and logical values.

MODE
Returns the most common value in a data set.

NEGBINOMDIST
Returns the negative binomial distribution.

NORMDIST
Returns the normal cumulative distribution.

NORMINV
Returns the inverse of the normal cumulative distribution.

NORMSDIST
Returns the standard normal cumulative distribution.

NORMSINV
Returns the inverse of the standard normal cumulative distribution.

PEARSON
Returns the Pearson product moment correlation coefficient.

PERCENTILE
Returns the kth percentile of values in a range.

PERCENTRANK
Returns the percentage rank of a value in a data set.

PERMUT
Returns the number of permutations for a given number of objects.

POISSON
Returns the Poisson distribution.

PROB
Returns the probability that values in a range are between two limits.

QUARTILE
Returns the quartile of a data set.

RANK
Returns the rank of a number in a list of numbers.

RSQ
Returns the square of the Pearson product moment correlation coefficient.

SKEW
Returns the skewness of a distribution.

SLOPE
Returns the slope of the linear regression line.

SMALL
Returns the kth smallest value in a data set.

SQRT
Returns the square root of a number.

STANDARDIZE
Returns a normalized value.

STDEV
Estimates standard deviation based on a sample.

STDEVA
Estimates standard deviation based on a sample, including numbers, text, and logical values.

STDEVP
Calculates standard deviation based on the entire population.

STDEVPA
Calculates standard deviation based on the entire population, including numbers, text, and logical values.

STEYX
Returns the standard error of the predicted y-value for each x in the regression.

TDIST
Returns the student's t-distribution.

TINV
Returns the inverse of the student's t-distribution.

TREND
Returns values along a linear trend.

TRIMMEAN
Returns the mean of the interior of a data set.

TTEST
Returns the probability associated with a student's t-test.

VAR
Estimates variance based on a sample.

VARA
Estimates variance based on a sample, including numbers, text, and logical values.

VARP
Calculates variance based on the entire population.

VARPA
Calculates variance based on the entire population, including numbers, text, and logical values.

WEIBULL
Returns the Weibull distribution.

ZTEST
Returns the one-tailed probability-value of a z-test.

E. Naming and Referencing Cells

You actually have experience in naming and referencing cells already. However, this will add a few helpful details to what you know. As shown in Exhibit 2.9, put your cursor in cell E11, and type in "=A2."

Now simply hit "Enter." You should see the number "5.00" displayed in cell E11 as shown in Exhibit 2.10. Basically, you copied the contents of cell A2 (5.00) into cell E11.

Exhibit 2.9. Naming and Referencing Cells, Part 1

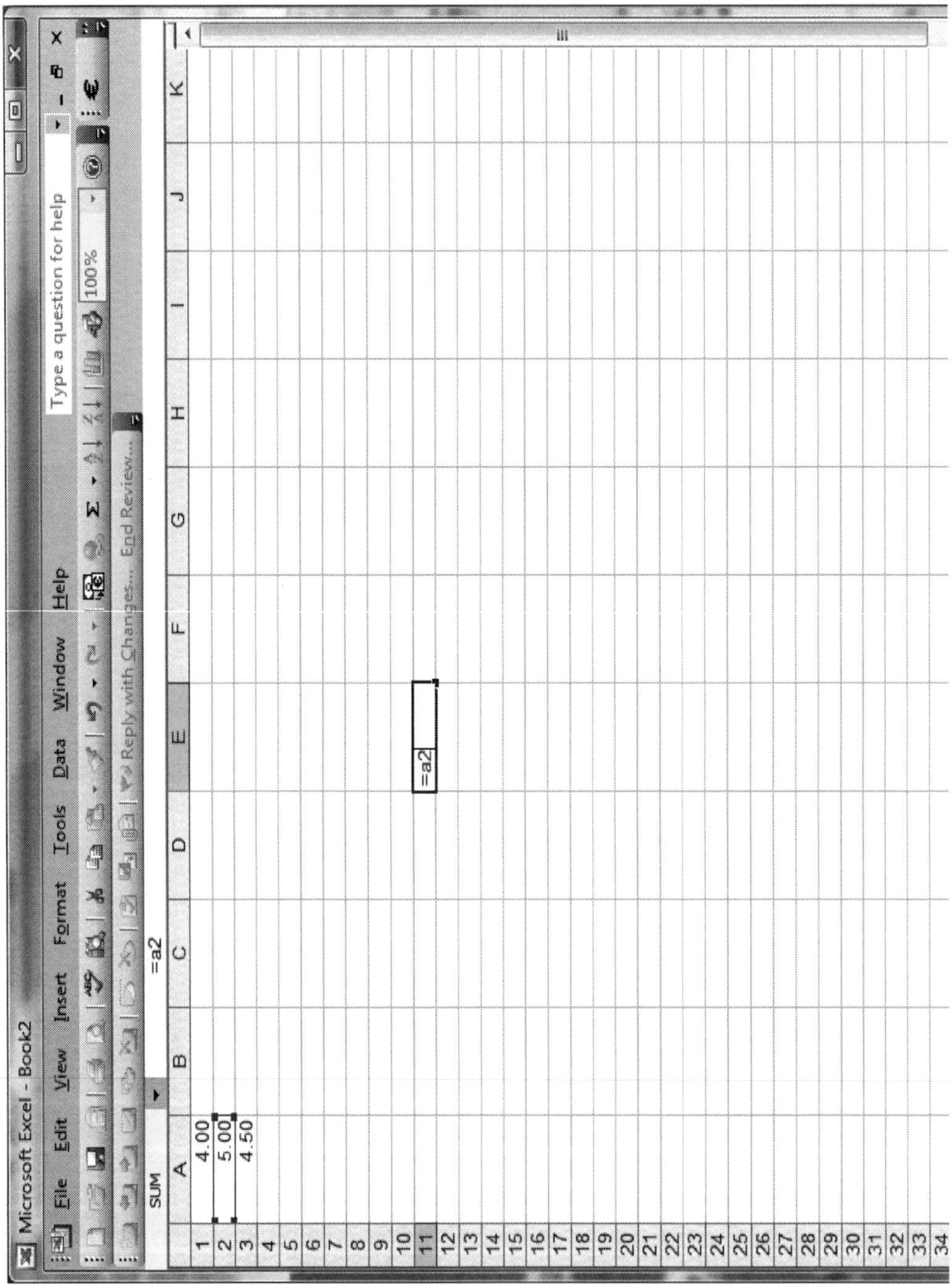

Exhibit 2.10. Naming and Referencing Cells, Part 2

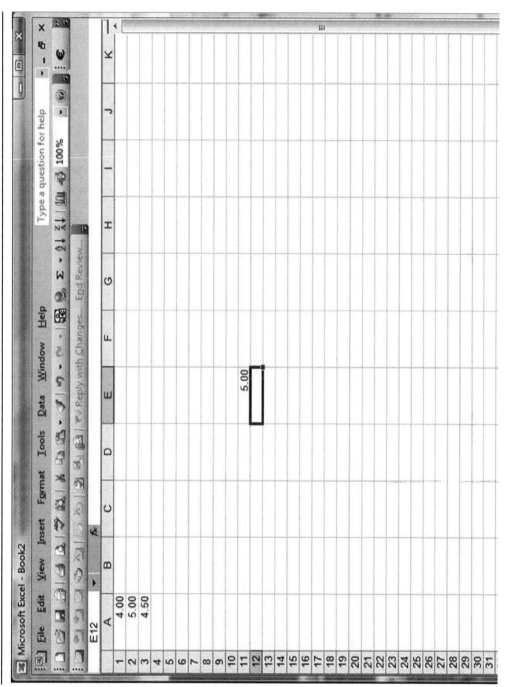

Exhibit 2.11. Entering the Phrase "Title Page" in Cell A1

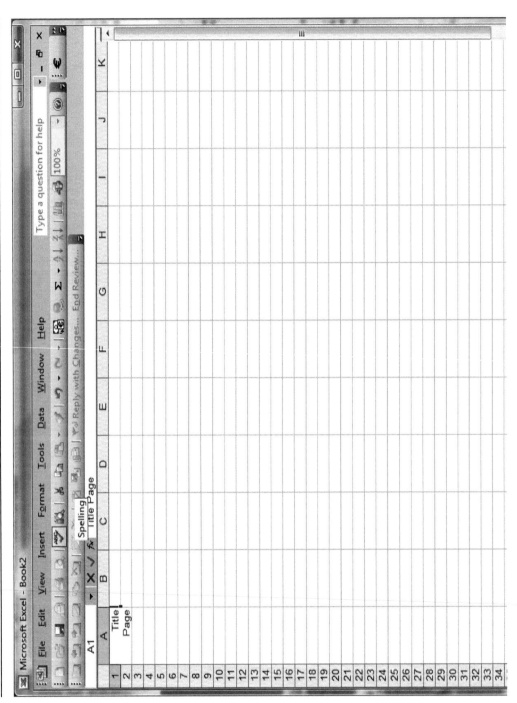

Exhibit 2.12. Formatting Cell Widths and Heights

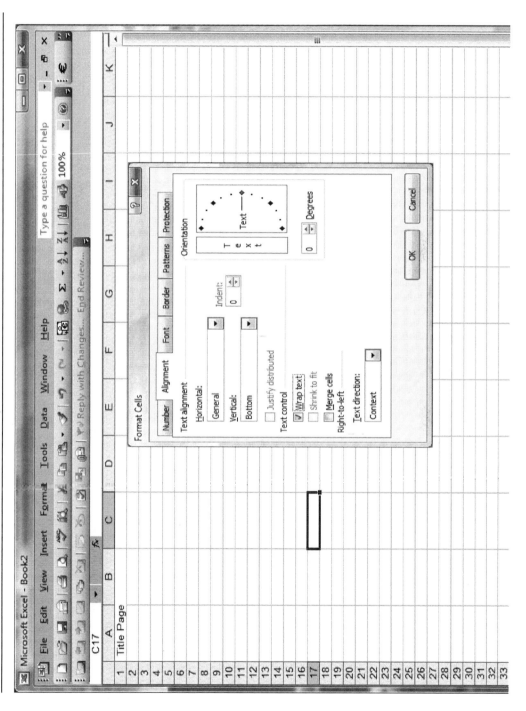

Exhibit 2.13. Adjustment to the Width of Column A So That the Phrase "Title Page" Can Be Seen in Cell A1

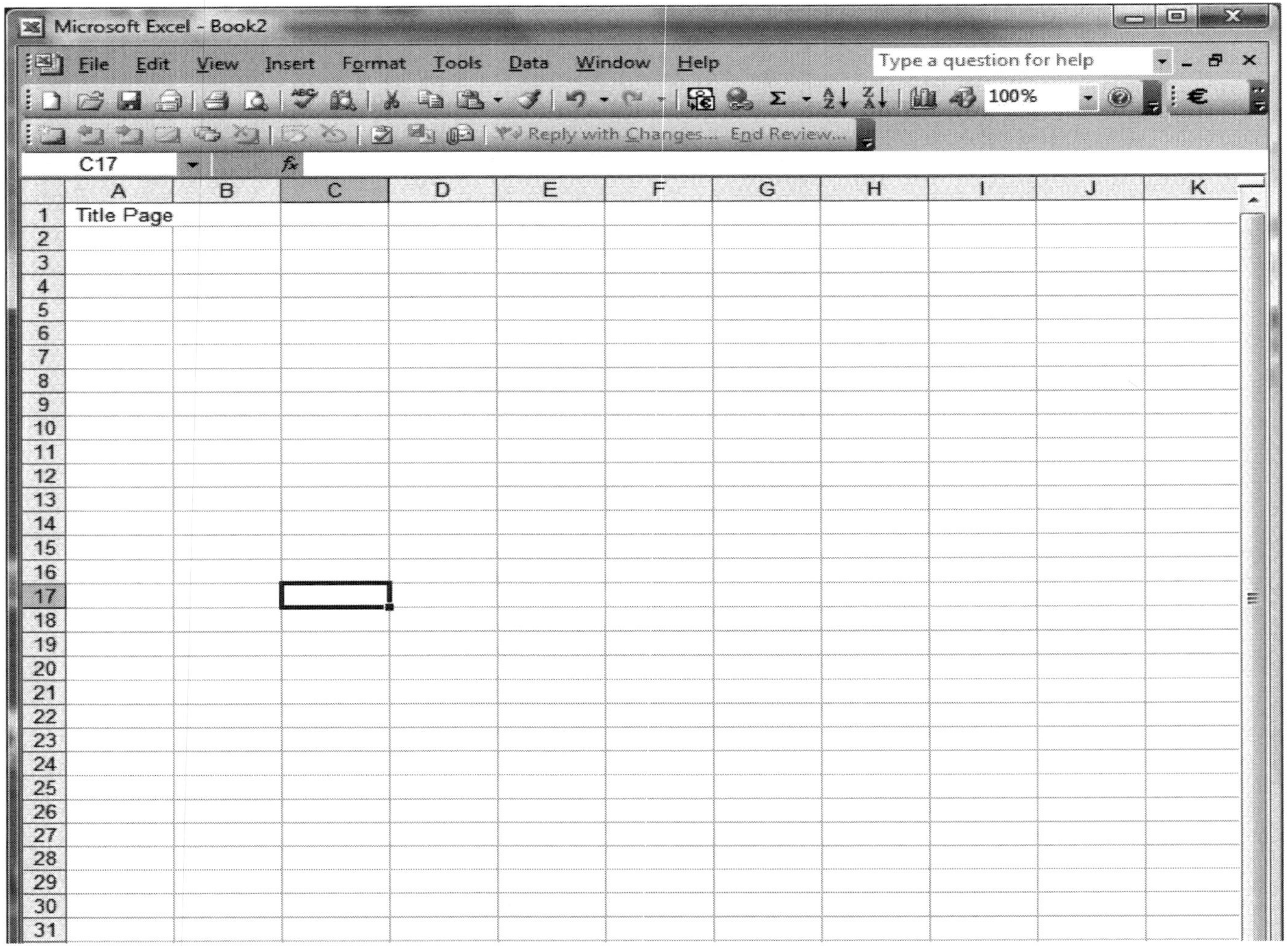

Exhibit 2.14. Adjustment to the Height of Row 1 to Give a New Display of the Phrase "Title Page" in Cell A1

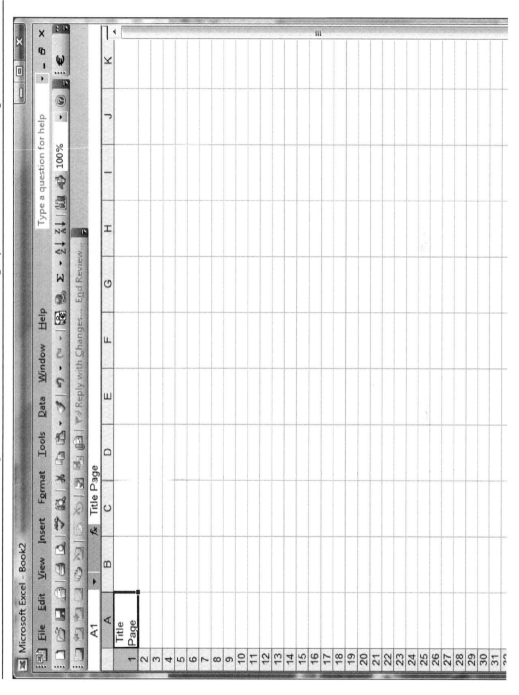

F. Entering Text and Other Symbols into a Worksheet

You also can enter text: that is, words and a wide range of symbols. Keep in mind that some symbols such as "=" entered in the first space in a given cell is interpreted by Excel as the start of a "function," and Excel will expect to find a built-in function (e.g., "=AVERAGE(A1:A4)") after the "=" sign. However, if you hit the space bar once after landing your cursor in a cell and then enter "=," the "=" symbol would now simply be interpreted by Excel as a symbol, as would be the case if you entered "=" anywhere in a cell other than the first space (e.g., "the arithmetic average =").

To get started, simply type in the phrase "Title Page" in cell A1 (where you have the number 4). If you already had an entry in this cell, the new entry for this cell, "Title Page," will simply replace it. After you have entered "Title Page" in cell A1, you will see "Title Page" appear in the toolbar area above the column headings (C, D, and so on) as is shown in Exhibit 2.11. Now, look to the left of this area, above cell A1, and you will see "A1" immediately above column A. The entry "A1" in this space is telling you that you are working in cell A1, and the entry "Title Page" in the area to its right tells you that you have entered "Title Page" in cell A1. These tools are designed to help you keep track of where you are in the worksheet.

Once you move your cursor from cell A1, you will not be able to see the entire phrase "Title Page" in cell A1, even though it is "entered" there. To see it, you can adjust the width of column A or the height of row 1, or do both. There are several ways to do this, but one way is to click on the "Format" tab in the toolbar and then click on "Format Cells." Once this screen comes up, click on the "Alignment" tab and you should see a screen "pop-up" similar to what is shown in Exhibit 2.12.

You can use the arrows to the right of the horizontal tab and the vertical tab, respectively, to change the width and height of specific cells and for columns and rows in general. See if you can adjust the width of column A so that the entire phrase "Title Page" can be seen, as is shown in Exhibit 2.13.

Now, adjust the height of row 1 so that cell A1 displays "Title Page" as shown in Exhibit 2.14. Here you can see that "Title" now sits above "Page" in cell A1.

Increase the width of column A once more, so that "Title" now longer sits above "Page," but precedes it as shown in Exhibit 2.15.

G. Saving Your Work

Now that you have learned some of Excel's basics, you do not want to lose this knowledge. You also are not going to want to lose data you have put into Excel once you start working on the projects (example assignments) discussed in this book. In this section, you will see how to save data that you have entered or computed in an Excel worksheet. To illustrate this, I will turn back to the example of the two numbers, 4 and 5, that you entered into cells A1 and A2 along with their arithmetic average (4.50), which you put

Exhibit 2.15. Another Adjustment to the Width of Column A to Give a New Display of the Phrase "Title Page" in Cell A1

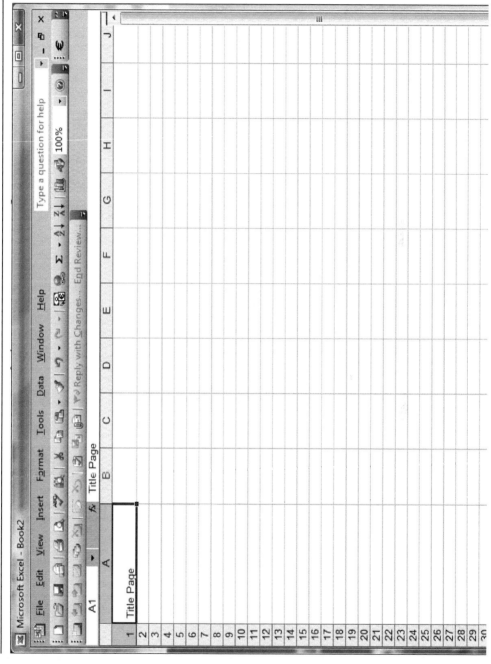

Exhibit 2.16. Saving an Excel Workbook, Step 1

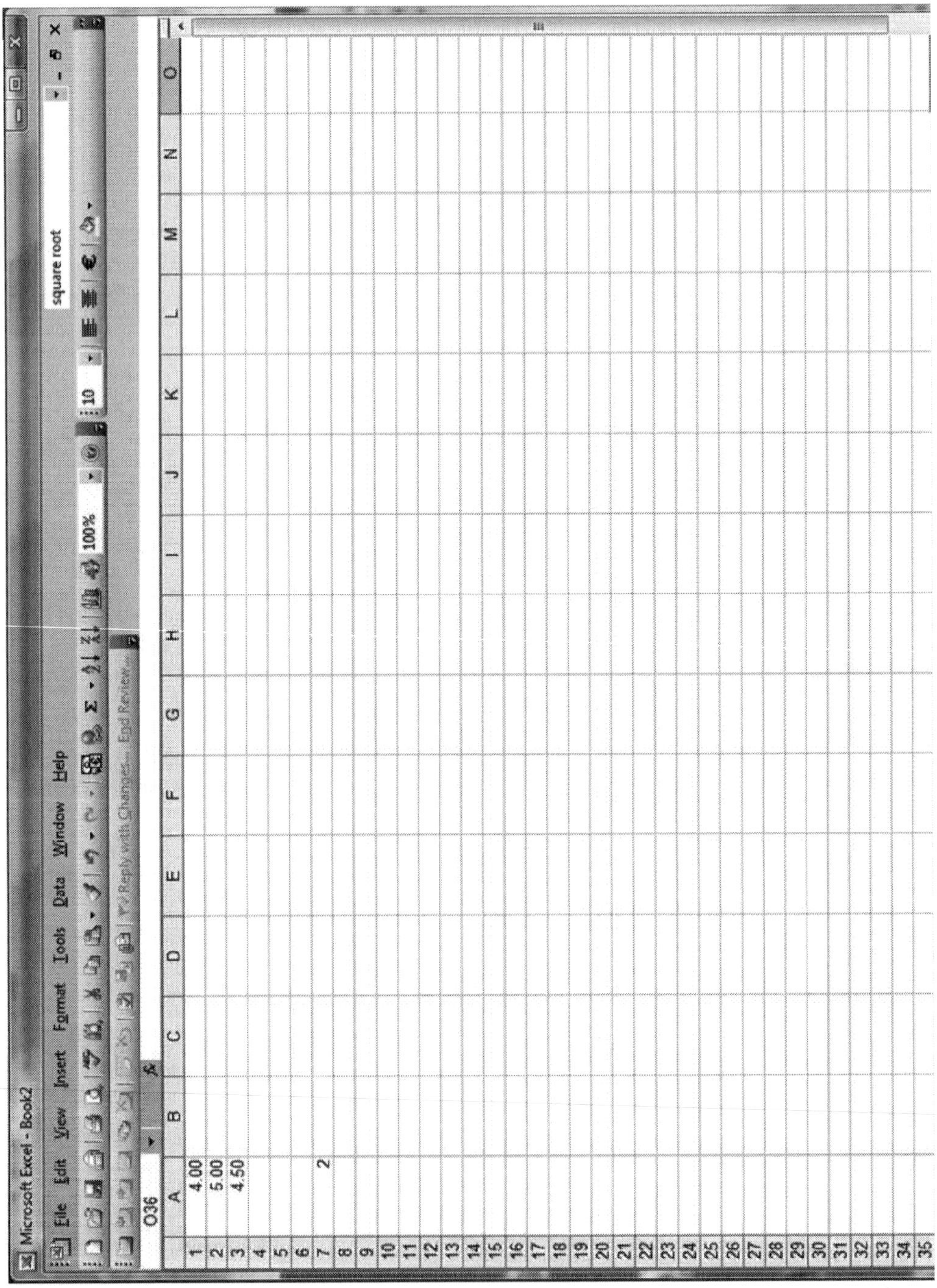

Exhibit 2.17. Saving an Excel Workbook, Step 2

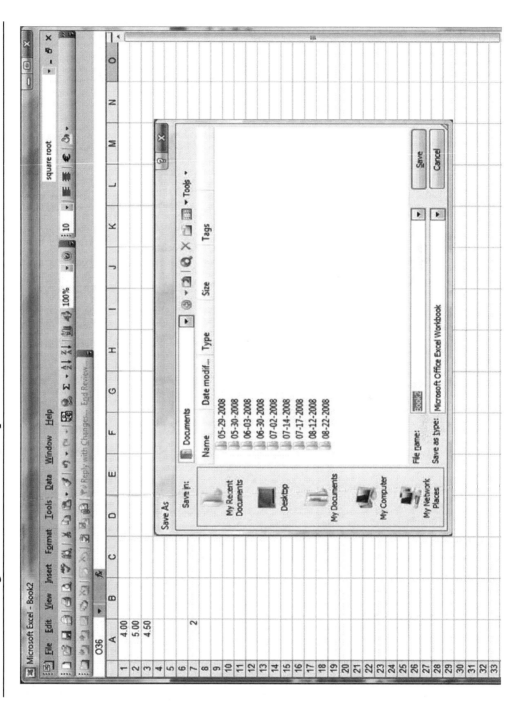

Exhibit 2.18. Saving an Excel Workbook, Step 3

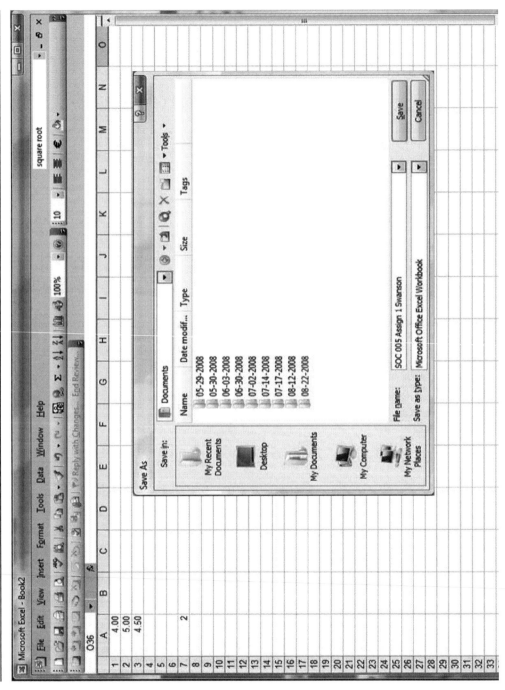

Exhibit 2.19. Saving an Excel Workbook, Step 4

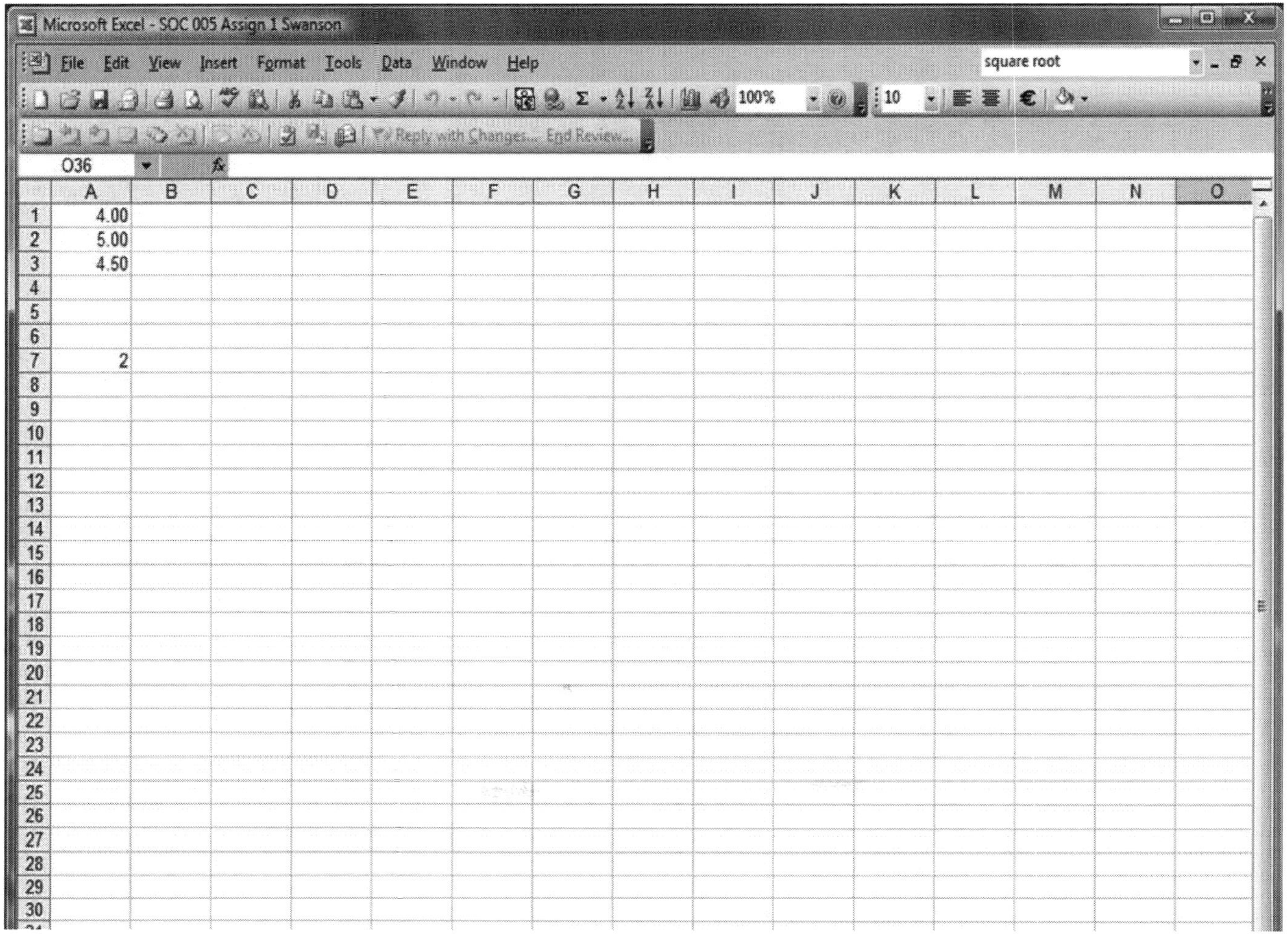

into cell A3. These results are shown in Exhibit 2.16 (without the numbers 9.00 in cell A4 and 5.00 in cell E11), along with a new number (2) in cell A7, which is the square root of 4 (cell A1). Before you save your worksheet, see if you can get Excel to put the square root of the contents of cell A1 in cell A7, and make sure you have deleted the number 9.00 from cell A4 and the number 5.00 from cell E11. (For assistance in getting Excel to find the square root of cell A2, see section H in this chapter.)

Once you have your worksheet looking like the one shown in Exhibit 2.16, point your cursor at the toolbar and click on the "File" tab located there. This will open a dropdown menu, on which you will see the tab "Save as." Move your cursor to this tab and click on it to open up the pop-up screen like you see in Exhibit 2.17.

In Exhibit 2.17, you see an area labeled "Documents" in the pop-up screen, while within the screen you see a set of nine folders stacked up, next to the name of each folder (e.g., the top folder is named "25-09-2008"), bottom of the pop-up screen, you will see two tabs in the lower right the "SAVE" tab, and below it, the "CANCEL" tab. At the far left of the "SAVE" tab is "File Name:" and below it is "Save as type:" In the space between the "File Name" and the "SAVE" tab, you will see "book2" highlighted in blue. It is in this area that you will provide a name for your workbook. Below it, you will see "Microsoft Office Excel Workbook" in the space between "Save as type"" and the "CANCEL" tab.

In Exhibit 2.18, you will see that I have given the name "SOC 005 Assign 2 Swanson" to the Excel file. After typing this name in and clicking on the "SAVE" tab, the file will be saved as SOC 005 Assign 2 Swanson.xls (where the suffix "xls" is automatically associated with an Excel file saved using the 2003 and earlier versions of Excel). Also, note that this file will be saved in my "C" drive in the "Documents" folder.

Once you have "saved" the file, you will see its name in the topmost right part of your screen where formerly "Microsoft Excel—Book1" appeared as the "default" name given by Excel to the workbook before you saved it under a specific name. You can see "Microsoft Excel SOC 005 Assign 2 Swanson" in this location in Exhibit 2.19. This indicates that the file was successfully saved.

H. The "Help" Facility in Excel

Excel has a built in "Help" facility. It is extremely useful. I often use it to refresh my memory of the exact names for functions that I do not remember off the top of my head. For example, if I forget the syntax of the formula for finding the square root of a number, I would simply type in "square root" in the box at the far upper right of the toolbar (where you can see "Type a question for help"). Once I do this, I hit the Enter key, which will reveal a dropdown menu associated with "square root" terms in Excel, as shown in Exhibit 2.20.

The first entry in the dropdown menu shown in Exhibit 2.20 is "SQRT," which I now remember is the formula for finding a square root in Excel. If I click on "SQRT," I will

Exhibit 2.20. The "Help" Facility in Excel: An Example for "Square Root"

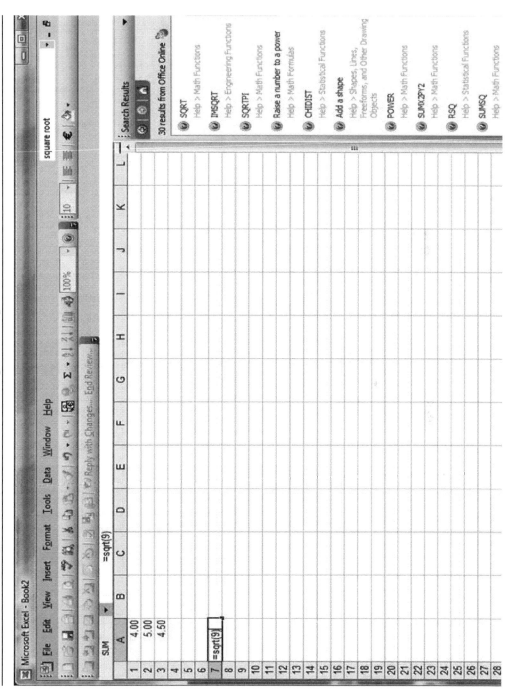

Exhibit 2.21. A "Grade Book" Example of Logical Functions

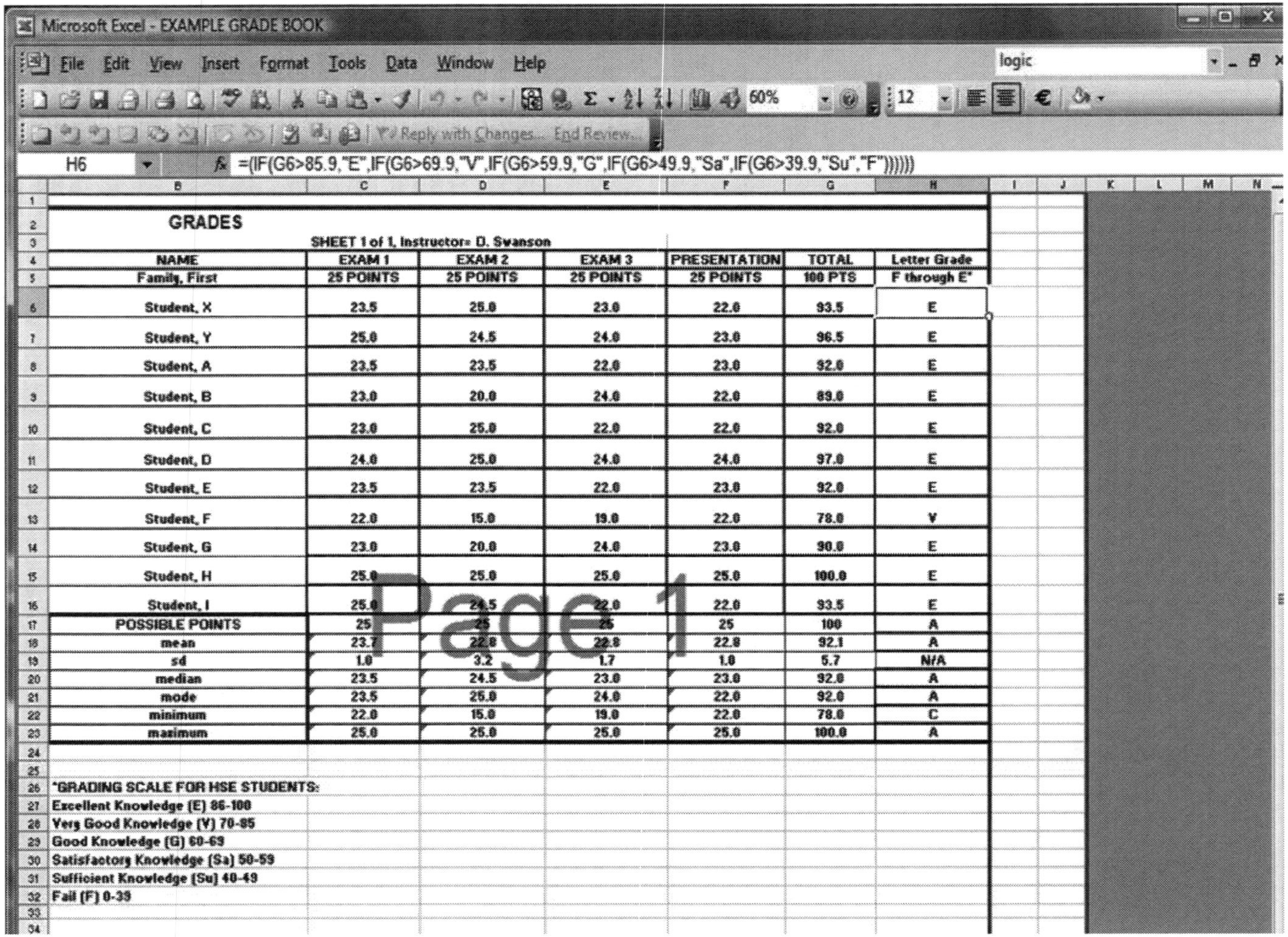

H6 =IF(G6>85.9,"E",IF(G6>69.9,"V",IF(G6>59.9,"G",IF(G6>49.9,"Sa",IF(G6>39.9,"Su","F"))))))

GRADES

SHEET 1 of 1, Instructor: D. Swanson

NAME Family, First	EXAM 1 25 POINTS	EXAM 2 25 POINTS	EXAM 3 25 POINTS	PRESENTATION 25 POINTS	TOTAL 100 PTS	Letter Grade F through E*
Student, X	23.5	25.0	23.0	22.0	93.5	E
Student, Y	25.0	24.5	24.0	23.0	96.5	E
Student, A	23.5	23.5	22.0	23.0	92.0	E
Student, B	23.0	20.0	24.0	22.0	89.0	E
Student, C	23.0	25.0	22.0	22.0	92.0	E
Student, D	24.0	25.0	24.0	24.0	97.0	E
Student, E	23.5	23.5	22.0	23.0	92.0	E
Student, F	22.0	15.0	19.0	22.0	78.0	V
Student, G	23.0	20.0	24.0	23.0	90.0	E
Student, H	25.0	25.0	25.0	25.0	100.0	E
Student, I	25.0	24.5	22.0	22.0	93.5	E
POSSIBLE POINTS	25	25	25	25	100	A
mean	23.7	22.8	22.8	22.8	92.1	A
sd	1.0	3.2	1.7	1.0	5.7	N/A
median	23.5	24.5	23.0	23.0	92.0	A
mode	23.5	25.0	24.0	22.0	92.0	A
minimum	22.0	15.0	19.0	22.0	78.0	C
maximum	25.0	25.0	25.0	25.0	100.0	A

*GRADING SCALE FOR HSE STUDENTS:
Excellent Knowledge (E) 86-100
Very Good Knowledge (V) 70-85
Good Knowledge (G) 60-69
Satisfactory Knowledge (Sa) 50-59
Sufficient Knowledge (Su) 40-49
Fail (F) 0-39

see more details, which will help me in putting the square root of the contents of cell A2, in cell A7, per the assignment given in section G.

I. Logical Functions in Excel

As you have seen already, Excel has mathematical functions, many more than shown here. You also have seen its many statistical functions. It also has built-in "Logical" functions. I am not going to go through them here in detail (you can learn about them through the online resources listed at the end of this chapter). However, to give you an example of their power, I will show you how I use them to determine letter grades from numerous scores of students that I input to a grading workbook. In Exhibit 2.21, you can see scores for exams inputted into an Excel workbook that are summed to get total points, which are then converted into letter grades. This example has the cursor in cell H6, which is where the summed scores for student X are converted into a letter grade of "E, which is "Excellent" and based on achieving 90 or more points. You can see the logic that does this in the area where the contents of a given cell are displayed in the toolbar (to the right of the "*fx*" sign in Exhibit 2.21. See if you can use the "Help" facility to figure out how this formula turns total scores (column G) into letter grades, where less than 49.9 points is turned into a letter grade of "F"; a score of 50 to 59.9 is turned into a letter grade of "Su"; a score of 60 to 69.9 becomes a letter grade of "Sa"; a score of 70 to 70.9 is turned into a letter grade of "G"; a score of 80 to 89.9 becomes a letter grade of "V"; and a score of 90 and over becomes a letter grade of "A."

J. Displaying Data in Excel: Graphs

This is an important aspect of Excel. Graphs represent a powerful tool for understanding data. Exhibit 2.22 shows a table of data in columns A and B, rows 1 through 7, and a "column chart" of these data in the area between columns E and L and rows 2 through 20, respectively. The graph was constructed using the "graph wizard" in Excel.

The data shown in columns A and B, rows 1 to 7, were entered first (which you should know how to do; it is a combination of text and numeric data). Once this was done, I clicked on the "chart wizard" in the toolbar area, which resulted in the screen shown in Exhibit 2.23.

Once the pop-up menu for the "chart wizard" comes up, select "Column Graph" and then click "Next," which will bring up the screen shown in Exhibit 2.24.

When you have the preceding screen up, put your cursor in cell A1 and "scroll" it over all the cells in columns A and B from row 1 to row 7. This will result in the screen shown in Exhibit 2.25, where you can see the column graph in the pop-up screen.

Now, all you need to do is select "Finish" in the pop-up box. This will yield a screen that looks like that shown in Exhibit 2.26.

Exhibit 2.22. Step 1 of Graphing Example, Data in Cells A1 to A11

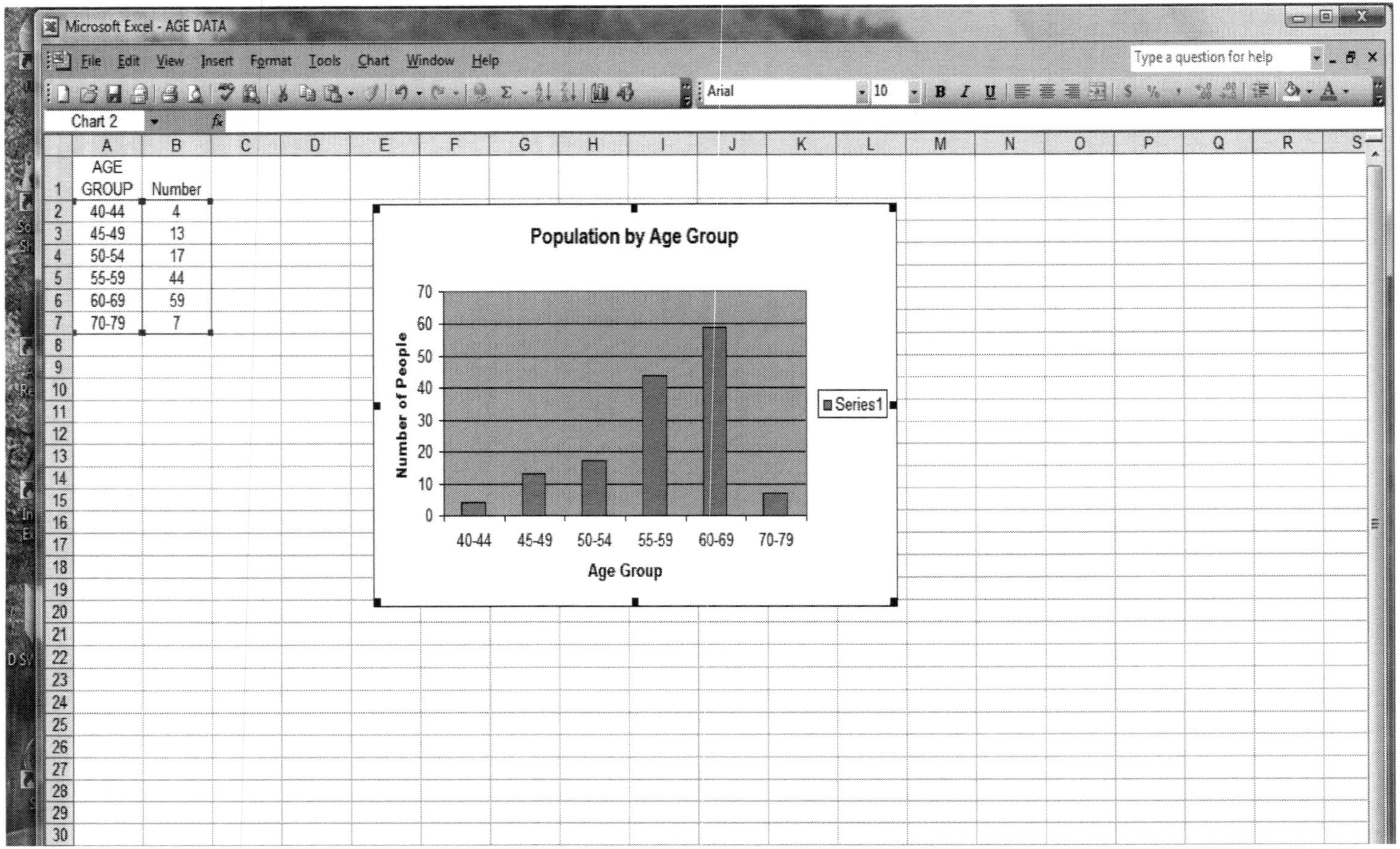

Exhibit 2.23. Step 2 of Graphing Example, Bringing up the Chart Wizard

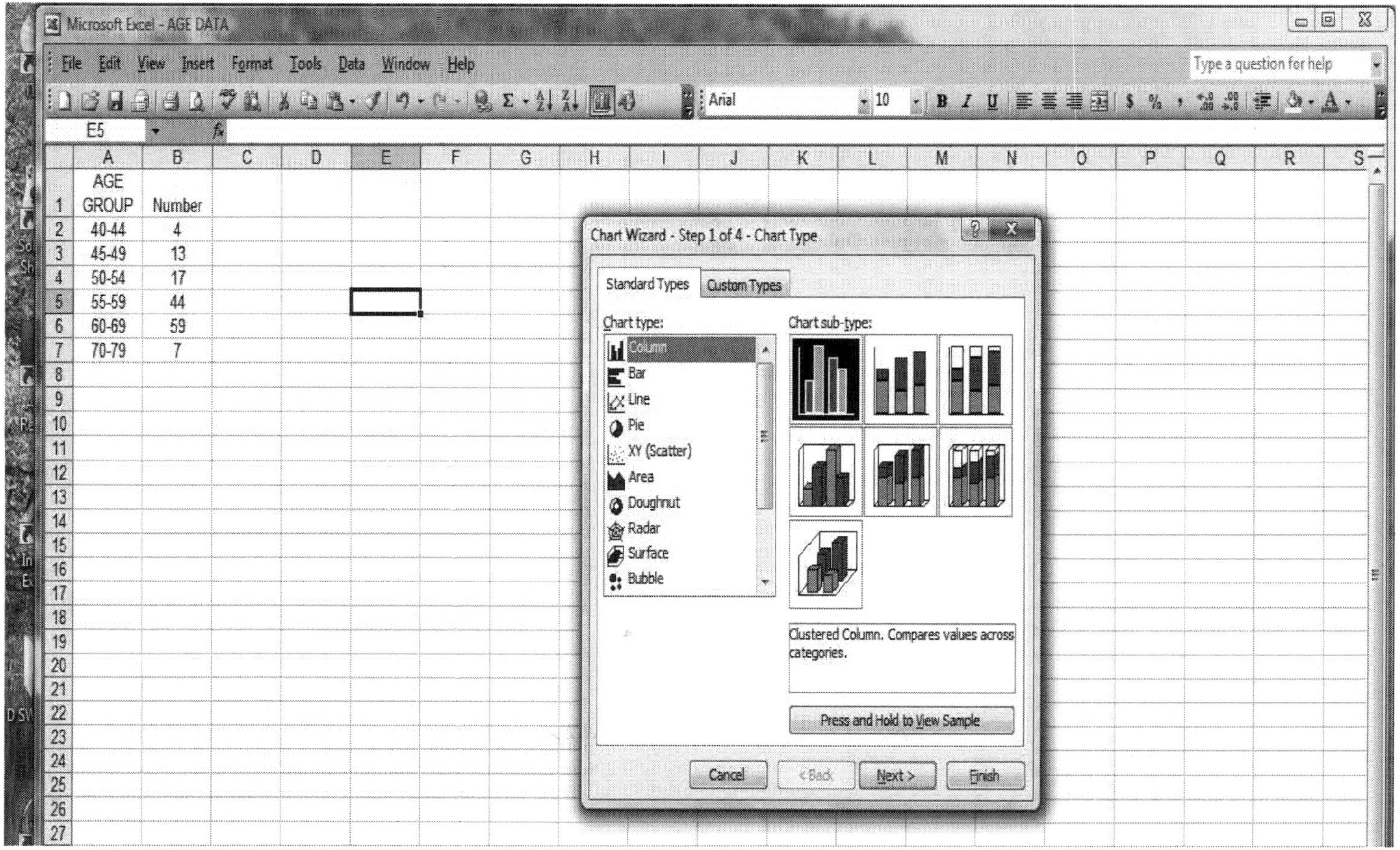

Exhibit 2.24. Step 3 of Graphing Example, Selecting the "Column Chart"

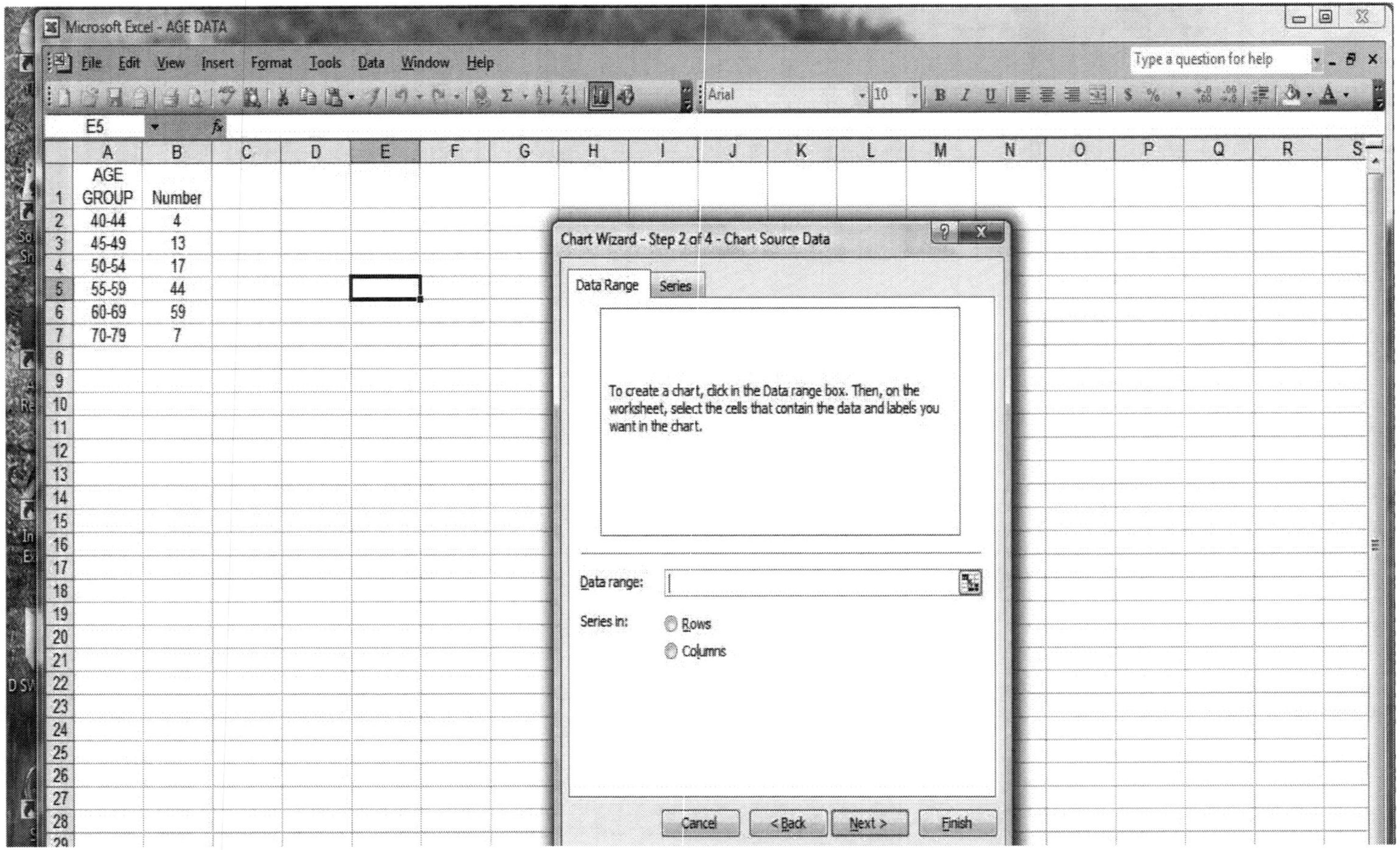

Exhibit 2.25. Step 4 of Graphing Example, Selecting the Data to Be Graphed

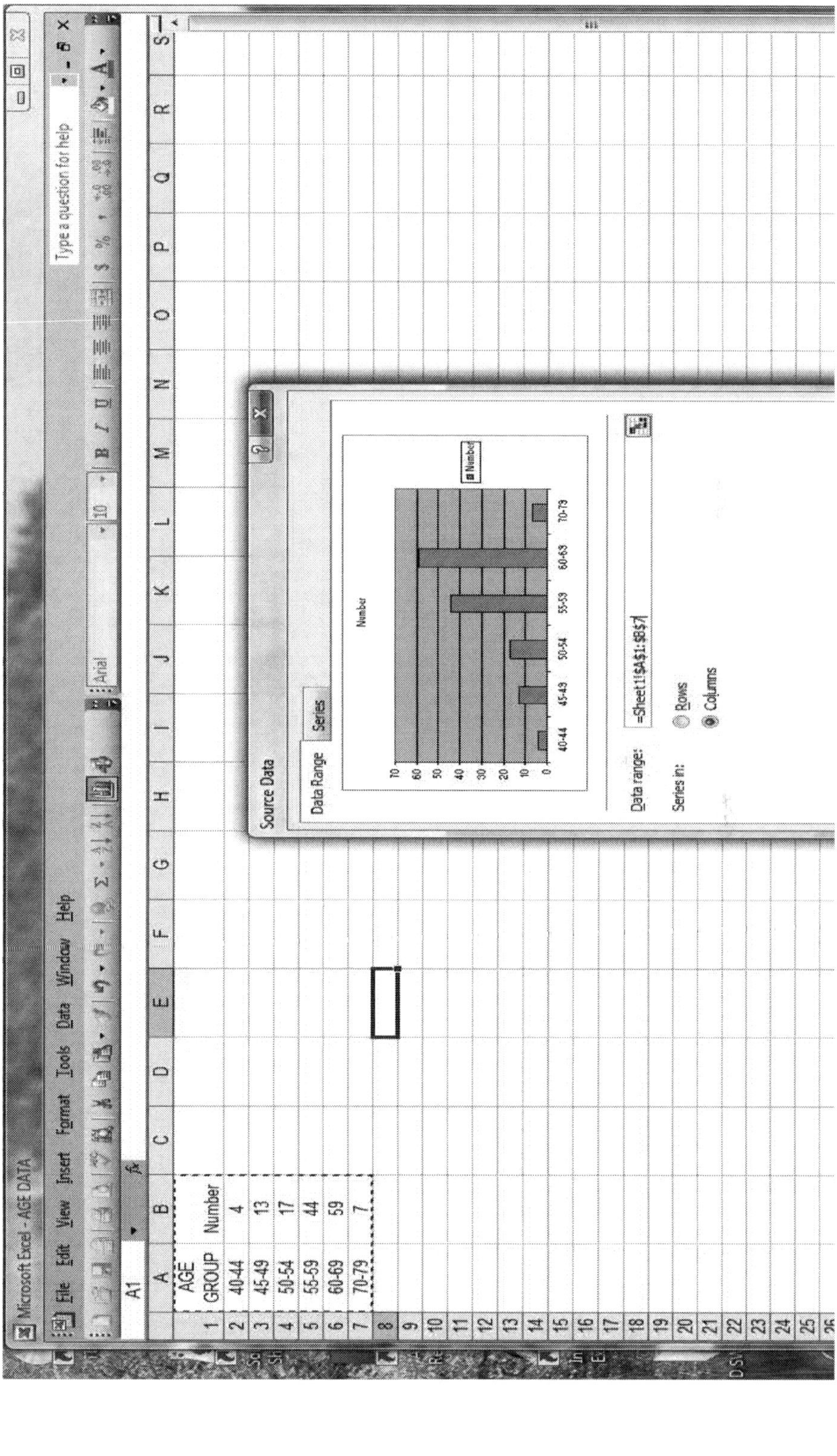

Exhibit 2.26. Step 5 of Graphing Example, Completing the Graph

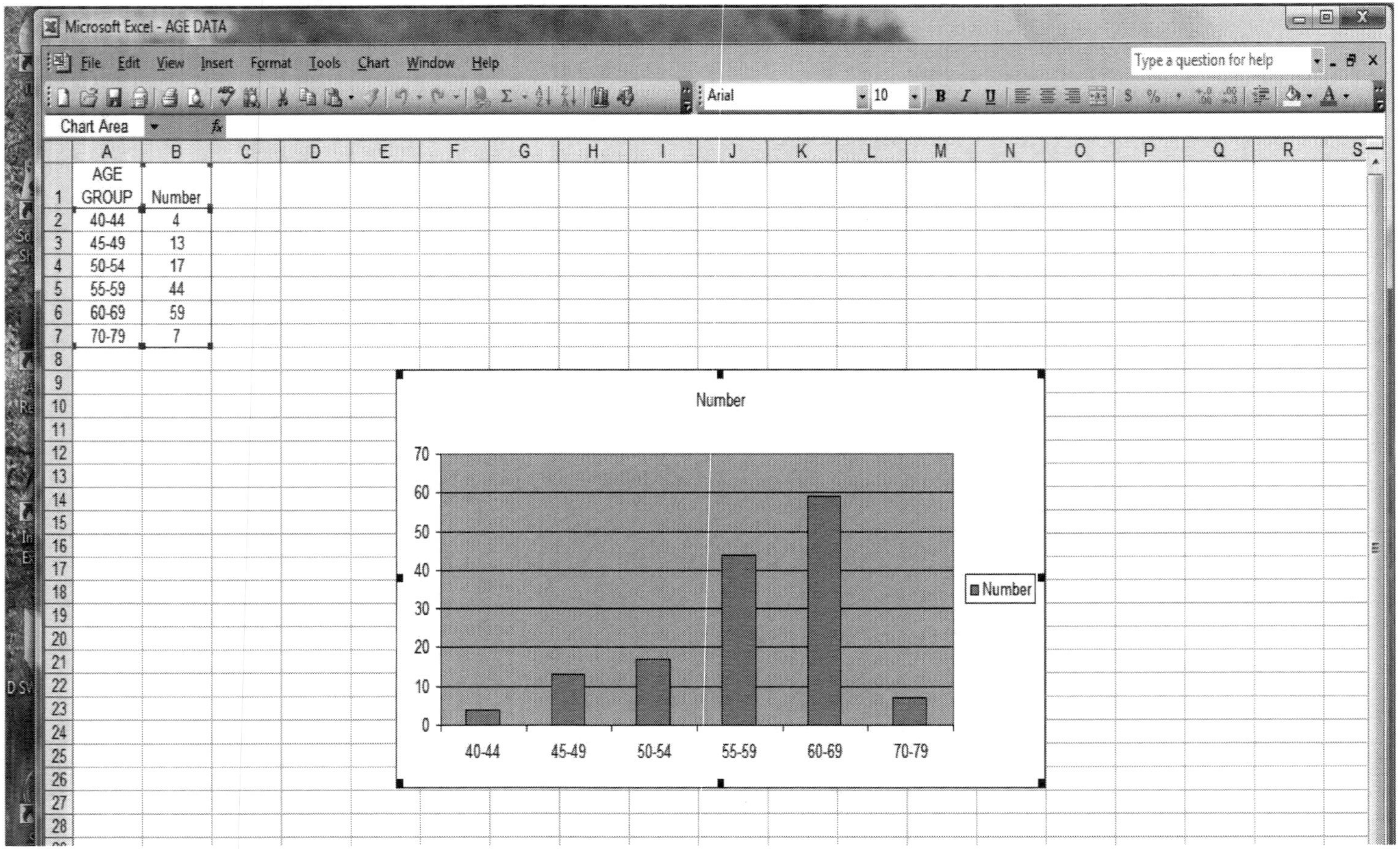

This was a "bare-bones" example. You can put titles, legends, and a host of other material in graphs. There are many more types of graphs you can do in Excel. This, however, should serve to get you started.

This covers the introduction to Excel. To become proficient in it, even in the limited way needed for the course this book is designed for, requires your engagement and hours of practice.

ASSIGNMENT FOR CHAPTER 2

1. Enter the numbers 5, 10, 5, 7, and 13 in column A, rows 1 through 5 in an Excel worksheet.
2. Find the arithmetic average of the numbers you entered and put it in cell A6.
3. Find the standard deviation of the numbers you entered and put it in cell A7.
4. Find the count of the number of numbers you entered in cells A1 through A5 and put the count in cell A8.
5. Find the square root of the number in cell A8 and put the result in cell A9.
6. Divide cell A7 by cell A9 and put the result in cell A10.
7. In cell B6, enter "mean" as text.
8. In cell B7, enter "standard deviation" as text.
9. In cell B8, enter "sample size" as text.
10. In cell B9, enter "standard error" as text.
11. Copy cells A1 through A9 and paste the results in cells C1 through C9.
12. Save your work using your name and "assignment 2" as part of the name of the file (e.g., Swanson.assign2.xls).

Appendix. Some Online Sites to Help You Get Started in Learning Excel

I have organized the sites into three major groups, listed below as A, B, and C. Note that these locations can change, especially as new versions of Excel are released. If the URLs below do not lead to the Excel tutorials, try doing a search in Youtube for "Excel."

A. Excel is Fun

http://www.youtube.com/user/ExcelIsFun

B. Excel Tutorials

Excel Tutorial 1: Intro
http://www.youtube.com/watch?v=X3jB4wncJp4

Once at the preceding site, you can work through all of the 20 videos available to find tutorials on specific aspects of Excel such as formatting, using functions, and so on.

C. Excel STATISTICAL MASTER SERIES (4 MANUALS, $19.95 to download)

http://Excelmasterseries.com/

The entire Excel STATISTICAL MASTER SERIES is described in a single YouTube Video
http://www.youtube.com/watch?v=4417HpAr2FU&feature=related

Endnote

1. COPYRIGHT NOTICE. © Microsoft Corporation. All rights reserved. Microsoft Excel is a copyrighted product of the Microsoft Corporation.

3. Data and Their Measurement

When learning something new, it is always best to start at the beginning!

A. What Are Data?

Both the counted ballots from our hypothetical election and the count in our hypothetical "exit sample" of voters in the preceding chapter are "data" sets. "Data" is the plural form of "datum," which is a single fact or observation. Thus, a set of data is a set of facts or observations. These facts or observations can be numbers, words, or other symbols. For data to be useful in any analysis, they need to be defined and organized. Table 3.1 shows a set of data, one that you will be using. This data set is organized into 50 cases, where each case represents a family. For each case (family),

Case	Monthly Family Food Expenditures	Annual Family Income	Family Size	Garden (1=yes; 0 = no)
	Table 3.1 Food Income Family Size and Garden Data Set			
1	$723.52	$41,230.00	1	1
2	$1,025.52	$59,110.00	1	1
3	$866.62	$71,940.00	1	1
4	$1,148.24	$81,420.00	1	0
5	$877.52	$94,540.00	1	1
6	$2,560.22	$127,110.00	1	0
7	$2,122.52	$134,260.00	1	0
8	$3,211.64	$148,120.00	1	0
9	$1,189.40	$53,130.00	2	1
10	$1,295.64	$54,920.00	2	1
11	$1,792.18	$62,660.00	2	0
12	$780.06	$66,100.00	2	1
13	$1,273.34	$69,730.00	2	1
14	$1,953.58	$71,030.00	2	0
15	$2,372.00	$75,160.00	2	0
16	$1,810.96	$85,620.00	2	0
17	$1,776.58	$86,510.00	2	0
18	$1,284.00	$94,610.00	2	0
19	$1,502.94	$96,650.00	2	1
20	$1,682.36	$110,600.00	2	0
21	$1,472.44	$116,440.00	2	0
22	$2,194.76	$117,940.00	2	0
23	$2,328.96	$119,540.00	2	0
24	$975.10	$132,950.00	2	1
25	$2,108.14	$83,320.00	3	0
26	$2,295.04	$91,270.00	3	0
27	$1,939.00	$100,540.00	3	0
28	$2,443.06	$103,000.00	3	0
29	$1,638.26	$118,540.00	3	1
30	$1,666.90	$121,080.00	3	1
31	$1,068.38	$135,730.00	3	1
32	$1,904.66	$144,370.00	3	0
33	$780.70	$43,710.00	4	1
34	$2,125.30	$73,110.00	4	0
35	$2,003.44	$106,190.00	4	0
36	$2,534.66	$116,580.00	4	0

37	$2,111.50	$147,250.00	4	0
38	$2,665.78	$148,450.00	4	0
39	$1,328.00	$64,760.00	5	1
40	$2,477.34	$75,860.00	5	0
41	$2,819.06	$131,430.00	5	0
42	$2,763.40	$142,780.00	5	0
43	$990.74	$45,240.00	6	1
44	$1,336.14	$66,930.00	6	1
45	$2,612.00	$119,150.00	6	0
46	$2,253.46	$139,680.00	6	0
47	$1,634.98	$52,920.00	7	1
48	$2,308.16	$112,260.00	7	0
49	$2,950.72	$68,730.00	8	1
50	$3,103.54	$127,520.00	9	1

we have information on four variables: (1) Monthly Family Food Expenditures; (2) Annual Family Income; (3) Family Size; and (4) if the family has a garden (Yes or No). Table 3.1 was copied directly from an Excel worksheet and pasted into this chapter when it was an MS-Word file. Exhibit 3.1 shows most (but not all, since the data set extends below the range of my computer screen) of the data set in its original Excel home. As you can see in Exhibit 3.1, the data set is named "Food Income Family Size and Garden.xls." These data came from a sample of families in a study that asked questions related to monthly food expenditures. In this study, measurement error, non-response error, coverage error, and coding/transcription error were kept to a very low level. Because it is a random sample, the data set is subject to sampling error, which we will look at in Chapter 7 and continue looking at through the remainder of the book.

Table 3.1 (and Exhibit 3.1) follows the typical pattern of organizing a data set in that it is composed of cases for which we have information on variables of interest.

In terms of Excel you now know some basic language about a data set—"case," "variable," and "value"—and some basic organization: Cases are found by row and variables by column. Thus, the value of a given variable for a specific case is found in the cell that represents the intersections of the rows and columns. Thus, the family represented as case no. 15 (found in row 17, which is highlighted) consists of two people who reported spending $2,372.00 monthly on food, an annual income of $75,160.00, and no garden.

In addition to knowing how a data set is organized and understanding the terms "case," "variable," and "value," you will need to know the principles of measurement before you can proceed to doing basic data analysis and statistical inference. These principles govern what you can and cannot do with numbers that are used as values for the variables you are studying.

Exhibit 3.1. A "Screen Shot" of Part of the Data Set in Table 3.1

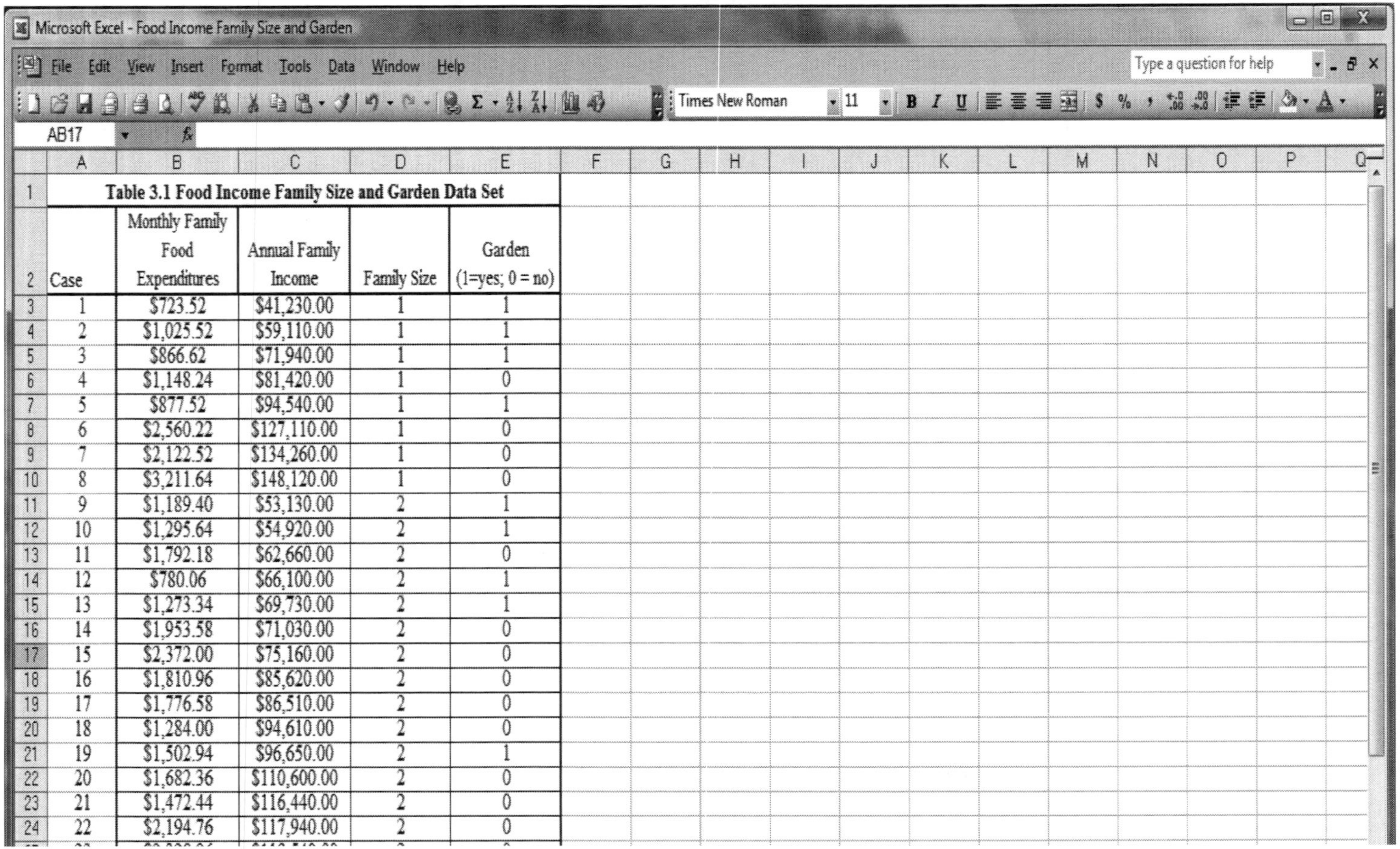

Microsoft Excel - Food Income Family Size and Garden

File   Edit   View   Insert   Format   Tools   Data   Window   Help   Type a question for help

Times New Roman   11   B   I   U

AB17

Table 3.1 Food Income Family Size and Garden Data Set

Case	Monthly Family Food Expenditures	Annual Family Income	Family Size	Garden (1=yes; 0 = no)
1	$723.52	$41,230.00	1	1
2	$1,025.52	$59,110.00	1	1
3	$866.62	$71,940.00	1	1
4	$1,148.24	$81,420.00	1	0
5	$877.52	$94,540.00	1	1
6	$2,560.22	$127,110.00	1	0
7	$2,122.52	$134,260.00	1	0
8	$3,211.64	$148,120.00	1	0
9	$1,189.40	$53,130.00	2	1
10	$1,295.64	$34,920.00	2	1
11	$1,792.18	$62,660.00	2	0
12	$780.06	$66,100.00	2	1
13	$1,273.34	$69,730.00	2	1
14	$1,953.58	$71,030.00	2	0
15	$2,372.00	$75,160.00	2	0
16	$1,810.96	$85,620.00	2	0
17	$1,776.58	$86,510.00	2	0
18	$1,284.00	$94,610.00	2	0
19	$1,502.94	$96,650.00	2	1
20	$1,682.36	$110,600.00	2	0
21	$1,472.44	$116,440.00	2	0
22	$2,194.76	$117,940.00	2	0

B. Levels of Measurement

The phrase "Level of Measurement" refers to a system of classifying numbers in terms of what operations can legitimately be done with them. Thus, knowing what level at which a variable is measured helps you decide what statistical analysis is appropriate on the values that were assigned to the variable and also helps you in interpreting the results of your analysis.

There are several ways the classification can be done. This book uses the fourfold classification system proposed by S. S. Stevens (1946), which classifies numbers as being (1) nominal; (2) ordinal; (3) interval; and (4) ratio. There are other systems such as the twofold classification of (1) discrete and (2) continuous. The system developed by Stevens is useful in that it points the way to specific measures to be used with numbers at given levels of measurement. For example, except in only the special case where a "nominal level" variable with two values is "dummy coded" as 1 and 0, it is not meaningful to find the arithmetic average for a nominal level variable.[1] In some situations, the arithmetic average for an ordinal level variable is meaningful, while in others it is not. It is always meaningful to have an arithmetic average for a variable at either the interval or ratio level of measurement.

Nominal Level of Measurement. This is known as the "lowest" level of measurement. Here, the values just "name" the attribute uniquely and they do not imply any ordering of the cases. For example, the variable "religion" is inherently nominal. Suppose we decide in a study that it is useful to have three values for this variable: Christian; Muslim; and All Other. Thus, we have three values (mutually exclusive and exhaustive). We could code these values as "C," "M," and "A," respectively. We also could code them as "1," "2," and "3," respectively. In the latter case, the numbers are really not numbers in the sense that we can add and subtract them. For example, it makes no sense to say that a "Christian" (coded as 1) is the result of subtracting "Muslim" (coded as 2) from "All Other" (coded as 3). Thus, numbers assigned to serve as values for nominal level variables such as "Religion" cannot be added, subtracted, multiplied, or divided in a meaningful way, with one important exception. The important exception is when we use "dummy coding" for a nominal level variable with two values (Reynolds, 1984). We discuss dummy coding in the following two chapters and give an example of using it in chapters 12 and 13.

Ordinal Level of Measurement. This is at a higher order level of measurement than is the nominal category, but it is still considered a "low level of measurement." It refers to the fact that attributes can be rank ordered, but that the distances between attributes are not fixed. For example, suppose we had a questionnaire in which we asked people if they thought statistics was a great subject to study, and had the following five response categories: (1) strongly disagree; (2) somewhat disagree; (3) neither disagree nor agree; (4) somewhat agree; and (5) strongly agree. We can see that a response coded as "5" ("strongly agree") indicates more agreement than does a response coded as "4" ("somewhat agree"), and so on. However, the "distance" between the categories is not fixed.

That is, we are not able to say if the "distance" from strongly disagree (coded as "1") to somewhat disagree (coded as "2") is the same as the distance from strongly agree (coded as "5") to somewhat agree (coded as "4"). All we can say is codes 1 through 5 preserve the order of agreement. The central issue is that the distances between the numbers are not fixed. It is as if we are using a rubber band for a ruler.

Numbers coded at the ordinal level occupy an interesting "gray area" between nominal level numbers, on the one hand (for which there is no meaningful addition, subtraction, multiplication, and division), and on the other hand, interval level numbers (for which there is meaningful addition and subtraction) and ratio level numbers (for which there is meaningful addition, subtraction, multiplication, and division). In some situations, one can treat numbers at the ordinal level as being interval, and in other situations, one cannot. The situations largely depend on the coding assigned to the attributes of ordinal level variables.

One of the reasons ordinal level variables are difficult to deal with is that they are often used to measure highly abstract concepts such as "social distance" (Bogardus, 1947). The process of trying to measure concepts like this usually involves a process known as "scaling," which can become quite complex (Edwards, 1957; Guttman, 1944; McIver and Carmines, 1981). While there is no clear-cut right or wrong answer for when to use the mean (or median) with ordinal level variables, it generally is true that it is easier to justify if the variable in question has been scaled and an appropriate response scale is used (Hildebrand, Laing, and Rosenthal, 1977). We return to this in the next two chapters, when we look at the mean and standard deviation, respectively, in a study of social distance.

Interval Level of Measurement. This is a much higher level of measurement than the ordinal level and very much higher than the nominal level. It refers to the types of numbers where the distance between attributes has meaning, which indicates we can do meaningful addition and subtraction. For example, the difference in temperature in Fahrenheit (which can be viewed as a variable) between 30 degrees and 40 degrees is the same as the distance from 70 degrees to 80 degrees. In both cases, the difference is 10 degrees. This means that we have a fixed distance between the points, which is like using a ruler. However, for interval level numbers, ratios don't make any sense. For example, 80 degrees is not twice as hot as 40 degrees. Thus, while we can say that the distance between 60 and 45 degrees is the same as the distance from 15 to 30 degrees, we cannot say that 60 degrees is twice as hot as 30. The ratio of 2 = 60/30 makes no sense, because in the Fahrenheit system for measuring temperature, zero is not the absence of heat. In the absence of a true "zero," numbers can be added and subtracted, but they cannot be multiplied or divided in a meaningful way.

Ratio Level of Measurement. This is the highest level of measurement. It refers to numbers at the interval level of measurement for which a "true zero" exists. This means that in addition to adding and subtracting numbers we also can divide and multiply them in a meaningful way. Thus, it is at the interval level of measurement, because the distance between the points is fixed. In the Kelvin system for measuring temperature, for example, there is an absolute zero at which molecular action ceases. Hence, we can say that 20 degrees Kelvin is twice as hot as 10 degrees Kelvin, since not only are the distances fixed (it is the same distance from 1 degree Kelvin to 2 degrees Kelvin as it is from 15 degrees Kelvin to 16 degrees Kelvin), but there also is a true zero. Thus, the Kelvin scale (a variable!) is at the ratio level of measurement.

Take a look at Table 3.1, and write down the level of measurement for each of the four variables: Monthly Family Food Expenditure, Annual Family Income, Family Size, and Presence of a Garden.

C. Tabulating Data

One the nice things about computers is that they can take the tedium out of a lot of tasks. In return, we have to learn their "language." The data shown in Table 3.1 (with the same data, in part, in Exhibit 3.1) are in "raw" form. Until we do some counting (or get Excel to do it for us), we do not know any of the basic characteristics of the data set. For example, how many of the families have two people? How many have a garden? How many spend more than $1,500 per month on food? Assembling numbers like these is known as tabulating because we can put the results into a "table." By tabulating, we also can see the distribution of values for a given variable. For example, we could look at all 50 families tabulated by size, which gives us the distribution of "Family Size" in this data set. As an example of what Excel can do, Table 3.2 shows the results of tabulating on "presence of Garden." This tabulation gives us the distribution of this variable for our data set.

Table 3.2. Presence of Garden

GARDEN		
YES	NO	TOTAL
20	30	50

From Table 3.2, we can see that 20 of the 50 families in our sample have a garden and 30 do not. How did we get Excel to do this for us? By setting up an area of the spreadsheet to use the "COUNTIF" function and formatting that same area to look like a table. For this simple example, I decided to put the table in columns J through L and rows 6 through 8. I then used the "FORMAT CELLS" function to put borders around this area that correspond to what you see in Table 3.2. Once I had the borders in place, I typed the word "GARDEN" in cell J6, the word "YES" in cell J7, the word "NO" in cell K7 and the word "TOTAL" in cell L7. I then used the "MERGE CELLS" command found in the "Alignment Tab" of the format cells function to merge the cell in which I typed "GARDEN" (J6) with the two cells to its right, K6 and L6. This allowed me to have a single "cell" in which to put the word GARDEN, one that spans the headings,

Exhibit 3.2. The "COUNTIF" Function in Cell J8

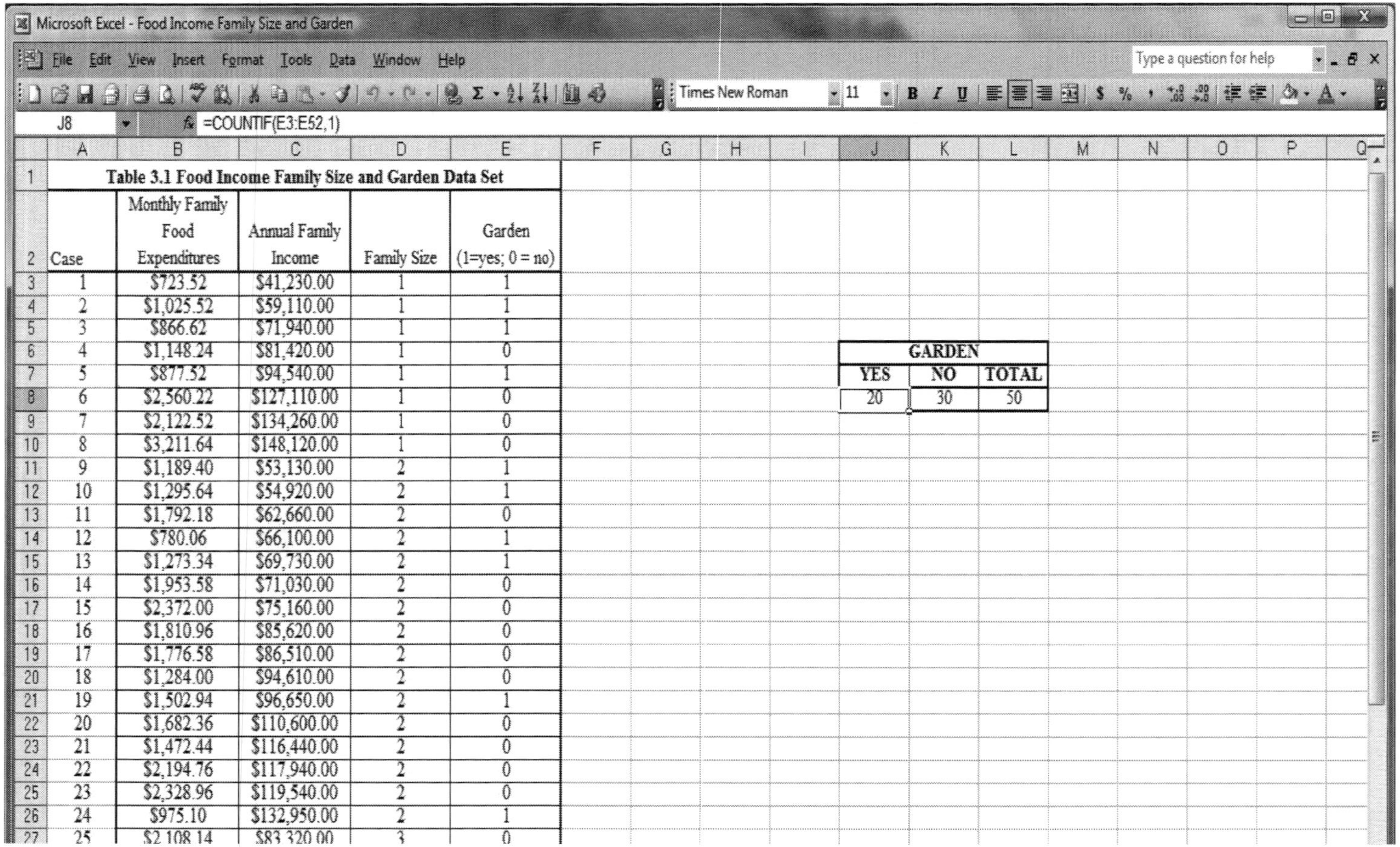

J8   =COUNTIF(E3:E52,1)

Table 3.1 Food Income Family Size and Garden Data Set

Case	Monthly Family Food Expenditures	Annual Family Income	Family Size	Garden (1=yes; 0 = no)
1	$723.52	$41,230.00	1	1
2	$1,025.52	$59,110.00	1	1
3	$866.62	$71,940.00	1	1
4	$1,148.24	$81,420.00	1	0
5	$877.52	$94,540.00	1	1
6	$2,560.22	$127,110.00	1	0
7	$2,122.52	$134,260.00	1	0
8	$3,211.64	$148,120.00	1	0
9	$1,189.40	$53,130.00	2	1
10	$1,295.64	$54,920.00	2	1
11	$1,792.18	$62,660.00	2	0
12	$780.06	$66,100.00	2	1
13	$1,273.34	$69,730.00	2	1
14	$1,953.58	$71,030.00	2	0
15	$2,372.00	$75,160.00	2	0
16	$1,810.96	$85,620.00	2	0
17	$1,776.58	$86,510.00	2	0
18	$1,284.00	$94,610.00	2	0
19	$1,502.94	$96,650.00	2	1
20	$1,682.36	$110,600.00	2	0
21	$1,472.44	$116,440.00	2	0
22	$2,194.76	$117,940.00	2	0
23	$2,328.96	$119,540.00	2	0
24	$975.10	$132,950.00	2	1
25	$2,108.14	$83,320.00	3	0

GARDEN		
YES	NO	TOTAL
20	30	50

YES, NO, and TOTAL. Now, how did I get Excel to count the number of families with gardens (30) and put this number in cell J8? The answer is provided in Exhibit 3.2, where, in the "Function" area of the toolbar, you can see the command that underlies the number 30 in cell J8.

In the "Function" area of the toolbar, you can see the command "=COUNTIF(E3:E52,1)." This tells Excel to count the number of times the number "1" occurs in cells E3 to E52 (where the values of the variable "Presence of Garden" are found) and put the result in cell J8. To count the number of families without a garden, I placed the following command in cell K8: "=COUNTIF(E3:E52,0)." Finally, to get the total number of families shown in cell L8, I placed the following command in cell L8: "=J8+K8."

See if you can replicate the table shown in Exhibit 3.3, which shows the distribution of families in our sample by size, where size has two values: (1) Less than 3; and 3 or more. Look in the function area of the toolbox in Exhibit 3.3 for a hint on how to do this.

Essentially, what I have done is "recoded" family size from its original range of values into two values, less than 3 and 3+. What level of measurement is my recoded family size?

One thing suggested by Exhibit 3.3 is that the notion of the "level of measurement" is flexible in that variables can be recoded. Indeed, this provides a really powerful tool for analysis. To answer the question about the level of measurement for family size as shown in Exhibit 3.3, by recoding it the way I did, it went from an interval level variable to an ordinal level variable. This can be generalized into the statement that variables can always be recoded into lower levels of measurement. Variables at either the ratio or interval level of measurement can be recoded into variables at either the ordinal or nominal level. Variables at the ordinal level of measurement can be recoded into nominal level variables. With the single exception of using dummy coding to make a nominal level variable into a limited form of the ratio level variables; variables at the lower levels cannot, however, be recoded into higher levels of measurement.

Two people and a gar-den...and one Statcat.

Exhibit 3.3. Families by Size

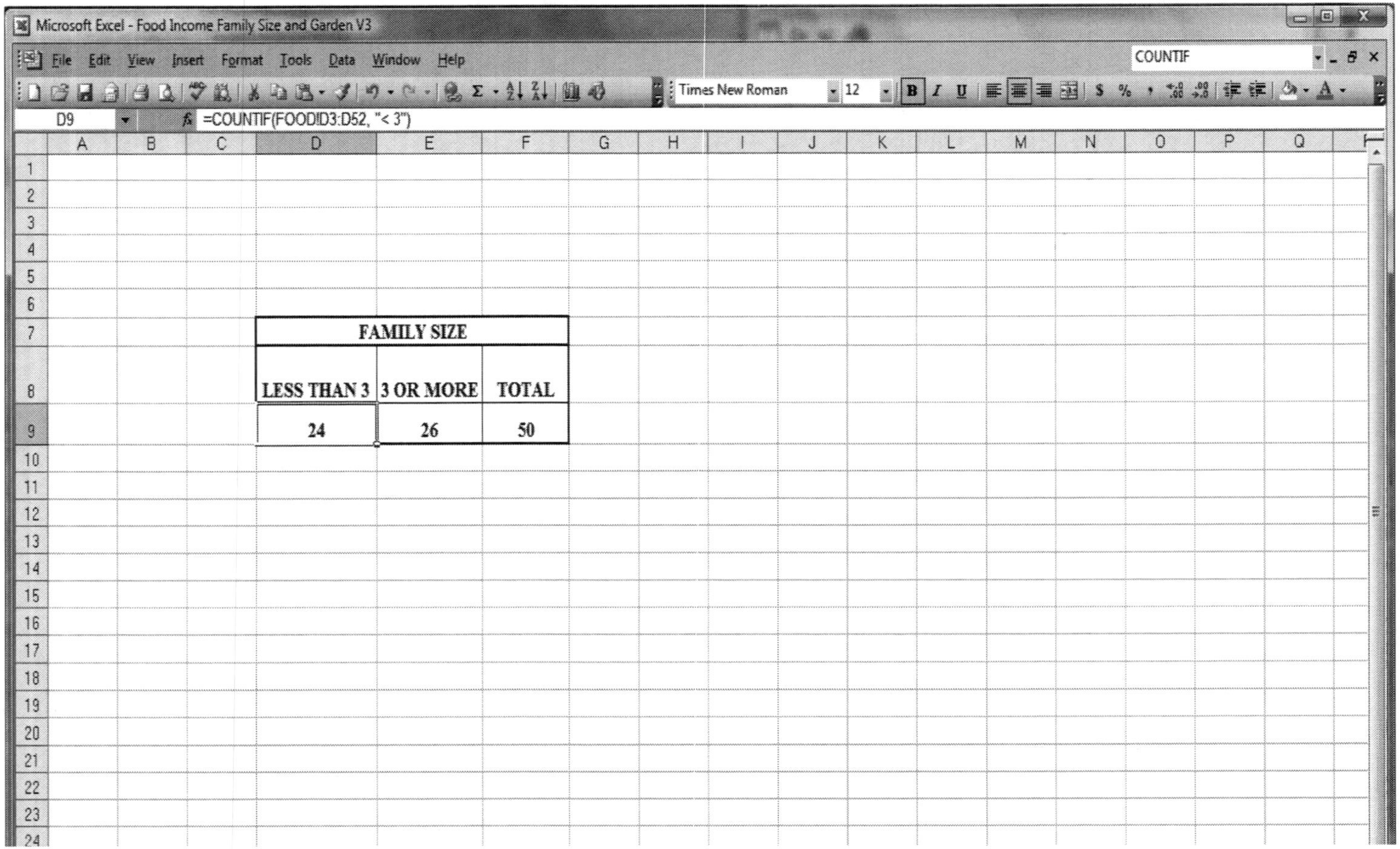

Microsoft Excel - Food Income Family Size and Garden V3

File Edit View Insert Format Tools Data Window Help

Times New Roman | 12 | **B** *I* U

D9 | fx =COUNTIF(FOODID3:D52, "< 3")

	FAMILY SIZE		
	LESS THAN 3	3 OR MORE	TOTAL
	24	26	50

You might ask why one would want to recode a ratio level variable into a lower level? The answer is to analyze its relationship with a lower level variable. For example, it does not make sense to have a table showing all 50 possible values of monthly family food expenditures relative to the presence of a garden. The table would have 50 rows and two columns (or 50 columns and two rows). However, by recoding month family food expenditures into say, three categories, high, medium, and low (thereby making it into an ordinal level variable), we can start to get a picture of the relationship between the presence of a garden and monthly family food expenditures. We will return to this subject in detail later in the book, but as a preview of things to come, take a look at Table 3.3, in which family food expenditures was recoded into three groups: Low (under $1,479); medium (between $1,479 and $2,149); and high ($2,149 and over). It shows that 88% (15 of 17) of the families with high food expenditures do not have a garden, and that 82% (14 of 17) of the families with low food expenditures have a garden. In this sample, there is clearly a relationship between the presence of a garden and monthly family food expenditures. We will turn again to this example when we discuss "inferring" from this sample to the population of families from which the sample was drawn.

Table 3.3. Presence of Garden by Monthly Family Food Expenditures

PRESENCE OF GARDEN	MONTHLY FAMILY FOOD EXPENDITURES			
	LOW (UNDER $1,479)	MEDIUM (BETWEEN $1,479 AND $2,149)	HIGH ($2,149 AND OVER)	TOTAL
YES	14	4	2	20
NO	3	12	15	30
TOTAL	17	16	17	50

D. Basic Mathematics (Fractions, Percents, Algebra)

If you need a review of basic mathematics, you should refer to a book. Here, I am only providing a refresher on some very simple concepts. To start, there are measures that focus on single numbers, such as the number of persons in a family and the total number of families in our sample data set. These are called absolute numbers. Another type of measure focuses on the relationship between two numbers. These are called relative numbers, and they are typically expressed as ratios, proportions, percentages, rates, or probabilities. All the relative measures are similar to each other, but each has a distinct meaning.

A ratio is simply one number divided by another. These could be any two numbers; they need not have any particular relationship to each other. To be useful, of course, the comparison of the two numbers should provide some type of meaningful information. For example, the ratio of gardens to families in our sample is 20/50.

A proportion is a special type of ratio in which the numerator is a subset of the denominator. Thus, we can view the ratio of gardens to families as the proportion of total families that have gardens, which is 0.40 = 20/50. If we multiply this proportion by 100, we have a "percent": 40% = 0.40*100. So, we can say that 40% of the families in our sample have gardens.

A rate is also a special type of ratio. Strictly speaking, a rate is the number of events occurring during a given time period divided by those at risk to the occurrence of those events. For example, the death rate is the number of deaths divided by the population exposed to the risk of dying and the birth rate is the number of births divided by the population exposed to the risk of giving birth over a given time period. The vacancy rate is the number of vacant housing units divided by the total number of housing units over a given time period. Can we call the 40% of families with gardens the "garden rate?"

ASSIGNMENT FOR CHAPTER 3

Enter the data found in Table 3.1 into a worksheet and save, using your name and assignment 3 as part of the file name (e.g., swanson.assign3.xls). Double check to make sure the data you entered match what is in Table 3.1.

Endnote

1. Dummy coding of a nominal level variables with two values (e.g., yes or no) makes the variable into a ratio level variable because there is a true zero (e.g., "no") and the distance between units is the same. A dummy-coded variable is, however, limited by the fact that it has only two values, which means that while some of the tools associated with numerical manipulation and inferential statistics can be used with it, not all can. As you will see in Chapter 12, "Relationships between Variables," you can use a dummy variable as the "independent variable" in a regression model, but not as the "dependent variable."

References

Bogardus, E. (1947). "Measurement of Personal-Group Relations." *Sociometry* 10: 306–11.
Edwards, A. (1957). *Techniques of Attitude Scale Construction*. Englewood Cliffs, NJ: Prentice-Hall.

Guttman, L. (1944). "A Basis for Scaling Qualitative Data." *American Sociological Review* 91: 139–50.

Hildebrand, D., J. Laing, and H. Rosenthal (1977). *The Analysis of Ordinal Data*. Beverly Hills, CA: Sage.

McIver, J., and E. Carmines (1981). *Unidimensional Scaling*. Beverly Hills, CA: Sage.

Reynolds, H. (1984). *The Analysis of Nominal Data*. Beverly Hills, CA: Sage.

Stevens, S. S. (1946). "On the Theory of Scales of Measurement." *Science* 103 (2684): 677–80.

4. Measuring the "Average" in a Set of Data

What's in a number? A rose by any other number would smell as sweet ... but zero still would not be a number.

A. What Is an "Average?"

An average is a number, and it can be just as mysterious as the idea of what a number is and simultaneously just as simple. The mystery underlying the idea of a number largely revolves around the necessity of including the concepts of zero and infinity (Reid, 2006; Seife, 2000). These two concepts lend a bit of perplexity to the question, "What is a number?" Not quite as mysterious as zero and infinity, but in many ways as equally perplexing as "What is a number?" is the question, "What is an average?" This perplexity exists despite the fact that just as we encounter numbers daily, we also hear the word "average" virtually every day—the temperature is below (or above) average for this time of year; your grade point average needs improvement; all of the children in this town are "above average," and so on.

From the perspective of this book, an average is a way to "summarize" data. What do I mean by "summarize?" Take a look again at Table 3.1. It has only 50 cases, but what can you tell me about this data set in five words or less? Not much, unless you "summarize" the data set. This is what averages do. For example, a nice way to summarize the variable "Family Size" is to look at its arithmetic mean, which is one of the three types of averages we will examine in this chapter. The arithmetic mean of family size is 3.26. This "average" provides a reference point for family size. For example, what is the size of your family? Is it above or below 3.26? The second type of average we will look at in this chapter is called the median. The median family size of our data set is 3.00. Finally, the third type of average we will look at is the mode. The mode for family size is 2.

So, we have three types of averages that we can use to summarize the variable of family size, the arithmetic mean (which I will shorten to simply "mean"), the median, and the mode. As you can see in our examples, they are not far apart, but none of them is equal to the other. The highest average family size, 3.26, is given by the mean, the lowest, 2.0, is given by the mode, and the average that falls in the middle for family size is the median, which is 3.00.

Let's look at each of these types of averages, starting with the mean.

Mean. This is the probably the most commonly used average. The mean is calculated by adding up the (interval or ratio) numbers in a set (e.g., a sample) and dividing that answer by the total number of cases. This is the only type of average that takes into account all the values of a given variable. To get mean family size, I simply had Excel sum up all of the 50 values of this variable and then divide that sum by 50. As you know, mean family size is 3.26. In essence, what the mean has done is allocate the total number of family members (169) equally across all the 50 families. We are stating this when we say that "on average, family size in our data set is 3.26." As you will see in Chapter 7, the formula for computing a mean is the same in a population as in a sample, but the notation differs so that one can quickly determine if a mean is from a sample or a population.

Recall Exhibit 3.1 in the preceding chapter, which showed (part of) the 50-family sample data set. The values for the variable "family size" are in column D, rows 3 to 52. To get Excel to calculate the mean of this variable, I used the command, "=AVERAGE(D2:D52)." This command can be placed in any cell in which you want mean family size to be displayed.

Two strong features of the mean are that it is easily calculated and has a straightforward interpretation. However, it has two weak features, both of which are linked to one another. The first weakness is that if you have a large number of small values and a few very large values in your data set, the mean becomes "skewed." This means that the few big numbers exert an extraordinary amount of influence. The result is that the mean is nearer to the bigger values, even though there are many more values that are small. It can also become "skewed" in the other direction if you have a few very small values and a lot of big numbers. In the case of family size, we can see that most of the families consist of two people.

However, the presence of the only four "big" families, two with seven, one with eight, and one with nine members, "pulls" the mean away from two. In fact, if these four families were not in our data set, the mean would be 2.87. The other weakness is that even only one value is really different from the rest, the mean average can be dramatically affected. In the example of family size, suppose that the family with nine members had instead 21 members. This single change would move the mean from 3.26 all the way up to 3.50. In statistical terms, the presence of a value dramatically different from the rest is called an "outlier." We can see that the mean is sensitive to outliers. It is the weak feature of the mean that leads to the use of the median, which is not sensitive to outliers.

The mean has a long history of use in the social sciences. In 1835, the Belgian Adolphe Quetelet (Stigler, 1986: 170–72) published data on the "average man." Interest in this type of analysis remains strong today; 170 years after Quetelet's work appeared, Kevin O'Keefe (2005) came out with "The Average American: The Extraordinary Search for the Nation's Most Ordinary Citizen." Quetelet's work also has a long history of use in astronomy and navigation (Stigler, 1986).

As an example of the use of the mean with ordinal data, I turn to a study of social distance conducted by Nix (1993) at the University of Mississippi. In the study, Nix used the social distance scale developed by Emory Bogardus (1947), which has a range from 1.0 to 7.0, with 1.0 representing the least social distance and 7.0 the most. Nix found that the mean social distance score was 2.43 for all students, while for the international students, it was 2.50. Thus, there was, on average, more social distance between the international students and other students, than for the student body as a whole.

Median. This type of average is the middle number in a data set. It simply finds the point at which half of the values are above it and half below it (or nearly so). Turning again to our example using family size, Excel finds the median to be 3.00. Note that this is less than the mean, 3.26. This is so because the median is not influenced by a few numbers that are different from the rest. It also is the case that it is not sensitive to outliers. If the family with nine members added 12 more people and became a family with 21 members, the median would still remain at 3.00—approximately one half of the families have more than three members and one half have fewer than three members. The term used by statisticians for this feature is "robustness." The median is a "robust" summary measure because it is not influenced by outliers. However, unlike the mean, the median does not take into account all of the values (e.g., it does not care that one family has nine, 21, or 230 members).

Recall again Exhibit 3.1, which has the values for the variable "family size" in column D, rows 3 to 52. To get Excel to calculate the median of this variable, I used the command, "=MEDIAN(D2:D52)." This command can be placed in any cell in which you want median family size to be displayed.

An early appearance of the median is found in the 80th annual report of the Massachusetts Board of Education (1917), where on page 104 the report discusses the median income of high school principals relative to their median years of experience, median years as principal, and median numbers of pupils in their schools.

Mode. This type of average is the value that occurs most often for a given variable. Unlike the mean, which can be influenced by outliers such that the mean may be not very "representative" of most of the values in the presence of outliers, the mode is very "representative," in the sense that it is totally focused on the values that occur most often and ignores other values. This can be a problem if the values are something like monthly family food expenditures and are carried out to two decimal points. For example, the family represented by case number 12 reports a monthly food expenditure of $780.06 while the family represented by case number 33 reports a monthly food expenditure of $780.70. For all practical purposes, these two values are the same, but to the mode, they are two different numbers. Thus, to use it effectively, the values of some variables may need to be "rounded" in some manner. In the case of these two families, the numbers could be rounded to the nearest $5.00, which would yield $780 for both. The mode does not have this kind of problem with a variable like "family size," which has a mode of 2.

Recall again Exhibit 3.1, which has the values for the variable "family size" in column D, rows 3 to 52. To get Excel to calculate the mode of this variable, I used the command "=MODE(D2:D52)." Just as getting Excel to calculate the mean and the median, this command can be placed in any cell in which you want the mode of family size to be displayed.

There are other types of "averages," but for purposes of this book, they are not used. Two others include the Harmonic Mean and the Geometric Mean. All of the types of averages are collectively referred to as "measures of central tendency," in that they are aimed at finding the center of a distribution of values for a given variable.

B. What Is the "Center of a Distribution?"

In considering the mean, median, and mode as measures of central tendency, the analogy of a teeter-totter is useful. Here, the mean would be the center point. That is, it represents the point at which the "weight" (values) of all the numbers is balanced. The median represents the point where half of the values are above it and half below it, but it may not be balanced. The mode, in turn, would be the place on the teeter-totter where most of the numbers are found, and like, the median, it would not necessarily be the point at which the teeter-totter is balanced. The relative positions of these three

summary measures, especially the mean and median, can tell us a great deal about the distribution of the values of a given variable.

Figure 4.1 shows the distribution of family size for our 50-case sample data set as a "bar chart" (called a "column chart" by Excel). It is the "center" of this distribution that our three types of averages are designed to get at. Recall that 3.26 is the mean, 3.00 is the median, and 2.00 is the mode. As you look at Figure 4.1, place these numbers mentally at the bottom of the chart according to the family size they fall closest to, respectively. It is clear that the mode and the median are closer to the family size of most of the families, while the mean is a bit higher. It is the presence of the "outlier" family sizes of 7, 8, and especially 9, that are "pulling" the mean away from the size of most of the families. This suggests something important about a distribution. If the mean is higher than the median, then the distribution is not symmetrical, but "skewed" to the right as is seen in Figure 4.1.

Figure 4.1. Family Size Distribution

As an example of the importance of the relative positions of the mean and median

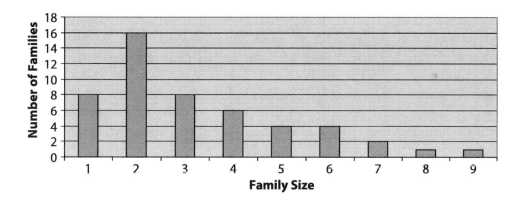

(and the mode) in saying something about the distribution of values for a given variable, suppose that the distribution of family size in our sample data was not skewed, but instead symmetrical as shown in Figure 4.2, which again is in the form of a bar chart. Can you tell where the mean, median, and mode are by looking at the graph shown in Figure 4.2? Here is a hint: They are all one and the same number (or very nearly so, given rounding error). This is the case in every "symmetrical" distribution.

We will return to the idea of the "shape" of a distribution in Chapter 5.

Figure 4.2. Example of a Symmetrical Distribution

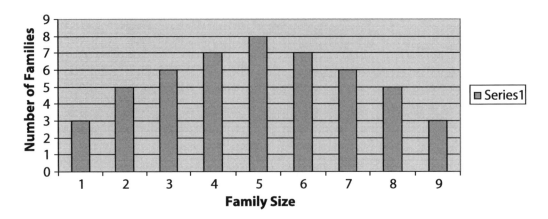

C. Averages and Level of Measurement

Recall from Chapter 3 that "Level of Measurement" refers to a system of classifying numbers in terms of what operations can legitimately be done with them. Recall also that this book uses the fourfold classification system developed by Stevens (1946), which classifies numbers as being (1) nominal; (2) ordinal; (3) interval; and (4) ratio. Where do the mean, median, and mode fit into this system? The mean can always be used with variables measured at the interval and ratio level and sometimes with variables measured at the ordinal level (I return to this subject later). Unless a nominal level variable is "dummy coded" into two values, 0 and 1, the arithmetic average makes no sense applied to nominal level variables. The median is much like the mean, in that it can always be used with variables measured at the interval and ratio level and sometimes with variables measured at the ordinal level. However, it makes no sense to apply the median to variables measured at the nominal level, even those that are dummy coded. The mode can be applied to variables measured at all four levels, nominal, ordinal, interval, and ratio.

In terms of ordinal level variables, the use of mean and the median depends greatly on how they are structured and whether or not they have been "scaled."

ASSIGNMENT FOR CHAPTER 4

Using Table 3.1 (which you put into a worksheet as assignment 3), calculate the mean, median, and mode of each of the variables and enter them in an appropriate place. Use the "Border" feature under the "Format" tab to create a nice-looking table for all of this work, and include labels for the variables (you may have to insert new rows above your first row of data). Print a hard copy of the table. Keep working on this table until it looks like something you could present or put in a paper. Save your file (e.g., swanson.assign4.xls) and print a hard copy of the final version of the table.

References

Bogardus, E. (1947). "Measurement of Personal-Group Relations." *Sociometry* 10: 306–11.

Massachusetts Board of Education. 1917. *Eightieth Annual Report of the Board of Education.* Public Document No. 2. Boston: Wright and Potter Printing Co. State Printers.

Nix, V. (1993). "Assessing the Existence of Social Distance and Factors That Affect Its Magnitude at a Southern University. Senior Undergraduate Thesis, Department of Sociology. Oxford, MS: University of Mississippi (http://socialdistancesurvey.com/data/SDSU.pdf).

O'Keefe, K. (2005). *The Average American: The Extraordinary Search for the Nation's Most Ordinary Citizen.* New York: Public Affairs Books.

Reid, C. *From Zero to Infinity: What Makes Numbers Interesting.* London, England: A. K. Peters Ltd.

Seife, C. (2000). *Zero: The Biography of a Dangerous Idea.* New York: Penguin Books.

Stigler, S. (1986). *The History of Statistics: The Measurement of Uncertainty Before 1900.* Cambridge, MA: Belknap Press.

5. Measuring the Dispersion of a Set of Data

A. What Is "Dispersion?"

Dispersion refers to the spread of values for a given variable. Suppose that we have the same variable, each with five numbers, from two different data sets as follows: (Data set 1) 10, 12, 10, 11, and 12; and (Data set 2) 10, 12, 15, 11, and 12. In comparing these two sets, we can see that all of the values are the same except that one of the "10" values in the first data set is replaced by the value "15" in

DISPERSION

the second one. The presence of the value "15" causes the second data set to have more dispersion in it than does the first. That is, the second data set is more "spread out." This simple example gives you an idea of what the concept of dispersion is, because it is easy to see that the second data set is more spread out than the first. But what if the two data sets had the following five values, respectively: (Revised Data set 1) 11, 13, 9, 12, and 13; and (Revised Data set 2) 10, 12, 13, 11, and 12? It is not as easy to see which of the two data sets is more spread out in the revised example. It is in answer to questions like the one just posed that measures of dispersion have been developed. Having a measure gives us a precise answer. In fact, I can tell you that in the revised example, the first data set has more dispersion than the second, as you will see later. We also will see later that the idea of dispersion is tied very closely to the idea of an "average."

As was the situation for measuring an average (mean, median, and mode) discussed in the preceding chapter, you will probably not be surprised to learn there are different ways to measure dispersion. You also will not be surprised to learn that the four levels of measurement (nominal, ordinal, interval, and ratio) also play a role in selecting which measure to use.

Range. The range is used to identify the highest and lowest scores. The range of the variable "family size" in the 50-family sample data set is 8 (8=9–1). Recall Exhibit 3.1 in the preceding chapter, which showed (part of) the 50-family sample data set. The values for the variable "family size" are in column D, rows 3 to 52. There is no "RANGE" function in Excel. So, to get Excel to calculate the range of this variable, I had to use two commands, MAX (which finds the maximum value) and MIN (which finds the minimum value), as follows, "=MAX(D2:D52) – MIN(D2:D53)." That is, I can subtract the minimum value from the maximum value. This command can be placed in any cell in which you want the range of family size to be displayed. As an example, the maximum value of the variable "Monthly Family Food Expenditures" is $3,211.64 ("=MAX(B3:B52)") and the minimum value is $732.52 ("=MIN(B3:B52)"), so the range is $3,211.64 – $732.52 = $2,488.12 ("=MAX(B3:B52) – MIN(B3:B52)").

Percentiles, Quartiles, and Quintiles. These are closely related in that percentiles divide a range of values into 100ths, quartiles into fourths, and quintiles divide a range of values into fifths. The idea is that if you divide the values into 100 (nearly) equal parts after ordering them, the values corresponding to these parts are the 1st, 2nd, 3rd, …, 100th percentiles. Similarly, the 25th, 50th, 75th, and 100th percentiles are the 1st, 2nd, 3rd, and 4th quartiles, while the 20th, 40th, 60th, 80th, and 100th percentiles correspond to the 1st, 2nd, 3rd, 4th, and 5th quintiles. Notice that the 50th percentile = the 2nd quartile = the median; and that the 100th percentile = the 4th quartile = the 5th quintile = the maximum value.

Again, using the family size variable from our 50-family sample data set (Table 3.1 and Exhibit 3.1 in the preceding chapter), where the values for the variable "family size" are in column D, rows 3 to 52, I can use the following Excel command to find the 50th percentile as follows: "=PERCENTILE(D3:D52, .5)." To find the 25th percentile, I would use "=PERCENTILE(D3:D52, .25) To find the 2nd quartile (which is also the median and the 50th percentile) I would use "=QUARTILE(D3:D52, 2)." To find the first quartile (which also is the 25th percentile), I would use "=QUARTILE(D3:D52, 1)."

Again, as actual examples of percentiles, quintiles, and quartiles, I will use the variable "monthly family food expenditures," which is found in cells B3 through B52 of the data set. The 50th percentile of this variable (which is the median and the 2nd quartile) is $1,857.61 ("=PERCENTILE(B3:B52, .5))." This tells us that 50% of the families spend less than $18,57.61 monthly on food. The 25th percentile (which is the 1st quartile) is $1,286.91 ("=PERCENTILE(B3:B52, .25)," which returns the same value as "=QUARTILE (B3:B52, 1)"). This tells us that 25% of the families spend less than

$1,286.91 monthly on food and 75% spend more. The fourth quintile (which also is the 80th percentile) is $2,449.92 ("=PERCENTILE(B3: B52, .8)"). This tells us that 80% of the families spend less than $2.449.92 monthly on food and 20% spend more than this amount. The fourth quartile is $3,211.64, which is equal to the maximum value, the 100th percentile, and the fifth quintile.

Standard Deviation. The standard deviation shows the relationship that all of the values have to their mean (I will explain more about this shortly).[1] The standard deviation is found by dividing the number of cases into the square root of the sum of the squared deviations from the mean of all the scores. Quite a mouthful to say, isn't it? This is why statisticians and mathematicians have developed a more concise "language" to show formulas. And this is as good a time as any to introduce some notation so that you can see how the preceding statement regarding the standard deviation is expressed much more concisely using mathematical terms.

Let

X = a "variable"

X_i = the value of case "i", where i = 1 to n: $X_1, X_2, X_3, ..., X_n$

n = the number of cases in our sample)

Σ = summation sign

ΣX_i = the sum of the values for variable x from 1 to n.

Using the five case example data set I introduced at the start of this chapter (which has the values 10, 12, 10, 11, and 12), the mean of this variable would be expressed as

$\Sigma X_i /n$ = (10+12+10+11+12)/5 = 55/5 = 11. Using the term "$\Sigma X_i /n$" is much more concise for defining the mean than writing "sum all of the values of a variable and then divide this sum by the number of cases."

The standard deviation of this variable would be expressed as

$$\{[\Sigma(X_i - mean)^2]/5\}^{.5} = \{[(10-11)^2 + (12-11)^2 + (10-11)^2 + (11-11)^2 + (12-11)^2]/5\}^{.5}$$
$$= \{[-1^2 +1^2 -1^2 + 0^2 +1^2]/5\}_{.5}$$
$$= \{[1+1+1+0+1]/5\}^{.5}$$
$$= \{[4]/5\}^{.5}$$
$$= \{0.80\}^{.5}$$
$$= 0.894$$

Using the term "$\{[\Sigma(X_i - mean)^2]/n\}^{.5}$" is much more concise for defining the standard deviation than writing "divide the number of cases into the square root of the sum of the squared deviations from the mean of all the variables in question."

As you can see in the preceding formula and its steps, the difference between each value and the mean is squared ($(10-11)^2$, $(12-11)^2$, $(10-11)^2$, $(11-11)^2$, $(12-11)^2$). This accounts for both positive and negative deviations from the mean. If we did not square these differences, the sum of the differences would equal zero (0 = (10–11) + (12–11) + (10–11) + (11–11) + (12–11) = (-1 +1 -1 +0 +1). The squared differences are then summed (1+ 1+1 +0 +1 = 4). The sum of these squared differences is then divided by the number of cases ((4/5) = .80). Finally, so that the result is expressed not in "squared values" but in the original values, the square root is taken of the quotient, formed by dividing the number of cases into the sum of the squared differences ($(.80)^{.5} = .894$) .

Recall Exhibit 3.1 in the preceding chapter, which showed (part of) the 50-family sample data set. The values for the variable "family size" are in column D, rows 3 to 52. To get Excel to calculate the standard deviation of this variable, I used the command "=STDEV(D3:D52)," which returned the number 2.00 as the standard deviation of family size. This command can be placed in any cell in which you want the standard deviation of family size to be displayed. The standard deviation of monthly family food expenditures is $670.20 ("=STDEV(B3:B52)").

The square of the standard deviation is called "variance." Again, using the family size variable, we could calculate its variance by placing the command "=VAR(D3:D52)" in any cell where we wanted to display the variance of family size. Doing this for family size reveals that its variance is 4.00 (the square of 2.00, the standard deviation). Doing this for monthly family food expenditures yields a really big number—$499,166.58—which is the square of $670.20, the standard deviation of monthly family food expenditures.

Both the variance and the standard deviation are actually types of averages. Compare the formula for the mean, ($\Sigma X_i/n$), to the formula for the standard deviation, ($\{[\Sigma(X_i - \text{mean})^2]/n\}^{.5}$). The relationship is perhaps even more clear if we rewrite the formula for the mean to an algebraic equivalent, $\{[\Sigma(X_i - 0)^2]/n\}^{.5}$. This is a "long way around" to get to the mean, but the formula will yield the same result as $\Sigma X_i/n$, and by displaying the mean the "long way around," we can see that the formula for the standard deviation is basically the same, except instead of subtracting zero from each X_i, we subtract the mean from each X_i.

In Chapter 7, I will show you that there is a slight difference in how the standard deviation is computed in a sample vs. a population. What you just saw is the formula for computing the standard deviation in a population. To help keep track of whether or not it is from a sample or a population, the notation is different as well.

The Coefficient of Variation. This is a measure of "relative dispersion." It takes a measure of "absolute dispersion," such as the standard deviation, and divides it by the average. It is used in comparisons. I will actually discuss this more in the next section.

C. The "Other Type" of Error

The preceding discussion brings us back to three points. The first is the one made in the last sentence of the first section of this chapter, which was that the idea of dispersion is tied very closely to the idea of an "average." The second is the point made earlier in this section, that the standard deviation shows the relationship between all of the values and their mean. In fact, it basically shows the mean of the differences between all of the values and their mean. The relationship between the standard deviation and the mean is not only very close, it also has a long history (Stigler, 1986). Relating some of this history will prepare you for the more conceptually difficult issues to come. This brings us to the third point, which is found at the end of Section C in Chapter 1 in regard to the "other type of error."

The "other type of error" to which I am referring is directly related to the mean and standard deviation. As an illustration of this type of error, think back to the first data set we used in this chapter as an example of spread: (Data set 1) 10, 12, 10, 11, and 12. Suppose that these five numbers represented five guesses from five different people on the distance from the floor to the ceiling of the living room in a friend's apartment. We can see that there is some "spread" in the guesses, but it looks like the ceiling is no less than 10 feet and no more than 12 feet from the floor. Further, suppose that the true height is between 10 and 12 feet. Knowing this, we would guess that the ceiling was neither less than 10 feet nor more than 12 feet high. If we guessed 12 and the actual distance was 10, we would be "long" by two feet. Similarly, if we guessed 10 and the true height was 12, we would be "short" by two feet. Given that the actual height is between 10 and 12 feet, +2 and -2 represent the range of our potential error. What if we want to "minimize" the error in our guess? How might we proceed? The answer is that we would take the mean of the 5 values, which we know is 11. How does this minimize error? The answer reveals something about the intimate relationship between the mean and the standard deviation, namely that the mean is the single number in a set of data for a given variable (or outside of it) that minimizes the sum of the squared differences between it and the rest of the values for this same variable in the data set. This means that when we get the standard deviation for a set of values, the minimum value is found when we use the mean: $\{[\Sigma(X_i - mean)^2]/5\}^{.5}$. If we substitute any other value for the mean in the preceding formula, the standard deviation will be larger. We return to this very important idea in the last section of this chapter. Before going there, however, let's look at some history of this type of error.

Back in the day when Europeans were navigating and otherwise observing celestial objects like stars with crude instruments, they discovered that their measurements were, not surprisingly, often in error. This was a major problem for sailors trying to find their way from one land mass to another. To minimize errors, it became common practice among oceangoing navigators by the middle of the 18th century to take several measurements with their crude instruments and then find the arithmetic mean of these measures (Stigler, 1986: 16). They were clever enough to make the repeated measurements under the same conditions (e.g., when the deck of the ship was at its high point while rolling and pitching and by the same person). They followed this practice for a very simple reason: They found that taking the mean of these repeated measurements under the same conditions and by the same person reduced the error. Does this sound like what you did to measure the height of your friend's living room ceiling? It is. In turn, the use of the mean led to the realization that "dispersion" should also be measured. After all, if the "spread" is very narrow (as is the situation with the height of the ceiling), we would have more confidence that the mean is close to the "true" value than would be the case if the spread was quite wide.

The idea of "combining data" (i.e., taking the mean) as a way of minimizing error was published posthumously in 1722 in a book on the "theory of errors," written by Roger Cotes, an English mathematician, before he died in 1766 (Stigler, 1986: 16). However, it appears that another English mathematician, Thomas Simpson, first applied the theory of probability to the discussion of errors of observation, and described a "probability curve" (Stigler, 1986: 88–90). This, in turn, led to a great deal of work, much of which culminated in the idea of "Least Squared Error." This is a topic we take up in discussing regression in Chapter 12, which, in turn, is yet another way in which the concept of "average error" associated with the standard deviation is used.

Now, let us return to discussing the coefficient of variation with your new knowledge of "average error" in hand. Suppose that you are a navigator on a sailing ship in 1850 that is bound for Pearl Harbor, Hawai'i, several days out of the San Francisco Bay. Per our discussion of early navigation, you have taken five measurements and find that the arithmetic mean of these five measurements is 2,000 miles, with a standard deviation of 20 miles. This is a case where "dispersion" can be interpreted as average error. That is, you have an "average error" of 20 miles in your five estimates of the distance to Pearl Harbor.

At the same time, suppose that another sailing ship is departing from the area of Hilo, Hawai'i, for Pearl Harbor (about 200 miles) and its navigator has estimated the distance at 200 miles using the mean of five measurements. Suppose further that the standard deviation of this estimate is also 20 miles. As you can see, the average distances are quite different, but the absolute average error is the same in that both you and the other navigator s have a standard deviation of 20 miles. You may be thinking, "Hey, I am doing a far better job in that I am estimating a distance that is about ten times that of the other navigator." This is where the coefficient of variation comes in, since you would use it for purposes of comparing your average error with that of the other navigator. That is, you want to measure your "relative average error" against the "relative average error" of the other navigator. For your ship out of San Francisco, the coefficient of variation is 0.001 (where 0.001 = 20/2,000), while for the ship from Hilo it is 0.10 (where 0.10 = 20/200). Relatively speaking, the "error" for the navigator bound for Pearl Harbor from Hilo is 100 times the average error in your estimate. You did some nice navigational work, relatively speaking.

D. Dispersion and Level of Measurement

You have probably figured out that like the mean, both the standard deviation and variance are always appropriate for use with ratio and interval level variables. They are sometimes appropriate for ordinal level variables, and they are never appropriate for use with nominal level variables, except in the case of nominal level variables with two values that have been "dummy coded" as 0 and 1. This also applies to the range, except in the case of dummy coded nominal level variables, where the range is always 1.00.

In terms of when the standard deviation can be used with ordinal level variables, recall the discussion in the preceding chapter, where if an ordinal variable has been scaled and an appropriate response scale is used with the ordinal variable in question, then it is easier to justify the use not only of the mean, but also the median (Hildebrand, Laing, and Rosenthal, 1977).

As an example of the use of the standard deviation with ordinal level data, recall the study by Nix (1993), who found that the mean social distance score was 2.43 for all students at the University of Mississippi, while for the international students, it was 2.50. From these mean scores, we concluded that the social distance for international students was greater, on average, than that for the students as a whole (and by deduction, the domestic students). We can now add to our analysis the standard deviations of the social distance scores for these two groups of students. For all students, the standard deviation was 1.29, while for the international students it was 1.31. Thus, we see that the international students not only have a higher average level of social distance than the general student body, but that as a group they vary more.

Taken as a group, percentiles, quintiles, and quartiles also are always appropriate for ratio and interval level variables, and sometimes with ordinal variables. They are never appropriate for nominal level variables, and if applied to a dummy coded nominal level variable, they are like the range: not very informative.

So what are we left with to describe dispersion in a nominal level variable? Not much. There is a measure called the Index of Qualitative Variation (IQV) that looks at the number of cases in each of the categories making up the values in a nominal level variable (Swanson, 1973, 1975). It works under the idea that "maximum dispersion occurs when the cases are spread equally across the categories" and minimum dispersion occurs when they are all concentrated in one of the categories. If we had 100 cases spread across four categories, maximum dispersion occurs when all four categories have 25 cases, and minimum dispersion occurs when one of the categories has all 100 cases in it while the other three have zero cases in each of them. The idea underlying IQV is that we divide a summary measure of the actual distribution of cases across the categories by a summary measure of the maximum possible distribution. It also operates under the idea that dispersion should be presented as a relative, not an absolute, measure, which means that IQV is zero when there is minimum dispersion and 1 when there is maximum dispersion.

Here is an example of how IQV works. Suppose we have 100 cases spread across four categories, A through D, as follows: 20 cases in category A; 40 cases in category B; 10 cases in category C; and 30 cases in category D. The "maximum dispersion" would occur if each of the four categories had 25 cases in it. This can be summarized immediately as 1/4 or .25. That is, maximum dispersion would take place in a nominal level variable with four categories if each category had 25% of the cases in it.

In regard to the actual dispersion component of the IQV measure, there are four steps. The first step is that IQV sums up the squared values of the number in each category. The second step is that the numbers in each category are summed, and the sum is then squared. The third step is to divide the sum of the squared values by the square of the summed values. The fourth and final step is to subtract the results of the previous step from 1.00.

With the summary measure of the maximum dispersion in hand as well as the summary measure of the actual dispersion, the next step is to subtract the former from 1 and divide the result into the results for the summary measure of the actual dispersion.

These steps can be more concisely presented using mathematical notation:

$$IQV = \{1 - [\Sigma(X_i)^2]/[(\Sigma X_i)^2]\}/[1 - 1/n]$$

Using our example, we find that

$$\Sigma(X_i)^2 \quad = (20)^2 + (40)^2 + (10)^2 + (30)^2$$
$$= 400 + 1,600 + 100 + 900$$
$$= 3,000$$
$$\Sigma X_i)^2 \quad = (20 + 40 + 10 + 30)^2$$
$$= (100)^2 = 10,000$$

and $\{1 - [\Sigma(Xi)2]/[(\Sigma Xi)2]\} = 1 - (3,000/10,000) = .70$

since $[1 - 1/n] = 1 - .25 = .75$

we have IQV = .70/.75 = .93.

We can interpret the "dispersion" of our hypothetical nominal variable with the 100 cases distributed among the four categories as shown above as follows: IQV shows that this variable is at 93% of its maximum variation. In other words, it is highly dispersed. Unfortunately, Excel does not have a function to calculate IQV. It can, however, be constructed using Excel formulas for summing, squaring, and the like.

E. The Shape of a Set of Data

Any discussion of the shape of a set of data is largely aimed at the distribution of values of a given variable measured at the interval or ratio level. The mean and the standard deviation are both important in shaping a distribution. The mean gives its "balance point," and the standard deviation, its spread. Two other measures are important in assessing the shape of a distribution, "skew" and "kurtosis."

"Skew" refers to the degree of asymmetry of a distribution. Recall Figure 4.1 in Chapter 4, which showed the distribution of family size for our 50-case sample data set as a "bar chart" (called a "column chart" by Excel). I have copied this same graph into this chapter as Figure 5.1. In looking at Figure 5.1, you can see the distribution is not symmetrical, but, in fact, skewed to the right. Also recall from the discussion in Chapter 4 that if the mean is higher than the median, then the distribution is not symmetrical, but "skewed" to the right. That is, it has a "tail" to the right. In regard to the variable family size, the mean (3.26) is, in fact, lager than the median (3.00). This is another confirmation that this variable is skewed to the right. But how skewed is it? To answer this question, we turn to the formula used by Excel to measure skew, which is defined as follows in mathematical terms:

$$\text{Skew} = [n/((n-1)*(n-2))*\{\Sigma[((x_i - \text{mean})/(\text{standard deviation}))^3]\}$$

Using the preceding definition, Excel finds the skew in Figure 5.1 to be equal to 1.0168, signifying a moderately right-skewed distribution.

Figure 5.1. Family Size Distribution

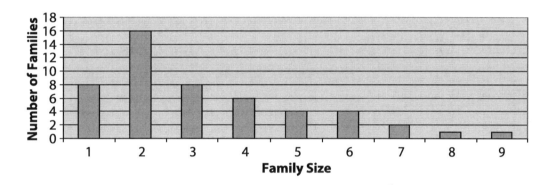

As an example of negative skew (a tail to the left), Figure 5.2 shows the distribution of monthly family food expenditures (recoded into "low," "medium," and "high") for families without a garden. The food expenditures were recoded using the 33rd and 66th percentiles so that the distribution would have three ordinal values, where "low" is less than \$1,479 spent monthly on food, "medium" is between \$1,479 and \$2,149 spent monthly on food, and "high" is more than \$2,149 spent monthly on food. Excel calculated the skew of the distribution shown in Figure 5.2 as -1.293, indicating a moderately left-skewed distribution.

Figure 5.2. Distribution of Family Food Expenditures for Families Without a Garden

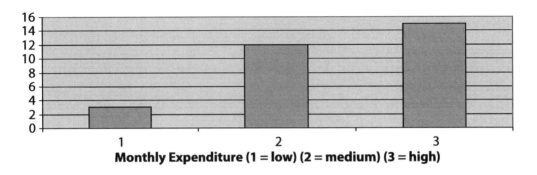

Monthly Expenditure (1 = low) (2 = medium) (3 = high)

If skew is equal to zero, then the distribution is symmetrical. As an example of this, I have copied Figure 4.2 (the hypothetical example of a symmetrical distribution of family size), here as Figure 5.3.

Figure 5.3. Example of a Symmetrical Distribution

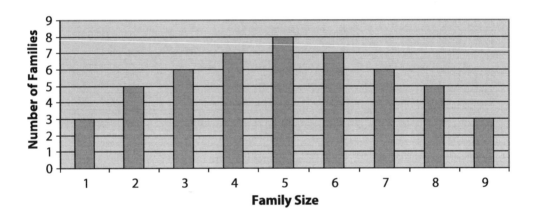

You may recall from Chapter 4 that in a symmetrical distribution, the mean, median, and mode are all equal. In this hypothetical distribution of family size, the mean, median, and mode are all equal (when the mean is rounded to the nearest whole number). The skew of this hypothetical distribution is zero when the Excel calculation (-0.06) is rounded to the nearest whole number. The mean (rounded from 5.04), median, and mode are all equal to 5.0.

The other measure of the shape of a distribution is kurtosis. This is a measure of the degree of "peakedness" of a distribution, usually taken relative to a symmetrical distribution . Distributions that are quite "peaked" are called leptokurtic. Those that are not very peaked at all, are called mesokurtic, and those that are neither leptokurtic nor mesokurtic are called platykurtic. Using again our example in Figure 5.3, Excel calculates the kurtosis for these data as -0.899.

The formula for kurtosis is pretty complicated. If you bring up "KURT" (Excel's name for its kurtosis function), you can see it. In general, a positive score indicates a relatively "peaked" distribution, while negative scores indicate more "flat" distributions. As we can see by the kurtosis score (-0.899) for the data in Figure 5.3, the distribution is not very peaked.

Figure 5.4. Hypothetical Leptokurtic Distribution of Family Size

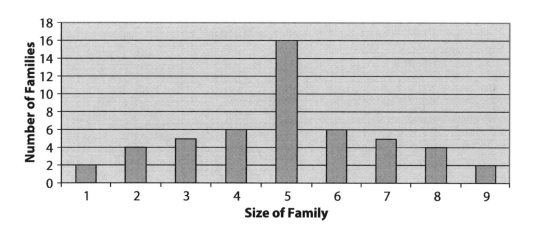

Figure 5.4 provides a revision of the data underlying Figure 5.3 so that they are more "peaked." Excel calculates the kurtosis of these data as -0.3032. Comparing this to the score for Figure 5.3 shows that as the distribution becomes more peaked (leptokurtic), the kurtosis score moves toward a positive score, although the data in Figure 5.4 are not sufficiently leptokurtic to bring its kurtosis score into the positive range.

F. Proof that the Mean Minimizes the "Sum of Squared Differences"[2]

The mean has a very important mathematical feature. It is the single number in a set of data for a given variable (or outside of it) that minimizes the sum of the squared differences (often called the sum of the squared errors) between it and the rest of the values for this same variable in the data set. The fact that the mean is the single number that minimizes variance and its square root, the standard deviation is very important in inferential statistics. As we go along in the book, this will become more apparent. To make sure you know that the mean does this (and to give you some practice reading mathematical and statistical notation), this section provides a simple algebraic proof that the mean is the unique estimate that minimizes the sum of squared errors. There are more sophisticated proofs using calculus, but this algebraic proof is useful for illustrating the fundamental concepts. I did not develop this proof. It is part of the general body of statistical knowledge. The basic form of the proof is to calculate the sum of squared errors for an arbitrary value, and then to show that it necessarily includes all the sum of squared errors for the mean plus some additional error.

Here, the arbitrary value is represented as "$\hat{Y}$," and the mean is defined as

$$\overline{Y} = \frac{\sum_{i=1}^{n} Y_i}{n}$$

Note that instead of using "X" to define a variable, "Y" is used.
For an arbitrary value, the sum of squared errors is

$$SSE = \sum_{i=1}^{n} (Y_i - \hat{Y})^2$$

Since $\overline{Y} - \overline{Y} = 0$, this representation of zero can be used within the parentheses without changing the sum of squared errors. That is,

$$SSE = \sum_{i=1}^{n} (Y_i + (\overline{Y} - \overline{Y}) - \hat{Y})^2$$

Rearranging the terms slightly and regrouping yields

$$SSE = \sum_{i=1}^{n} [(Y_i - \overline{Y}) + (\overline{Y} - \hat{Y})]^2$$

Squaring inside the summation gives

$$SSE = \sum_{i=1}^{n} [(Y_i - \overline{Y})^2 + (Y_i - \overline{Y})(\overline{Y} - \hat{Y}) + (\overline{Y} - \hat{Y})^2]$$

Breaking the sums apart yields

$$SSE = \sum_{i=1}^{n} (Y_i - \overline{Y})^2 + \sum_{i=1}^{n} 2(Y_i - \overline{Y})(\overline{Y} - \hat{Y}) + \sum_{i=1}^{n} (\overline{Y} - \hat{Y})^2$$

The last term contains no subscripts, which allows this sum to be replaced with

$$n(\overline{Y}_i - \hat{Y})^2$$

and the factor with no subscripts in the second term can be moved outside the summation, giving

$$SSE = \sum_{i=1}^{n}(Y_i - \overline{Y})^2 + 2(Y - \hat{Y})\left[\sum_{i=1}^{n}(Y_i - \overline{Y})\right] + n(\overline{Y}_i - \hat{Y})^2$$

The bracketed term is the sum of the deviations about the mean and must therefore equal zero. So, the preceding equation reduces to

$$SSE = \sum_{i=1}^{n}(Y_i - \overline{Y})^2 + n(\overline{Y} - \hat{Y})^2$$

If the arbitrary value equals the mean, then $\overline{Y}_i - \hat{Y} = \overline{Y} - \overline{Y} = 0$ and the last term in the prior equation is zero. Thus, when the arbitrary value is the mean,

$$SSE = \sum_{i=1}^{n}(Y_i - \overline{Y})^2$$

and if the arbitrary value equals anything other than the mean, the sum of the squared difference is increased by

$$n(\overline{Y}_i - \hat{Y})^2$$

Hence, the mean is the single number that minimizes the sum of squared differences; any other value necessarily gives a larger sum of squared differences. At the same time, the mean is the single number that minimizes both the variance and the standard deviation. Any other arbitrary value increases them by the factor, $n(\overline{Y}_i - \hat{Y})^2$, where $\hat{Y}$ is the arbitrary value.

ASSIGNMENT FOR CHAPTER 5

1. Using the table that resulted from your work on assignment 4, calculate the standard deviation, maximum, minimum, range, kurtosis, and skew of each of the variables and enter them in an appropriate place. Revise your table accordingly, using the "Border" feature under the "Format" tab and "Text" to create a nice-looking table for all of this work. Print a hard copy of the table. Keep working on this table until it looks like something you could present or put in a paper. Save your file (e.g., swanson.assign5.xls), and print a hard copy of the final version of the revised table.

2. Using MS-Word, write a short essay on the variables in your table and their summary statistics. This should cover about two or three pages. When done, save the MS-Word file (e.g., swanson.assign5.docx).

Endnotes

1. According to Stigler (1986: 328), the pioneering English statistician Karl Pearson introduced the term "standard deviation" around 1892 or 1893.

2. This proof is adapted from one provided by Gary H. McCelland, Department of Psychology, University of Colorado, http://samiam.colorado.edu/~mcclella/twt/sseproof.pdf.

References

Hildebrand, D., J. Laing, and H. Rosenthal (1977). *The Analysis of Ordinal Data*. Beverly Hills, CA: Sage.

Nix, V. (1993). "Assessing the Existence of Social Distance and Factors That Affect Its Magnitude at a Southern University. Senior Undergraduate Thesis, Department of Sociology. Oxford, MS: University of Mississippi (http://socialdistancesurvey.com/data/SDSU.pdf).

Stigler, S. (1986). *The History of Statistics: The Measurement of Uncertainty Before 1900*. Cambridge, MA: Belknap Press.

Swanson, D. A. (1975). "The Division of Labor: Further Exploration in the Analysis of an Ecological Concept." *Western Sociological Review* 6 (summer): 72–82.

Swanson, D. A. (1973). "A Comment on the Clemente and Gibbs-Martin Measures of the Division of Labor: Their Relation to Amemiya's Index of Economic Differentiation." *Pacific Sociological Review* 16 (July): 401–405.

6. Data from the Probability Perspective

Pascal says his probability of winning is nil.

A. What Is Probability?

The easy answer is that it is a number from zero to one. However, getting to this "easy answer" was not an easy task. There is a lot of history behind it. An important piece of this history took place in 1654, when the French mathematician Blaise Pascal wrote a letter to his colleague, Pierre De Fermat. In this letter, Pascal described a method for predicting mathematical futures (Devlin, 2008). Although it is clear that the idea of probability is an old one (Ceccarelli, 2007; Stigler, 1986, 1999), the modern foundations can be traced to Pascal's letter. The correspondence between Pascal and Fermat developed into the modern concept of risk management, which permeates the modern world. As the correspondence between Pascal and Fermat suggests, probability theory arose in the 17th century, but even they were not unaware of their predecessors, such as the Italian Pacciolo, who wrote the first book we know of on probability in 1494 (David, 1962).

The letter from Pascal to Fermat was sparked by a question from a gambler (Chevalier de Méré) on why a new way he was betting on certain rolls of dice was not as profitable as an older way he had used. Pascal worked through the problem and found that the probability of winning using the new approach was only 49.1%, compared to 51.8% using the old approach (Devlin, 2008). The problem proposed by the gambling nobleman was the start of correspondence between Pascal and Pierre de Fermat. They continued to exchange their thoughts on mathematical principles and problems through a series of letters.

Not long after learning about the correspondence between Pascal and Fermat, the Dutch mathematician and scientist, Christian Huygens, published the first book on probability in 1657, which was focused on problems associated with gambling (Apostol, 1969). This focus fit in with the times, in that there was a lot of gambling and interest in making money from it. The gamblers soon made books on probability theory quite popular.

A turning point in the orientation toward gambling occurred for probability theory when Pierre Laplace came out with a book in 1812, *Théorie Analytique des Probabilités*, in which he applied the ideas of probability to a wide range of scientific and mathematical problems (Apostol, 1969). A difficulty that emerged in Laplace's work was the conflict between trying to define probability sufficiently narrow enough to satisfy mathematicians, while remaining sufficiently broad so that it would apply to a wide range of phenomena (Apostol, 1969). In 1933, a monograph by a Russian mathematician, Andrey N. Kolmogorov, proposed an "axiomatic" approach as the basis for probability and its definition, which became the basis for the modern theory of probability (Apostol, 1969).

You need to have a basic idea of what probability is—and isn't—since it is a fundamental component of inferential statistics. For purposes of the book, I use what is known as the "frequentist" perspective (Lehmann, 2011). This perspective sees "probability" as a way of expressing knowledge as opposed to the more "personal belief" used by Bayesians that some event will occur, or has occurred (Lehmann, 2011; Savage, 1972). The frequentist approach sees probability as based in data and uses statistical inference and inductive logic to arrive at decisions under conditions of uncertainty generated by the use of sampling to gather data. In concert with this approach is the idea that the data are drawn from a random process, which yields a random "event." In turn, the probability of this event occurring is found in the "relative frequency" (hence the name "frequentist") of its occurrence under repeated drawings "in the long run."

How does relative frequency work? Consider a set of "draws" that can produce a number of results. The collection of all results is called the sample space. We start to form the sample space by considering all different collections of possible results. For example, rolling a die can produce six possible results—this is the starting point. One set of possible results is made up of the even numbers on a die (2, 4, and 6). This is an element of the sample space of die rolls. These sets are called "events." In this case, (2,

4, and 6) represent the event that the die falls on any of the three even numbers. If the results that actually occur fall in a given event, the event is said to have occurred.

As stated at the outset of this chapter, a "probability" is the assignment of a value from zero to 1.0 for every event. We now add to that the requirement that the event made up of all possible results must be assigned a probability of 1.0. In the example of rolling a single die, the event (1, 2, 3, 4, 5, 6) is assigned 1.0, since when you roll the die, one of these six possibilities will come up with 100% certainty. We also need to define the events that have a probability of zero. The number 7 would have a probability of zero assigned to it, since it does not appear on a six-sided die.

The relative frequency approach is usually based on empirical (real-life) frequencies, but uses theory as well. For example, we might toss a coin ten times and get heads six times. However, if we do this ten-time coin toss 1,000,000 times, we would find in the long run that we have exactly or very close to an average of five heads per ten-toss set. Theory says that if you do this an infinite number of times, we will get exactly an average of five heads per ten-toss set.

B. Basic Probability Concepts

You will need to spend some time on the definitions and terms that are covered in this section. Understanding them is essential to your ability to get through the rest of the book. We start with some terms:

Let

$P(A)$ = Probability of event A

$P(B)$ = Probability of event B.

With these terms we can now define one of two fundamental rules in probability, the "Mutually Exclusive Events" rule, also known as the "OR" rule:

$$P(A) \text{ OR } P(B) = P(A) + P(B)$$
$$P(A \text{ OR } B) = P(A) + P(B) - P(C)$$
$$\text{where } C = P(AB).$$

Venn diagrams can be used to show the preceding ideas in graphic form (Venn, 1888). By looking at the Venn diagram in Exhibit 6.1, can you "see" the difference between $P(A) \text{ OR } P(B) = P(A) + P(B)$, on the one hand, and $P(A \text{ OR } B) = P(A) + P(B) - P(C)$, on the other? Part of being able to see this difference is understanding "c = P(AB)."

Exhibit 6.1. A Venn Diagram Showing Mutually Exclusive Events

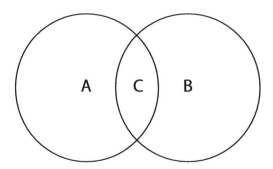

In addition to the "OR" rule, the second important rule in probability is called the "Independent Events" rule or "AND" rule. It is defined as follows:

P(A) AND P(B) = P(A)* P(B).

What do the "OR" and "AND" rules actually mean, you may ask? Let's look at this from the standpoint of those 17th-century gamblers who got Pascal and Fermat on the road to providing a modern foundation for probability theory. To start, suppose that we have a standard deck of playing cards (N = 52), in which there are four aces, four kings, four queens, …, and so on, down to four 2s. There also are 26 red cards (13 hearts + 13 diamonds) and 26 black cards (13 spades + 13 clubs). Now, suppose I ask you to choose a card at random from the deck. Can you tell me what the probability is that you will pick out a jack (of any suit)? How about using 4/52 = .08? What is the probability it is a red card? How about 26/52 = .50? Now, what is the probability of drawing either an ace or a jack? Using the "OR" rule, it turns out to be (4/52) + (4/52) = .08 + .08 = .16. What is the probability of drawing a red jack? Using the "AND" rule, it is (26/52)*(4/52) = .04 = (2/52).

Are you ready for some more? What is the probability of drawing either an ace or a spade? This is where we would use P(A OR B) = P(A) + P(B) – P(C), where C = P(AB), as follows: (4/52) + (13/52) – (1/52) = .08 + .25 – .02 = .31 Why do we subtract (1/52) ?

Because P (ace) and P (spade) are not mutually exclusive (i.e., C = P(AB)). The ace of spades can be drawn (1/52). Thus, we need to eliminate it so that we have only the probability of drawing an ace or a spade.

What is the probability of drawing a family with a garden from our sample of 50 families? Exhibit 3.1 shows that 20 of the 50 families have a garden, so the probability of drawing one of them is .40 = 20/50. What is the probability of drawing a family with three members or a family with five members? This requires use of the "OR" rule in the form of P(A) OR P(B) = P(A) + P(B). What is the probability of drawing a family with a garden or a family with four members from our sample? This also requires use of the "OR" rule, but in the from of P(A OR B) = P(A) + P(B) – P(C).

C. The Concept of a Random Variable and Expectation

A random variable is a variable whose value results from a measurement on some type of random process. It is a numerical description of an outcome. If you roll a die, the outcome is between 1 and 6, but it is not fixed. (If it were, those casinos in Las Vegas would not be there.) So, you can look at a random variable as something that is not fixed, but can take on different values. "Family Size" in our 50-family data set is another example of a random variable. If you randomly selected a family from this data set, its size will neither be less than one nor greater than nine, but other than this we do not know in advance which size you will get until you draw a given family. However, we could give the probabilities of drawing different family sizes (e.g., the probability of drawing a family of nine is .02 = 1/50). Hence, "Family Size" is a random variable.

So, what is the "expected value" of family size? To find this, we would multiply the different values of family size by their probability of occurrence, which is the proportion of times they occur (as shown in Figure 4.2, for example). In the sample, eight of the 50 families have one member, 16 have two members, eight have three members, six have four members, four have five members, four have six, two have seven, one has eight, and one family has nine members. Thus, the expected value of family size is = [1*(8/50)] + [2*(16/50)] + [3*(8/50)] + [4*(6/50)] + [5*(4/50)] + [6*(4/50)] + [7*(2/50)] + (8*(1/50)] + [9*(1/50)] = [1*.16] + [2*.32] + [3*.16] + [4*.12] + [5*.08] + [6*.08] + [7*.04] = [8*.02] + [9*.02] = [.16] + [.64] + [.48] = [.48] + [.40] + [.48] + [.28] + [.16] + [.18] = 3.26. Does this number look familiar? It should—it is mean family size. Thus, viewed from the probability perspective, the mean of a given variable is the "expected value" from a data set (distribution) of the values for a given variable. The preceding calculation also shows that the mean is a "weighted" average of the values of a variable, where the "weights" are given by the relative frequency of each value (e.g., the relative frequency of a family size of 3 is 8/50 = .16). We will never see a family size of 3.26, but if we drew a lot of samples of, say, size 20 from our 50-family data set, the average of all of the sample averages would tend toward 3.26 (the "long run" view from the frequentist perspective). The value may not be expected in the general sense—the "expected value" itself may be unlikely or even impossible (such as having 2.5 children), just like the sample mean. As we will see later, this example of the "long run" average is an important part of the mathematical theory underlying statistical inference. That is, the "hypothetical" mean of the means found in an infinite number of samples of size n is a random variable.

D. Probability Distributions: Concepts and Examples

What is a probability distribution? In large respect, you already know the answer based on what you read in the preceding sections. Using again the "relative frequency" definition of probability (from the frequentist perspective), there are two fundamental types:

discrete (nominal, ordinal) and continuous (ratio, interval). In a discrete probability distribution, if a variable, "x," has a set of k values, x_1, x_2, x_3, ..., x_k, with probabilities p_1, p_2, p_3, ..., p_k, where $p_1 + p_2 + p_3 +, ..., + p_k = 1.00$, we can say that a discrete probability distribution for x has been defined. The function p(x) which has the respective values p_1, p_2, p_3, ..., p_k for x = x_1, x_2, x_3, ..., x_k is called the probability function or frequency function of x. Returning to another example from gambling, consider now not just a single die but a pair, and let the sum of the "points" obtained in rolling the dice be denoted by x. Thus, the (discrete) probability distribution for it is given in Exhibit 6.2.

Exhibit 6.2. The Probability Distribution for Rolling a Pair of Dice

x	P(x)
2	1/36
3	2/36
4	3/36
5	4/36
6	5/36
7	6/36
8	5/36
9	4/36
10	3/36
11	2/36
12	1/36

Because x can assume certain values with given probabilities, you already know that it is a random variable. It is "discrete" because only whole numbers are in it.

The preceding ideas can be extended to the case where a variable, "x," has a "continuous" set of values. That is, x can take on values like 2.3, 3.001, and so on. The relative frequencies of these values become in the theoretical or limiting case a continuous curve. The total area under the curve (see Exhibit 6.3) bounded by the x axis is equal to 1.0, and the area under the curve between lines x = a and x = b is the probability that x is between values a and b.

Exhibit 6.3. Areas Under a Curve as Probabilities

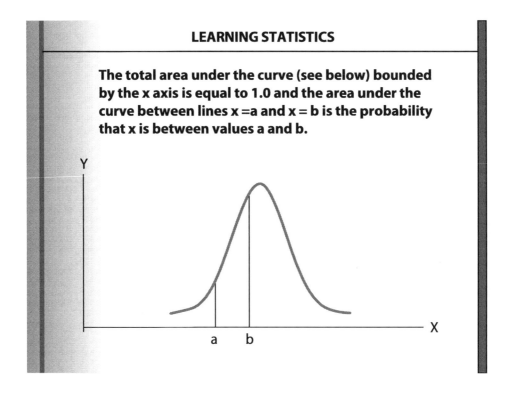

LEARNING STATISTICS

The total area under the curve (see below) bounded by the x axis is equal to 1.0 and the area under the curve between lines x = a and x = b is the probability that x is between values a and b.

P(x) is called the probability density function, and when such a function is found, we say that a continuous probability density function for x has been defined. X is then often called a "continuous random variable."

We can think of probability distributions as theoretical or "ideal limiting forms" of relative frequency distributions when the number of observations is very large (think of an infinite number of ten-toss coin flips). For this reason, we can think of a given probability distribution as being a distribution for a given population, while a given relative frequency distribution can be viewed as a sample drawn from a given population.

E. The Normal Curve

A very important type of continuous probability distribution in inferential statistics is a mound-shaped, symmetrical curve that is called the "normal curve." It is defined by the rather complex formula: $P(X) = \{1/((2\Pi\sigma2)(.5))\}\ \{e^{(-(X-\mu)2/(2\sigma2))}\}$. However, with this formula, you only need to know the mean (μ) and the standard deviation (σ) of a set of numbers to create the curve. As you will see in Chapter 9, you will find that you are using the sample mean ($\bar{X}$) for the population mean (μ) and the sample's standard error (se) for the population standard deviation (σ) in order to do statistical reference. Exhibit 6.3 gave an example of the normal curve, as do Exhibits 6.4 and 6.5.

Exhibit 6.4. An Example of the Normal Curve

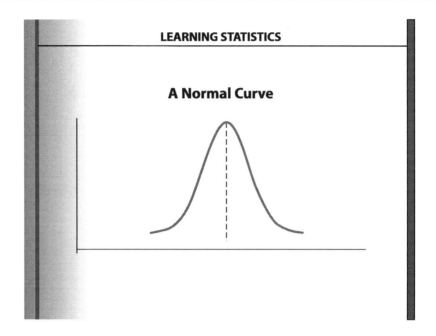

Exhibit 6.5. Another Example of the Normal Curve

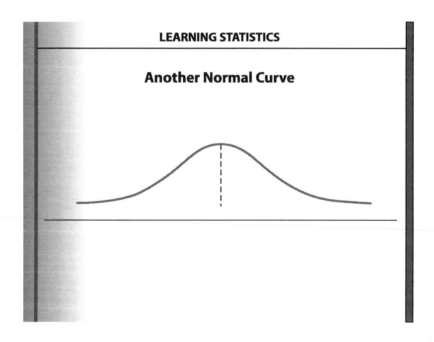

Both of the preceding normal curves were generated from the formula P(X) = {1/ ((2Пσ2)(.5))} {e$^{(-(X-\mu)2/(2\sigma2))}$}, using the mean (μ) and the standard deviation (σ). In the case of the example found in Exhibit 6.5, its standard deviation was greater than the standard deviation of the normal curve shown in Exhibit 6.4.

As suggested by Exhibit 6.3 and the discussion of means and standard deviations, we can find locations in the normal curve, a feature that is used in inferential statistics. For example, if we have a set of values of a random variable that is normally distributed (whether condensed as is shown in Exhibit 6.4 or spread out as is shown in Exhibit 6.5), then approximately 67% of the sample scores fall within one standard deviation of the mean (plus or minus). Approximately 95% of the scores would then fall within two standard deviations of the mean (plus or minus), and 99% of them fall within three standard deviations of the mean (plus or minus), as is shown in Exhibit 6.6. Note also that in a normal curve, the mean, median, and mode are all one and the same number.

Exhibit 6.6. The Mean, Median, and Mode in the Normal Curve and Approximate Areas Under it Defined by 1, 2, and 3 Standard Deviations

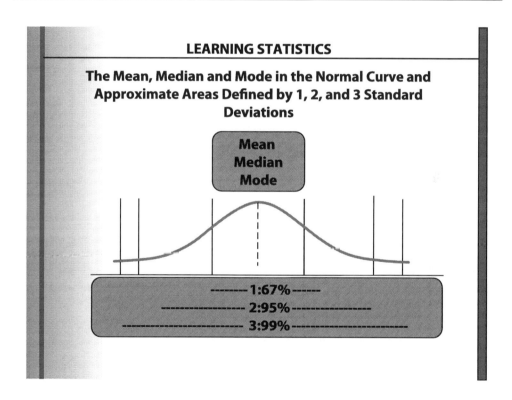

The preceding can be used to find a variable value when probability is known. First, we transform the values of the variable X into the number of standard deviations from the mean into a "Z" score, as follows: $Z_i = (Xi - \mu)/\sigma$. You can see in Exhibit 6.7 how the Z score is related to the standard deviation in a normal curve. The Z scores (i.e., 1, 2, and 3) at the bottom of the normal curve shown in Exhibit 6.6 correspond approximately to 67%, 95%, and 99% of the area under the normal curve, respectively. Similarly, in

Exhibit 6.7, the "standard error" scores (i.e., 1, 2, and 3) at the bottom of the normal curve shown in Exhibit 6.7 also correspond approximately to 67%, 95%, and 99% of the area under the normal curve, respectively.

Exhibit 6.7. Z Scores as Standard Errors (SE) and Areas Under the Standard Normal Curve

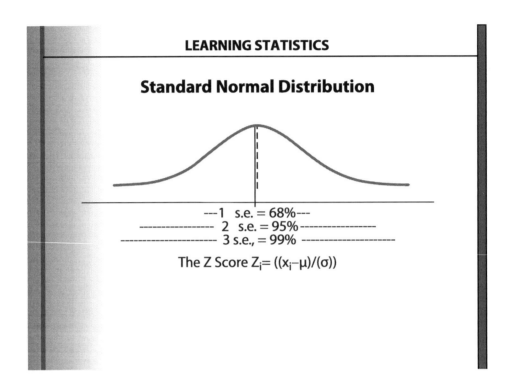

Once you have a Z score, you can use a "table of probabilities" associated with it. An example of such a table is given in Exhibit 6.8, where the shaded area in the normal curve depicted at the top of the table represents the probability associated with a given Z score. In this particular table, the area associated with a Z score is given from the center of the normal curve and the Z score. As an example of the use of the kind of table shown in Exhibit 6.8, suppose we want to know the probability of having more than 115 students show up for a lecture, given that the distribution is normal with a mean of 75 and a standard deviation of 20? First, we find the Z score associated with 115, which is $Z = [(x_1 - \mu)/\sigma] = [(115 - 75)/20] = +2$. Once we have this score, we find it on the type of table shown in Exhibit 6.8 and look at the "probability" associated with it. Doing this, we see that a standard (Z) score of +2 relates to approximately 0.4772 of the area between the center of the distribution (the mean is at the center, which in this case is 75) and the Z score. If we wanted the probability of having less than 115 students show up, we would have to add the area to the left of the center to the 0.4472, which yields 0.9772 (where .5 +.4772 = .9772). However, we want the probability that 115 or more would show up. Thus, we want the area to the right of the Z score. To get this, we subtract all of the area to the left (.9772) from 1.000, which yields 0.0228. Thus, we expect the probability of having more than 115 students show up for a lecture to be about 2.3% (where 2.3 ≈ 0.0228*100).

What if I wanted the probability that between 75 and 115 students would show up? The answer is .4472, or about a 44.72% probability. What is the probability that less than 115 show up? The answer is 0.9772, or about a 97.72% probability. What is the probability that between 100 and 115 show up? To get this, we need the Z score for 115, which we know is 2.0, and the Z score for 100, which is 1.25 = (100–75)/20). The probability shown in the table in Exhibit 6.8 associated with a Z score is .3944. This gives the probability of having between 75 and 100 students show up. We already know that the probability of having between 75 and 115 students show up is 0.4472. By subtracting 0.3994 from 0.4472, we get the probability that between 100 and 115 will show up, or 0.0478 (where 0.0478 = 0.4472 – 0.3994). Thus, the probability of having between 100 and 115 students show up is about 4.8%.

Excel has a "distribution function" for the standardized normal distribution, which means that you do not have to find a table like the one shown in Exhibit 6.8, but instead you can use this function to get the probability of a given value. The function is called "NORMDIST." Here is an example of using it with the number of students expected to show up for a lecture (e.g., the probability of having 115 or more show up is about 2.3%). First, we need to put the numbers in Excel. Suppose we put the number 115 in cell R5, the mean (75) in cell R6 and the standard deviation (20) in R7. I would then turn to the "NORMDIST" function. Its format is "=NORMDIST(value, mean, standard deviation, cumulative)." The term "value" corresponds to the value that you want to find the probability for (e.g., 115). The term "mean" corresponds to the mean (e.g., 75) of the variable for which you want to find the value, while the term "standard deviation" corresponds to the variable's standard deviation (e.g., 20). The term "cumulative" corresponds to the choice of having the probability returned that represents all of the area to the left of the Z score or the probability returned that represents "exact probability area." We want the former, so we would use "TRUE" in the "cumulative" location (if you want the latter, you use "FALSE" in the "cumulative" location). However, as was the case in using the table in Exhibit 6.8, we have to subtract the probability we obtain from "NORMDIST" to get the probability to the right of the Z score. So, to get the probability of having 115 or more show in up in cell R8, here is the statement that goes into cell R7: "=1 – (NORMDIST(R5, R6, R7, TRUE))." Doing this would return "0.02275" in cell R7, which we can round to 0.023. Multiplying this by 100 yields 2.3%, which matches what we got from the table in Exhibit 6.8.

Exhibit 6.8. Probabilities Associated with Z Scores in the Normal Distribution[1]

Areas under the Standard Normal curve from 0 to Z

z	0	1	2	3	4	5	6	7	8	9
0.0	0.0000	0.0040	0.0080	0.0120	0.0160	0.0199	0.0239	0.0279	0.0319	0.0359
0.1	0.0398	0.0438	0.0478	0.0517	0.0557	0.0596	0.0636	0.0675	0.0714	0.0754
0.2	0.0793	0.0832	0.0871	0.0910	0.0948	0.0987	0.1026	0.1064	0.1103	0.1141
0.3	0.1179	0.1217	0.1255	0.1293	0.1331	0.1368	0.1406	0.1443	0.1480	0.1517
0.4	0.1554	0.1591	0.1628	0.1664	0.1700	0.1736	0.1772	0.1808	0.1844	0.1879
0.5	0.1915	0.1950	0.1985	0.2019	0.2054	0.2088	0.2123	0.2157	0.2190	0.2224
0.6	0.2258	0.2291	0.2324	0.2357	0.2389	0.2422	0.2454	0.2486	0.2518	0.2549
0.7	0.2580	0.2612	0.2642	0.2673	0.2704	0.2734	0.2764	0.2794	0.2823	0.2852
0.8	0.2881	0.2910	0.2939	0.2967	0.2996	0.3023	0.3051	0.3078	0.3106	0.3133
0.9	0.3159	0.3186	0.3212	0.3238	0.3264	0.3289	0.3315	0.3340	0.3365	0.3389
1.0	0.3413	0.3438	0.3461	0.3485	0.3508	0.3531	0.3554	0.3577	0.3599	0.3621
1.1	0.3643	0.3665	0.3686	0.3708	0.3729	0.3749	0.3770	0.3790	0.3810	0.3830
1.2	0.3849	0.3869	0.3888	0.3907	0.3925	0.3944	0.3962	0.3980	0.3997	0.4015
1.3	0.4032	0.4049	0.4066	0.4082	0.4099	0.4115	0.4131	0.4147	0.4162	0.4177
1.4	0.4192	0.4207	0.4222	0.4236	0.4251	0.4265	0.4279	0.4292	0.4306	0.4319
1.5	0.4332	0.4345	0.4357	0.4370	0.4382	0.4394	0.4406	0.4418	0.4429	0.4441
1.6	0.4452	0.4463	0.4474	0.4484	0.4495	0.4505	0.4515	0.4525	0.4535	0.4545
1.7	0.4554	0.4564	0.4573	0.4582	0.4591	0.4599	0.4608	0.4616	0.4625	0.4633
1.8	0.4641	0.4649	0.4656	0.4664	0.4671	0.4678	0.4686	0.4693	0.4699	0.4706
1.9	0.4713	0.4719	0.4726	0.4732	0.4738	0.4744	0.4750	0.4756	0.4761	0.4767
2.0	0.4772	0.4778	0.4783	0.4788	0.4793	0.4798	0.4803	0.4808	0.4812	0.4817
2.1	0.4821	0.4826	0.4830	0.4834	0.4838	0.4842	0.4846	0.4850	0.4854	0.4857
2.2	0.4861	0.4864	0.4868	0.4871	0.4875	0.4878	0.4881	0.4884	0.4887	0.4890
2.3	0.4893	0.4896	0.4898	0.4901	0.4904	0.4906	0.4909	0.4911	0.4913	0.4916
2.4	0.4918	0.4920	0.4922	0.4925	0.4927	0.4929	0.4931	0.4932	0.4934	0.4936
2.5	0.4938	0.4940	0.4941	0.4943	0.4945	0.4946	0.4948	0.4949	0.4951	0.4952
2.6	0.4953	0.4955	0.4956	0.4957	0.4959	0.4960	0.4961	0.4962	0.4963	0.4964
2.7	0.4965	0.4966	0.4967	0.4968	0.4969	0.4970	0.4971	0.4972	0.4973	0.4974
2.8	0.4974	0.4975	0.4976	0.4977	0.4977	0.4978	0.4979	0.4979	0.4980	0.4981
2.9	0.4981	0.4982	0.4982	0.4983	0.4984	0.4984	0.4985	0.4985	0.4986	0.4986
3.0	0.4987	0.4987	0.4987	0.4988	0.4988	0.4989	0.4989	0.4989	0.4990	0.4990
3.1	0.4990	0.4991	0.4991	0.4991	0.4992	0.4992	0.4992	0.4992	0.4993	0.4993
3.2	0.4993	0.4993	0.4994	0.4994	0.4994	0.4994	0.4994	0.4995	0.4995	0.4995
3.3	0.4995	0.4995	0.4995	0.4996	0.4996	0.4996	0.4996	0.4996	0.4996	0.4997
3.4	0.4997	0.4997	0.4997	0.4997	0.4997	0.4997	0.4997	0.4997	0.4997	0.4998
3.5	0.4998	0.4998	0.4998	0.4998	0.4998	0.4998	0.4998	0.4998	0.4998	0.4998
3.6	0.4998	0.4998	0.4999	0.4999	0.4999	0.4999	0.4999	0.4999	0.4999	0.4999
3.7	0.4999	0.4999	0.4999	0.4999	0.4999	0.4999	0.4999	0.4999	0.4999	0.4999
3.8	0.4999	0.4999	0.4999	0.4999	0.4999	0.4999	0.4999	0.4999	0.4999	0.4999
3.9	0.5000	0.5000	0.5000	0.5000	0.5000	0.5000	0.5000	0.5000	0.5000	0.5000

ASSIGNMENT FOR CHAPTER 6

1. Open the Excel file you created in assignment 5 and find the probability of having:
   a. $3,000 or more in monthly family food expenditures;
   b. Less than $3,000 in monthly family food expenditures;
   c. Having between $2,000 and $3,000 in monthly family food expenditures.
2. Save your results (e.g., swanson.assign6.xls).

Endnote

1. Adapted from Appendix Table 2 in Zelditch (1959).

References

Apostol, T. (1969). *Calculus, Volume II, 2nd ed.* New York: John Wiley and Sons.

Ceccarelli, G. (2007). "The Price for Risk-Taking: Marine Insurance and Probability Calculus in the Late Middle Ages." *Electronic Journal for History of Probability and Statistics* 3: 1–26 (http://www.jehps.net/Juin2007/Ceccarelli_Risk.pdf).

David, F. N. (1962). *Games, Gods, and Gambling.* London, England: Charles Griffin and Co. Ltd.

Devlin, K. (2008). *The Unfinished Game: Pascal, Fermat, and the 17th Century Letter That Made the World Modern.* Philadelphia: Perseus Books.

Lehmann, E. (2011). *Fisher, Neyman, and the Creation of Classical Statistics.* Dordrecht, The Netherlands: Springer.

Savage, R. (1972). *The Foundations of Statistics, 2nd rev. ed.* New York: Dover Publications.

Stigler, S. (1999). *Statistics on the Table: The History of Statistical Concepts and Methods.* Cambridge, MA: Harvard University Press.

Stigler, S. (1986). *The History of Statistics: The Measurement of Uncertainty Before 1900.* Cambridge, MA: Belknap Press.

Venn, J. (1888). *The Logic of Chance: An Essay on the Foundations and Province of the Theory of Probability with Especial Reference to Its Logical Bearings and Its Application to Moral and Social Science, and to Statistics, 3rd Edition Rewritten and Enlarged.* London, England: MacMillan.

Zelditch, M. 1959. *A Basic Course in Social Statistics.* New York: Henry Holt and Company.

7. Data Collected in Samples

A. What Is a Sample?

In Chapter 1, we looked at the five types of error that can occur in the collection and assembly of data, one of which only occurs in samples. This brought up the question: Why not eliminate samples, so we could focus on the other four types of error? The answer was that the driving force behind using samples is the cost of collecting data, and keeping costs down is important when it comes to assembling data. As an example of cost, the 2000 U.S. Census cost about $6.5 billion (Yacyshyn and Swanson, 2011). This comes out to $23.29 per person, given that 281,421,906 people were counted. As you can see, collecting and assembling information on an entire "population" of interest can be quite costly. It also requires a lot of planning. Even before the 2000 census was completed, the staff at the U.S. Census Bureau was working on plans for the 2010 census.

As you can guess, it is simply neither practical nor financially feasible to conduct an annual census for the United States. It is, however, both practical and financially feasible to conduct sample surveys much more frequently than once every ten years. The "American Community Survey" is one such survey that the U.S. Census conducts on a "rolling" basis throughout a given year. It collects information that is very similar to what has been collected in the U.S Census. The U.S. Government Accountability Office (2004) reports that having an annual sample of about 4.9 million households for the American Community Survey costs about $750 million. At about 11% of the cost of the 2000 census, over the course of once every ten years, this sample allows data to be collected much more frequently than the census for about the same cost as the decennial census.

So, what is a sample, exactly? It is a subset of a population, where a "population" represents a collection of items of interest, such as people, families, households, all of the caribou in Alaska, all of the computer chips coming off an assembly line, and so on. The idea of a population can become very abstract, but even so, the population in question usually has some attachment to what we call reality, since sampling is used to make decisions. Typically, the population from which the sample is drawn is very large. Samples are designed, data are collected, and "statistics" are calculated from the sample data in order to make inferences from the sample to the population from which it is drawn. The idea is that we can make decisions about the population as a whole by using information from a sample.

A complete sample is a set of objects from a population that includes all of the objects that satisfy a set of well-defined selection criteria. That is, a complete sample is a "census." For instance, a complete sample of the housing stock in the United States would include all the housing units, vacant and occupied, single family and multifamily, permanent and temporary, within the boundaries of the United States. This basically is what the U.S. Census does every ten years, as it counts all of the people who reside in the country.

The idea of a population is flexible, not fixed. For example, I can view all of the students in a statistics course as the "population" of interest for some purposes, but for other purposes, I might view them as one component of the population of students found across all of the courses I am teaching in a given term. We also can take samples from samples. For instance, we can take a random sample of 10 families from our sample of 50, and treat the entire sample of 50 as a "population" from which our sample of 10 is taken.

A desirable characteristic of a sample is one that is "representative" of the population from which it is drawn. For example, if we wanted a representative sample of adults (18 years and over) residing in Hawai'i in terms of age, we would like to have about 81% of the sample be aged 18–64 and the remaining 19% age 65 and over, since these percentages would match the 2010 census distribution for adults in Hawai'i. We could, of course, more finely tune our idea of "representativeness" in terms of age groups and also combine age with sex, race, and ethnicity, if we were seeking a sample representative of the adult population of Hawai'i in terms of its age-sex-race-ethnic composition.

Even more important than the idea of "representativeness" is the idea of having an "unbiased" sample. This means that the sample has not "excluded" anybody in principle. In other words, there is no "coverage error." One of the best ways to get a representative and unbiased sample is to use "random sampling," which is a sample in which each member of the population has a known, nonzero chance of being selected. There are several variations on "random" sampling that can accomplish this, including simple random samples, systematic samples, stratified random samples, and cluster random samples. As a result, an important part of a sample is how the data are collected.

B. Sample Types

There are two major types of samples: (1) "Probability"; and (2) "Nonprobability." A probability sample—also known more commonly as a random sample or a scientific sample—is one in which each item in the population from which the sample is drawn has a known, nonzero chance of being selected as part of the sample. A nonprobability sample is simply any sample in which each item in the population may have a nonzero change of being selected in a sample, but the probability of selection is not known. That is, a nonprobability sample is any that is not a probability sample.

There are several types of probability samples, including simple random samples, stratified random samples, cluster random samples, and systematic samples. To describe this in sampling terms, let me start with the following definitions.

Let
N = the number of cases in the sampling frame (the population);
n = the number of cases in the sample;
$f = n/N$ = the sampling fraction.

With the preceding in hand, we can now look at a simple random sample, a stratified random sample, a systematic sample, and a cluster random sample.

Simple Random Sample. The objective is to select n units out of N, such that every member of N has an equal chance. To do this, one would use a table of random numbers, computer random number generator, or mechanical device. Sampling can be done with or without replacement, where $f=n/N$ is the sampling fraction. Sampling without replacement refers to the fact that once a member of the population is selected, it is not eligible to be selected again. Sampling with replacement refers to the fact that a member remains eligible to be selected even if it has already been selected. Sampling with replacement is especially useful for "small" populations.

<u>Stratified Random Sampling</u>. Sometimes called "proportional" or "quota" random sampling, where the population of N units is divided into non-overlapping "strata," N_1, N_2, N_3, ..., N_i, such that $N_1 + N_2 + N_3 ... + N_i = N$, then do simple random sample of n/N in each stratum. Using the family food expenditures data set, we might first divide the population into those that have gardens and those that do not and then select a random sample from within each of these two "strata." Why use stratification? It is usually used to make sure that each of the strata are represented in the final result. For example, it may be the case that it is important to have good representation of all adults by age in a sample, but the population from which the sample is to be drawn is believed to have only a few young adults. In this case, the population could be stratified into young adults, middle-aged adults, and old-age adults, and random samples taken from each of these three strata to ensure that an adequate representation of the young adults was in the final sample. Also, it may be the case that variation of a variable of interest is less within each stratum than it is across the strata, which can be used to increase "efficiency" (a statistical term meaning the reduction of variation).

For example, in the 50-family data set, there is more variation in food expenditures in the whole data set (standard deviation = $670.20) than there is if it is stratified into: (1) Those with a garden (standard deviation = $456.82); and (2) those without a garden (standard deviation = $645.35). There are two ways in which a stratified random sample can be implemented: proportional and disproportional. A proportional stratified random sample is where the sampling fraction is equal across all strata; a disproportional stratified random sample is where the sampling fraction is not equal across all strata. The former might be used in terms of having a garden or not in the family food expenditure data set, and the latter might be used in terms of the sample of adults such that the young adults would have a higher sampling frequency than the middle-aged or old adults.

Samples also can be "post-stratified," which means that the results are "weighted" by using auxiliary data. For example, in a telephone-based random sample of households in a rural area of southwest Nevada done in the early 1990s, there was a much higher proportion of adult females as responders in the survey than found in the 1990 census. Using the 1990 census data, the results were weighted so that the proportion of adult females in the sample matched that of the 1990 census (Swanson, 2008). Since some of the answers given by adult females were different from those given by adult males, the "post-stratification" provided a better picture of the responses of the adult population as a whole.

<u>Systematic Random Sampling</u>. In this type of sampling, you would select every "kth" member of a population. For example if you have 1,000 names on a list and you want a sample of 100, then you want to get every "10th" member in your sample. Clearly, to do this, you must have a way to "order" the population. For example, you would be able to number the members of the population from 1 to N, decide on the n that you want or need, and then the "interval," where k = N/n. Typically, this begins with a "random start." This means you would randomly select a number from 1 to k. Once you have

selected "k," then you would take every "kth" member of the population. This way of sampling operates under the assumption that the population is randomly ordered.

I once provided assistance (pro bono) to a public interest group in the South San Francisco Bay area that involved taking a systematic random sample from local telephone books to get a sample of 250 completed interviews. We estimated that there were 100,000 listed personal phone numbers in the books that covered the area we defined as the population (this was back before mobile telephones), and that to get 250 completed interviews we needed 4,000 numbers. We also knew that not all numbers were listed in the phone books, so we used what was known as the "plus 1" technique to get unlisted numbers in our sample. (This works by adding "1" to the last digit of the telephone number selected if the last digit is from 1 to 8, and if the last digit is 9, turning it into zero.)

We found our "kth" sampling fraction by dividing 100,000 by 4,000, which gave us k = 25. We then put the numbers 1 through 25 on separate slips of paper of equal size, which we placed into a small box (this, indeed, was a high-tech operation). We shuffled the slips around and then drew one (I believe it was 13). With the telephone books in order, we then went to the first one and counted 13 personal listings into it. The 13th listing was our selection. We modified the telephone number selected using the "plus 1" technique, and recorded it in our set of call sheets. We then selected every 25th number thereafter and modified it by the "plus 1" technique, until we had worked our way through all of the telephone books and had about 4,000 telephone numbers.

Cluster Random (Area) Sampling divides a population into clusters randomly sampled and measures all units within sampled clusters. It is usually used with face-to-face interviews. Its main advantage is a huge cost saving when the population is spread over a big geographic area. The University of Alaska's Institute for Social and Economic Research used this technique when it evaluated the results of the 1980 census in Alaska (Kruse and Travis, 1981). This approach also was used in a study of the effects of Hurricane Katrina on the Mississippi Gulf Coast (Henderson et al., 2009).

The four methods I have covered so far—simple, stratified, systematic, and cluster—are the simplest random sampling strategies. In most real applied social research, we would use sampling methods that are considerably more complex than these simple variations. The idea is that these simple methods can be combined in a range of different ways that facilitate data collection and keep costs down. Combining the simple methods leads to what is called "multi-stage" sampling. For example, if one wanted to do a study involving face-to-face interviews of households in a given state where distances are great and transportation expensive, one might first stratify the state into towns and rural places, then randomly select five towns in the towns stratum and ten rural places in the rural places stratum. This could be followed by randomly selected blocks of homes within each of the five towns and the ten rural places. The sample of villages could be disproportionately higher than that for towns, to make sure an adequate number of rural residents is in the sample. Examples of these complex approaches are provided by Farley, Krysan, and Couper (2004), Kruse and Travis (1981), and Swanson (2008).

Nonprobability Sampling is where selection is anything other than "random." This lack of "randomness" translates into the fact that we have little, if any, idea of what the probability is that a given member of the population of interest will be selected. And without having an idea of the probability of selection, we cannot legitimately use inferential statistics. There are several major types of nonprobability sampling, including purposive, quota, and convenience.

Purposive sampling involves sampling with a purpose in mind. We usually would have one or more specific predefined groups we are seeking. For instance, have you ever run into people in a mall or on the street who are carrying a clipboard and who are stopping various people and asking if they could interview them? Most likely they are conducting a purposive sample (and most likely they are engaged in market research). They might be looking for Asian females between 20 to 30 years old. They size up the people passing by, and anyone who looks to be in that category they stop to ask if they will participate. One of the first things they're likely to do is verify that the respondent does in fact meet the criteria for being in the sample. Purposive sampling can be very useful for situations where you need to reach a targeted sample quickly and where sampling for proportionality is not the primary concern. With a purposive sample, you are likely to get the opinions of your target population, but you are also likely to overweight subgroups in your population that are more readily accessible.

Quota sampling involves selecting ample members nonrandomly according to some fixed quota. There are two types of quota sampling: proportional and nonproportional. In proportional quota sampling, you want to represent the major characteristics of the population by sampling a proportional amount of each. For instance, if you know the population has 40% women and 60% men and that you want a total sample size of 100, you will continue sampling until you get those percentages, and then you will stop. So, if you've already got the 40 women for your sample but not the 60 men, you will continue to sample men, but even if legitimate women respondents come along, you will not sample them because you have already "met your quota."

Convenience sampling is done in such a way that a "convenient sample" is selected. For example, I could distribute a questionnaire to everybody in my statistics course on a given day, but this would not be a random sample of all the students in the course, much less students in general. As this example suggests, this type of sample is selected in places where at least some members of the population of interest tend to congregate such that access to them is convenient.

The major difference between nonrandom and random sampling is that the former does not involve random selection and probability sampling does. This does not mean that a given nonrandom sample is not representative of the population it is supposed to represent, but it does mean that the methods of statistical inference cannot be legitimately applied to nonrandom samples. Nonrandom samples are most effective when they are used to give an idea of how random sampling of a given population may be accomplished and how to structure questions. That is, when they are used as pilot studies. Focus groups are an example of this use of nonrandom sampling (Swanson, Schiller, and McDade, 1992).

As an example of what is to come, here is something you can do with a probability sample, but not with a nonprobability sample. In the 50-family data set, we know that the mean monthly expenditure of food is $1841.65. However, we do not "know" what the mean expenditure is in the population of families from which our sample was taken. What we can do, however, is get a good idea of where the mean is by constructing a "confidence interval" around the mean in our sample. Using the sample size (50) and standard deviation in the sample for monthly food expenditure ($670.20), I can create a 95% confidence interval for the mean monthly food expenditures for the entire population of families and make the following statement: "I am 95% certain that the mean monthly food expenditures for all families is between $1,655 and $2,028." This gives us an idea of what the mean monthly expenditure is for all families in that we are 95% certain it falls within a range of about $186 (plus and minus) of the mean. It is an example of what you can do with inferential statistics. You cannot make this statement if the 50-family sample was not "random."

C. Averages and Dispersion in Samples

Before you get to leave this chapter, you need to know some terminology, definitions, and notation in regard to the mean and the standard deviation for a population vs. a sample. First, in a population, let

X = a "variable"
X_i = the value of case "i," where i = 1 to N, $X_1, X_2, X_3, ...,X_N$
N = population size
Σ = summation sign
ΣX_i = the sum of the values for variable x from 1 to N.

In a population, the mean of a given variable X is equal to

$$\mu = \Sigma X_i /N$$

and the standard deviation of a given variable X in a population is equal to

$$\sigma = \{[\Sigma(X_i - \mu)^2]/N\}^{.5}$$

As you can see, the arithmetic mean of a variable measured over an entire population is denoted by the symbol μ (Greek, "mu") and the standard deviation of a variable measured over the entire population is denoted by the symbol σ (Greek, "sigma").

Second, in a sample, let

x = a "variable"

x_i = the value of case "i," where i = 1 to n $x_1, x_2, x_3, ..., x_N$

n = sample size

Σ = summation sign

ΣX_i = the sum of the values for variable x from 1 to n.

In a sample, the arithmetic mean is equal to

$$\bar{X} = (x_1 + x_2 + x_3... + x_n)/n = (\Sigma x_i)/n$$

and the standard deviation of a given variable X in a population is equal to

$$s = \{[\Sigma(x_i - \bar{X})^2]/n-1\}^{.5}$$

As you can see, the arithmetic mean of a variable measured over a sample is denoted by the symbol "$\bar{X}$" (a horizontal bar over the variable, enunciated as "x bar") and the standard deviation of a variable measured over the entire population is denoted by the letter "s." As you can also see, the formula for calculating the mean in a population is the same as calculating the mean in a sample. However, the formula for calculating the standard deviation in a sample is slightly different from the formula for calculating the standard deviation in a population. In a population, we divide the sum of the "squared differences" by N, and in a sample we divide it by n–1. Not surprisingly, Excel has two different formulas for calculating the standard deviation. In a population, you use "STDEVP," and in a sample you use "STDEV." In Chapter 5, you saw that the former calculated the standard deviation of monthly family food expenditures as $670.20 ("=STDEV(B3:B52)"), which you now know is for a sample (as is appropriate for this data set). If the 50-family data set had been the entire population, the standard deviation of monthly family food expenditures would have been $663.46 ("=STDEVP(B3:B52)").

ASSIGNMENT FOR CHAPTER 7

1. Open the MS-Word file you created in assignment 5, and add to your essay a description of the 50-family sample data set using the ideals of a good sample. Do not forget to include all of the measures of error in your revised essay.
2. Save your updated results (e.g., swanson.assign7.docx).

References

Farley, R., M. Krysan, and M. Couper. (2004). *Detroit Area Study, 2004.* Ann Arbor, MI: Inter-university Consortium for Political and Social Research, 2009-04-09.10.3886/ICPSR23820.

Henderson, T., M. Sirois, A. Chia-Chen Chen, C. Airress, D. A. Swanson, and D. Banks. (2009). "After a Disaster: Lessons in Survey Methodology from Hurricane Katrina." *Population Research and Policy Review* 28: 67–92.

Kruse, J., and R. Travis. (1981). *A Technical Review of the 1980 U.S. Census in Alaska: Interviews with Census Workers.* Institute for Social and Economic Research. Anchorage: University of Alaska.

Swanson, D. (2008). "Applied Demography in Action: A Case Study of Population Identification." *Canadian Studies in Population* 35 (1): 133–58.

Swanson, D., J. Schiller, and K. McDade. (1992). *Final Report: Tacoma-Pierce County Employment and Training Consortium Job Retention Research Project.* Center for Social Research. Tacoma, WA: Pacific Lutheran University.

U.S. Government Accountability Office. 2004. *American Community Survey: Key Unresolved Issues.* GAO-05-82 (October). Washington, DC: U.S. Government Accountability Office.

Yacyshyn, A., and D. A. Swanson. (2011). "The Costs of Conducting a National Census: Rationale for Re-Designing Current Census Methodology." Presented at the 21st Annual Warren E. Kalbach Population Conference at the University of Alberta, Edmonton, Canada, March 18, 2011.

8. Making Decisions from Data: Single Variables

Now that's what I'm talking about!

A. Simple Is as Simple Does

Our discussion in this chapter will cover some areas that are common to both data representing an entire population and data representing a sample from a given population, but there are some issues specific to each. In this chapter, you will learn how decisions are made using examples of single variables in regard to both types of data sets, population and sample.

The discussion will be simple and not quite realistic ... by necessity. For example, what if we wanted to make a decision about how to price a house that we want to put up for sale? We would likely want to take into account the age of the house, its location, its size, the number of bathrooms and bedrooms, size of the lot, selling prices of similar homes that are nearby, how many cars can be parked in the garage, and so on. These are all variables that would be used in the real world, and there are statistical methods that can take them all into account simultaneously—"multivariate analysis." However, the examples in this chapter will only take into account one variable at a time because you are just starting to learn how to do statistics. Take heart, though—when you move on to take more advanced statistics courses, you will learn how to use a number of variables to set the price of a house by using a multivariate technique such as multiple regression. For now, however, we will make do with the simplistic examples as you get behind the wheel of this car we call statistics.

B. Your Old Friends: The Mean, Median, Mode, Dispersion, and Shape

OK, so you know now we will be looking only at one variable at a time to get you started. You are probably wondering what exactly we should look at, however. The key is to use your new "old friends," the summary measures, including those of "central tendency," the mean, median, and mode, and those of "dispersion," including the standard deviation, range, and quartiles. We also will look at the "shape" of the data. That is, we will look at skew and kurtosis, the two measures commonly used to look at "shape." You also will need to keep in mind the "level of measurement" issue for the single variables we use as examples in this chapter.

You might be asking yourself why we need to use the summary measures, since there often is a lot of information that they cannot take into account, information you might want to know as you make a decision about something using a single variable. The reason is that in a given distribution of values of a given variable, there is too much information. It can easily become overwhelming. As an example, suppose that as a traffic analyst for the Riverside City Planning Department, you were given the task of determining the commuting distances of a random sample of 900 people who reside in Riverside and drive alone to work. You could look at the driving distances of all 900 commuters and put them in a table, which would tell you something, but without much clarity or precision. However, what if I told you that the mean, median, and standard deviation ("Commute Distance" would be a variable measured at the ratio level, right?) are 19.56 miles, 12 miles, and 69.07 miles, respectively. These are "facts" you not only can remember, but ones that you can use to get an idea of what is going on. You know, for example, that the mean is larger than the median, which tells you that the distribution of this variable is skewed right by a few "outliers" who are driving long distances. So, you also know something about the "shape" of this data set.

Suppose the Los Angeles City Planning Department had done a similar study of its residents who commute to work alone and found in a sample of 900 commuters that the mean distance was 12 miles, the median was 12, and the standard deviation 2.847 miles. Clearly, there is one similarity in that the medians are both the same. However, there are some striking differences. First, the average distance driven by Riverside residents is about 7.6 miles more than that of Los Angeles residents. Second, the standard deviation for Riverside residents is 69.07, which is about 24 times larger than the one for Los Angeles residents. Third, we know that the distribution of driving times by Riverside residents is skewed right and we also know that the distribution of driving times by Los Angeles residents is symmetrical (how do we know this?). Fourth, if we look at the coefficients of variation for both sets of drivers, we can see that both the "absolute" and "relative" dispersion is higher among Riverside residents compared to Los Angeles residents: The coefficient of variation for Riverside is 3.53 miles (where 3.53 = 69.07/19.56), while for Los Angeles residents it is 0.237 miles (where 0.237 = 2.847/12). Thus, we can say that the relative dispersion of driving times among Riverside residents is about 15 times that of Los Angeles residents.

How would this type of information help you make a decision? Suppose that the state of California had implemented a plan aimed at reducing average commuting distances in order to cut down on smog in the Los Angeles Basin (which would include the city of Riverside), and you as the Riverside City Traffic Planner were teamed with other city planners, including your counterpart from Los Angeles. Because the Riverside data are "skewed right," you know that there are some (but not likely many) commuters driving really long distances compared to most of the Riverside commuters. This is not the case for the data representing Los Angeles, where there is about the same number of drivers commuting more than 12 miles as there are commuting less than 12 miles. If you were tasked with a plan for reducing the average commute time of Riverside residents who drive alone, you might think about targeting the few people who have really long commuting distances, whereas the Los Angeles planner might be more inclined to having a plan aimed at all drivers. Given the information in the samples, the two different approaches would represent a better use of (scarce) resources in order to reduce average commuting distances.

C. More Old Friends: The Five Types of Error

As you know by now, there is absolutely no statistical uncertainty when the data you have represent the entire population. That is, there is no sampling error. How can there be sampling error if there is there is no sample? However, we always are left with the uncertainty about the "true value" due to the other four sources of error: (1) Measurement error; (2) non-response error; (3) coverage error; and (4) coding/transcription error. Because these errors are difficult to measure, they tend to be ignored in most discussions. Even when attempts are made to measure some, if not all, of these types of errors, they tend to be ignored by users unless what the user sees is contrary to his or her opinion. However, even if we cannot "measure" errors like these, all is not lost. We can use Excel and its tools to help us understand these errors, which is the first step in dealing with them.

As an example, think back to our sample of 900 residents of Riverside who drive alone to work. We know that the distribution is skewed to the right because the mean is larger than the median. This indicates that we have "outliers." Whenever there are outliers, it is good to have an idea of how many there are and their size. One immediate way Excel can help is to find the maximum commute time. To do this, we would use the "MAX" function. Since I have the Riverside data in column D of a worksheet in rows 2 to 901, I could get Excel to find the maximum value and place it, for example, in cell

D909 by putting the following function in cell D909: "=MAX(d2:d901)." Doing this, I find that the maximum commute distance for the Riverside drivers is 2,000 miles and that there is only one driver with this distance.

Does this seem a bit suspicious to you? It does to me. I could do some further investigation by getting Excel to "sort" the Riverside data so I could quickly see how many "outliers" I have that go along with the person for whom we have a driving commute distance of 2,000 miles. Using the "SORT" function (under the "DATA" tab in the toolbar), I find that there are 19 drivers for whom the reported commuting distance is more than one standard deviation larger than the mean, which is 88.63 (where 88.63 = 19.56 + 69.07). Of these 19 drivers, there are six who report driving 90 miles, seven who report 120 miles, five who report 200 miles, and the one for whom we have a distance of 2,000 miles. Since these are driving (not "flying") distances, it appears that 2,000 miles is a mistake and given that there are five who report 200 miles, I would now be working on the idea that this is a coding/transcription error that added an extra zero to a reported distance of 200 miles. With this knowledge in hand, I could go back through the original questionnaires to find this person to see what was recorded. Suppose I did that and found that this Riverside resident reported a commute distance of 200 miles and during transcription it was miscoded as 2,000. I would then update my Excel file by replacing the incorrectly transcribed value of 2,000 miles with the correct one of 200 miles.

With this correction, I would revise my statistics for Riverside County accordingly, which would reveal that the mean, median, and standard deviation are 17.58, 12, and 20.97, respectively. I could then make corrections to my comparison of Riverside commuters with Los Angeles commuters, which would now reveal that the mean for Riverside is 5.58 miles more, not 7.56 miles; the standard deviation is about 7.4 times higher, not 24 times higher; and the coefficient of variation for Riverside is 1.193 (where 1.193 = 20.97/17.58), which is about five times larger than the one for Los Angeles drivers (.237), not 15 times larger.

As you can guess from this example, there are more tools to evaluate the quality of data, including the all-important graphs, but this should give you an idea of how you can use Excel to help make sure that your data are "clean" in regard to the four types of error, even though we cannot precisely "measure" any of these four types of error (Beimer and Lyberg, 2003; Lessler and Kalsbeek, 1992). So, assuming our data are as clean as they can be, we can turn to looking at decision making, starting with data representing an entire population.

D. The Population Perspective

In making decisions with data representing an entire population of interest, we do not have to worry about sampling error, so there is no "uncertainty." This means that we do not need any of the tools of statistical inference, such as confidence intervals or hypothesis tests. All we need is a "clean" set of data, an understanding of "descriptive" statistics—such as the mean, median, standard deviation, and "shape"—and how to use them to make decisions.

Unlike the simple problems used in this book to help you learn statistics, problems in real life tend to be messy. As I wrote in the preface, "About this Book," there are questions and problems that have no absolute answers, and to make things worse, some of them are often not structured very well. What does it mean to have a question or problem that is not structured very well? What if I assigned you to write a paper on something "statistical" as a requirement in a course worth 25% of your grade and left it at that? Your reaction might be "That's nice—now what am I supposed to do?" You would likely start asking me questions such as what is the topic, how long is the paper, what kind of format is needed, and when is it due? In asking these questions you would be following a set of criteria: (1) Identifying the problem; (2) enumerating possible solutions; (3) establishing criteria to be incorporated in the solution that is selected; and (4) selecting the solution along with a description of why you selected your particular solution. If you are working in a group, all of these criteria would have to be worked out to your mutual agreement.

One way to describe the population perspective is to look at an example "case study" (Patten and Swanson, 2003). Suppose that "Lucky Bamboo, Ltd.," a company based in Vietnam, is investigating the optimal pricing for fish paste that it plans to sell in Singapore, where the market consists of 2 million households (the "population" of interest). It does not have any experience with sampling, and it knows that trying to survey all 2 million households in Singapore about its fish paste would be very costly. So, it uses its past experience with other products in the Singaporean market and its experience selling fish paste in Vietnam to set up a market research plan to determine the optimal pricing of its fish paste.

Here is how Lucky Bamboo proceeds: It knows that it has to sell its fish paste for at least S$1.00 per tube to make a profit in Singapore, and it believes that the maximum price it can sell it for is S$1.50 per tube (note that "S$" stands for "Singapore dollar"). Thus, these two price points represent the management team's judgment on the range of prices that households in Singapore would be willing to pay for a 190-gram tube of Lucky Bamboo fish paste. In past market research it has done in breaking into a new market, it has found that the arithmetic average is a good third choice between the lower and upper range, which in this case would be S$1.25.

Lucky Bamboo follows a policy of maximizing gross sales revenue in terms of selling price when it opens a new market, but it is very conservative in terms of pricing. Thus, in Singapore, the company would select a price that generates the maximum amount of sales revenue, with a lower price preferable to a higher price, all else equal. The company's management team then applies several "rules of thumb" to make a decision based on its experience. The most important one is that it believes that about 25% of the households in Singapore will buy its fish paste at S$1.00 per tube, about 15% would buy it for S$1.50 per tube, and about 20% will buy it at S$1.35 per tube. Lucky Bamboo proceeded by selling its fish paste at the two different prices it selected as the lower and upper range in a mix of retail outlets for a month. After one month, it found that it had sold 12,000 tubes of fish paste, where 7,500 tubes were sold at S$1.00 and 4,500 at S$1.50.

Because the ratio of sales at the lower price to sales at the higher price is 1.7 (where $1.7 = 7,500/4,500$), the management team is very comfortable with the results of its monthlong test, since the ratio of sales approximates its belief that about 25% of households will purchase its fish paste at the lower price and 15% at the higher price (where $1.7 = .25/.15$). So, using its rules of thumb and information on its sales, Lucky Bamboo's management team constructs the table shown in Exhibit 8.1 as part of a presentation it will make to the company's board of directors, who will make the final decision in regard to the team's recommendations on where to set the sales price.

Exhibit 8.1. Expected Gross Sales Revenues under the Company's Traditional Approach

Total Households	Price (P)	Proportion Purchasing	Total Purchasing (T)	Gross Sales Revenues (GSR) (GSR = T * P)
2,000,000	S$1.50	.15	300,000	S$450,000
2,000,000	S$1.25	.20	400,000	S$500,000
2,000,000	S$1.00	.25	500,000	S$500,000

Based on the information presented to them in Exhibit 8.1, Lucky Bamboo's Board of Directors decided to set the price at S$1.00, which is in line with its conservative policy. As you can see, Lucky Bamboo used some classic tools of descriptive statistics in combination with experience and judgment to arrive at the decision to set its price at S$1.00 per tube. Although the details may vary from company to company, this example describes a type of decision-making process that is widely used in conjunction with data that represent an entire population. Information is assembled, some descriptive statistics are calculated, and in combination with experience and judgment, they are used to make a decision.

Unknown to Lucky Bamboo, however, a competitor also is looking at opening up the market in Singapore to its fish paste. The competitor, "Morning Star, Ltd.," has experience with sampling and statistical inference through its longtime research partner, VGRC, Ltd. ("Very Good Research Company, Limited"). Let's see how they develop Morning Star's pricing strategy.

E. The Sample Perspective

Morning Star and VGRC know from experience that sampling represents a cost-effective way to get precisely the data needed to make a decision in regard to marketing questions and problems. VGRC and Morning Star also know that, unlike the situation where one may have information that represents the entire population of interest, with sample data one has to deal with sampling error, "statistical uncertainty." This means that in addition to the understanding of data analysis illustrated in the preceding section on "the Population Perspective," as well as using experience and judgment, one must now turn to tools of statistical inference, such as confidence intervals or hypothesis tests. However, they have learned to use statistical inference very effectively in combination with statistics, experience, and judgment to make marketing decisions.

Like Lucky Bamboo, both VGRC and Morning Star know that the total potential market in Singapore is composed of 2,000,000 households. Unlike Lucky Bamboo, Morning Star also has the results of a random survey of 600 households, conducted under the auspices of VGRC, in Singapore. Because this sample survey followed the principles of the "Tailored Design Method" (Dillman, 2000) it is thought by both VGRC and Morning Star to have data of good quality, minimally affected by measurement, coverage, non-response, and coding/transcription error. Moreover, VGRC conducted an analysis of data quality that supports this belief (Beimer and Lyberg, 2003; Lessler and Kalsbeek, 1992). Thus, both VGRC and Morning Star know that the only source of "error" they need to deal with is statistical. In addition, Morning Star also knows how to exploit measures of this type of error in making decisions. This gives it a competitive advantage over its rivals, such as Lucky Bamboo. Its game plan is shown as Exhibit 8.2.

Exhibit 8.2. The Morning Star Game Plan

1. The Decision Maker: The Board of Directors, with recommendations from the Morning Star Management Team and VGRC analysts.

2. Identify alternative decisions (courses of action): The decision involves selecting one of two or more identified courses of action. The goal is to choose the course of action that is "best."

3. Identify Events: These are occurrences that are beyond the control of the decision maker, yet can have an effect on the course of action selected. The events are subject to uncertainty, but ideally they are mutually exclusive and exhaustive so that one, and only one, can occur.

4. Return or Payoff: A measure of net benefit to the decision maker used to make a decision.

5. Uncertainty: A measure by the probabilities assigned to the identified events. This can include both objective and subjective.

In the sample survey, a set of questions was asked about two different prices that people would be willing to pay for a 190-gram tube of fish paste. The summary statistics from the sample survey are shown in Exhibit 8.3. Keep in mind that you do not yet know what the "inferential" components are of Exhibit 8.3, which are under the headings, "Standard Error" and "95% C. I.," respectively. Without going into the details (which will be covered in the next chapter), all you need to know at this point is that Morning Star is (1) 95% certain that between 67% and 83% of all households in Singapore would be willing to pay S$1.00 per tube; and (2) 95% certain that between 43% and 63% of all households would be willing to pay S$1.50 per tube.

Exhibit 8.3. Case Study Data

How much would you be willing
to pay for a 190-gr. tube of
high-quality Baltic Roe Paste?

	Proportion Willing to Pay This Amount	Standard Error	95% C. I. Proportion of Households That Would Buy, by Price		
			High	Average	Low
S$ 1.00	.75	.04	.83	.75	.67
S$ 1.50	.53	.05	.63	.53	.43

Not surprisingly, Morning Star follows a policy of maximizing gross sales revenue in terms of selling price when it opens a new market, and like its competitor, Lucky Bamboo, it does so using a conservative approach. Also not surprisingly, Morning Star knows that it has to sell its fish paste for at least S$1.00 per tube to make a profit in Singapore, and it believes that the maximum price it can sell it for is S$1.50 per tube. Thus, these two price points represent the management team's judgment on the range of prices that households in Singapore would be willing to pay for a 190-gram tube of Morning Star's fish paste.

As a result, Morning Star would select a price that generates the maximum amount of sales revenue, given the probability of expected sales at a given price. Because it is experienced with sampling and in working with VGRC, the management team at Morning Star knows that a standard tool of statistical inference, the "95% confidence interval," is extremely useful in establishing three potential levels of gross sale revenues (high, average, and low) when using survey data to forecast expected sales revenue. The management team then applies a "rule of thumb" (i.e., a judgment based on ex-perience) that assigns probabilities to the attainment of high, average, and low gross sales revenues. This rule of thumb is based on the cumulative experience gained from entering new markets and has worked well. It is comprised of three decision points: (1) There is a 20% chance of obtaining high gross sales revenues; (2) a 50% chance of obtaining average gross sales revenues; and (3) a 30% chance of obtaining low gross sales revenues.

For Morning Star, the "alternative acts" described in Exhibit 8.2 are the two different selling prices, S$1.00 and $1.50. The "events" (Exhibit 8.2) are represented by the high, average, and low estimates of gross sales revenues generated by the proportion of households willing to buy at each price as measured by the high and low ends of the 95% confidence interval of the estimated (average) market share in the survey. For example, the "low" estimate of gross sales that would result from pricing the roe paste at S$1.00 is (2,000,000) *(.75 − (2*.04))*S$1.00 = S$1,340,000. This value reflects the objective probability (sampling error) of the low value of market share. That is, we are 95% certain that at least this gross level of sales will be achieved. From the preceding information, we can construct a table that shows the "Expected Gross Sales Revenues under Uncertainty," as shown in Exhibit 8.4. This table will yield the expected gross revenues under each of the alternative prices, taking into account the statistical uncertainty resulting from the use of a sample.

Exhibit 8.4. Expected Gross Sales Revenues Under Uncertainty

		Alternative Act 1 (Price= S$1.00)	
		Gross Sales Revenues	Weighted Gross Sales Revenues
Event (E)	Probability (P)	(GSR=E*S$1.00)	(WGSR)=P*GSR
(High Sales) 2,000,000* .83	.20	S$1,660,000	S$332,000
(Average Sales) 2,000,000* .75	.50	S$1,500,000	S$750,000
(Low Sales) 2,000,000* .67	.30	S$1,340,000	S$402,000

Expected Gross Sales Revenues: S$1,484,000

		Alternative Act 2 (Price= S$1.50)	
		Gross Sales Revenues	Weighted Gross Sales Revenues
Event (E)	Probability (P)	(GSR=E*S$1.00)	(WGSR)=P*GSR
(High Sales) 2,000,000* .63	.20	S$1,260,000	S$252,000
(Average Sales) 2,000,000* .53	.50	S$1,060,000	S$530,000
(Low Sales) 2,000,000* .43	.30	S$860,000	S$258,000

Expected Gross Sales Revenues: S$1,040,000

The events are very simple as are the acts, and they remain so even when coupled with the uncertainty associated with the estimated market share and the management's rule of thumb. You can see from the table that no information is available for certain combinations of events and acts because of how the survey was constructed and the criteria used by the company. For example, no gross sales revenues are "expected" in excess of S$166,000 if the price is set at S$1.00. In principle, of course, an unlimited number of events could occur that would affect the payoffs of alternative decisions. These would affect the payoffs of alternative decisions. However, to make the problem manageable, the company has established a range of potential prices that it believes is realistic and subjected this range of prices to an empirical examination—a sample survey of 600 households randomly selected from the 2 million households in Singapore.

Consequently, you can think of "demand" as being represented by only three levels—high, average, and low—that are taken from the sample of households and translated via the 95% confidence interval apparatus into the numbers expected to purchase the paste at the two prices preselected by the company as being realistic. Note that these levels of demand are set up to correspond with the "rule of thumb" probabilities used by the company to gauge potential gross sales revenues. How do you compare the alternative acts? A number of different criteria exists for selecting the "best alternative course of action," given uncertainty. If the company knew with exact certainty what the payoff outcomes would be, the decision procedure would be very simple: Select the act that yielded the highest payoff. Unfortunately, "certainty" does not exist. This is where statistical inference can help in combination with the policies used by the company and the rule-of-thumb probabilities used by its management team.

Morning Star may not know with exact certainty what will happen, but it does have some guidance from the sample survey and the experience summarized in the rule-of-thumb probabilities. One choice that could be made is for the decision maker to assume that once a course of action is selected, things could turn out to be terrible, and the "real world" may turn out to be the worst possible for the decision maker. If this was the company's policy, then the choice would be based on the assumption that only 43% of all households would purchase (the worst set of events), which happens when the price is set at S$1.50. This yields an expected payoff of S$860,000 in gross sales revenues.

Because we are using information from a random sample, we are not limited to assuming the worst. We can be very confident that, in fact, more than 43% of the households will purchase the roe paste, given that we sell it at S$1.00 instead of S$1.50. By selling at S$1.00, we are 95% certain that at least 67% of the households will purchase. At this sales level, we minimally expect gross sales revenues of S$1,340,000, which exceeds the minimal gross sales revenue of S$860,000 expected if we price the paste at S$1.50. Given company policy, it appears that choosing a price of S$1.00 is the best "act."

A quick example of yet another way to make the choice is to take into account the probabilities (based on prior experience) assigned by the company executives to the high, average, and low sales. By summing up the "weighted gross revenues" by sales level, we can obtain an "average" for "expected gross sales revenues" for each of the two prices. Doing this, we see that by setting the price at S$1.00, we "expect" an average gross sales revenue of S$1,484,000. This figure is higher than the expected gross sales revenues that result by summing up the weighted gross revenues by sales level at the S$1.50 price, which yields an S$1,040,000. This suggests that by taking into account both the objective probabilities associated with the survey and the more subjective probabilities used in the rule of thumb to estimate sales levels, the price to select would be S$1.00. Why? Because it yields a higher average gross sales revenue figure than would the price of S$1.50, given the experience of the company and its rules of thumb.

Are you ready to get behind the wheel and do some inferential statistics?

ASSIGNMENT FOR CHAPTER 8

Open the MS-Word file you created in assignment 6 and the Excel file that goes with it. Pretend you are a research analyst working for a food retailer and that your management wants to know the financial impact of gardens on how much people spend monthly on food. For purposes of this assignment, ignore the fact that the 50-family data set is a random sample and write something in MS-Word about the impact of gardens on food expenditures as if the sample represented the entire population. Include in your two- to three-page essay what the financial impact is. Whatever new work is not in your file, save it in your updated files (e.g., swanson.assign8.xls and e.g., swanson.assign8.docx).

References

Biemer, P., and L. E. Lyberg (2003). *Introduction to Survey Quality*. New York: Wiley.

Dillman, D. (2000). *Mail and Internet Surveys: The Tailored Design Method, 2nd ed.* New York: John Wiley and Sons.

Lessler, J., and W. Kalsbeek (1992). *Nonsampling Errors in Surveys*. New York: John Wiley & Sons.

Patten, R., and D. A. Swanson (2003). "Using Cases in the Teaching of Statistics." Paper presented at the annual conference of the World Association for Case Method Research and Application (WACRA 2003), Bordeaux, France, June 29 to July 3.

9. Making Decisions from Samples: Single Variables

Just one key can unlock a whole other world!

A. Introduction

In terms of understanding inferential statistics, you need to master this chapter. It is aimed at you gaining a conceptual framework as opposed to memorizing formulas. However, there are key concepts you have to know to gain this conceptual framework. One of them involves a formula that you not only need to memorize, but also use to "see" the foundation of inferential statistics. To do this, you will need to spend time on this chapter as you read, think about what you have read, develop questions, and go back and read again. You also will need to "do" statistics as you strive to learn this conceptual framework.

B. Statistical Uncertainty: A Function of Sample Size and Variation

To deal with statistical uncertainty, you need to use statistical inference, which for those of us doing nonexperimental research is the process of inferring from a random sample to the population from which the sample was drawn. In a more general sense, the term is used to describe sets of rules (procedures) that can be used to draw conclusions from data sets arising from systems affected by random variation. The results of the sets of rules are designed to make a data-based decision in regard to some problem or question. The decision to be made may involve doing more research or the implementation of a marketing strategy by a business or a policy by a governmental entity. The process of statistical inference typically starts with descriptive statistics, which were discussed in Chapter 8. Statistical inference is then typically applied to selected descriptive statistics (e.g., the mean). It is based on assumptions, and for the process to work, the assumptions must be correct or nearly so.

Incorrect assumptions can invalidate the entire process of statistical inference. For example, if you assume that a data set is a random sample and it is not, in fact, then none of the inference tools is valid.

There are two major approaches to the process of statistical inference: (1) Confidence intervals; and (2) hypothesis testing. The former is used when you are trying to estimate something in a population of interest such as a mean; the latter is used to make comparisons (across populations or against a standard) in regard to a statistic of interest, such as the mean. You would use a confidence interval to estimate the mean monthly food expenditure in the population from which our 50-family sample was drawn. However, you would use a hypothesis test in regard to comparing the mean month food expenditure for families with gardens to the mean for families without gardens.

These two approaches are essentially two sides of the same coin. The fundamental foundation they share is that statistical uncertainty is a function of two—and only two—things: (1) Sample size; and (2) dispersion (variation). In regard to sample size, we have this information directly at hand, since we know how big a sample we have drawn. In regard to dispersion, we do not know what level of variation there is in a population of interest (if we did, we also would know a lot of other things, such as the mean, which suggests that we would not bother with taking a sample), so we have to estimate it from the sample.

In thinking about the role that sample size and variation play in statistical uncertainty, let's start with sample size. What would we have if we drew a sample that included all of the elements of the population of interest? We would have no statistical uncertainty, and therefore would not have to use statistical inference. If the population of families from which we drew our random sample of 50 had 10,000 members (i.e., there were 10,000 families) and we found that the mean monthly expenditure on food was $1,500, then there is nothing to "estimate" in a statistical sense. Similarly, if we drew a random sample of 9,999 from this population, it is pretty likely that we would get the same mean, $1,500. Even if we drew a sample of 9,000, its mean would likely be very close to that of the population. However, as sample size gets smaller, it becomes more likely that our sample mean might be different from the population mean. Why? Because not all families spend the same amount on food. In fact, we know from our sample that, in the population from which it was drawn, there is at least a difference of $2,488.12 between the family that spends the highest and the family that spends the lowest, because the maximum in our sample is $3,211.64 and the minimum is $723.52. This and the standard deviation in our sample ($663.46) suggest that there is, in fact, quite a bit of variation in the population. Knowing that there is variation in monthly food expenditures and having an idea of how large it is in the population based on what we see in our sample, we can see that the mean of a small sample can be considerably different from the mean for the population as a whole.

This brings us to the second factor that determines statistical uncertainty, variation. If all families spent the same amount monthly on food, there is no variation, and any random (or otherwise) selected sample would reflect this fact. If there is no variation in a population, then there is no variation in any sample selected from it, regardless of how big it is. If there was no variation, we could estimate monthly food expenditures from a sample of one, two, three, or 10,000 families. Thus, the lack of variation leads to the fact that there is no statistical uncertainty.

So, statistical uncertainty is a function of sample size and variation. If you hold variation constant, as sample size increases, statistical uncertainty decreases. If you hold sample size constant, as variation increases, so does statistical uncertainty. Thus, the level of statistical uncertainty in a given sample is a function of its size and its variation.

C. Measuring Statistical Uncertainty

Now that you know statistical uncertainty is determined by sample size and variation, you are probably thinking that it could be measured—and you are absolutely right. A common way to measure it is to use the "standard error," which was introduced by G. U. Yule in 1897 and later refined in such a way that is consistent with the way it is used here, which is in terms of the arithmetic mean (Yule, 1919). The standard error (of the mean) also is easy to calculate. We divide a measure of variation by sample size. The most common way to do this is to divide the standard deviation by the square root of the sample size. Why take the square root, you may well ask? The answer is that the standard deviation is the square root of variance, so it is natural to use the square root of the sample size. The formula is

s.e. = $s/(n)^{.5}$
where
s.e. = standard error (of the mean)
s = the standard deviation in the sample
n = the size of the sample.

This formula is not only easy, but elegant. It captures all of the information about statistical uncertainty from the sample itself. As such, it is critically important that you not only memorize this formula, but also understand what it is telling you about statistical uncertainty. As an example of what it is telling you, suppose that we hold s constant and allow n to increase. What will happen to s.e.? It decreases. As you already know, as sample size increases, then statistical uncertainty decreases if variation is held constant. If we allow s to increase and hold n constant, then s.e. increases. That is, as s increases, then statistical uncertainty increases if n is held constant. By computing the standard error of any given sample, we have a measure of the level of statistical uncertainty inherent in it.

In our sample of 50 families, the statistical uncertainty in the mean monthly family expenditures on food is s.e. = \$93.83 (where \$93.83 = \$663.46/$(50)^{.5}$). Suppose that we had a sample of 100 instead of 50, and that the standard deviation was the same. In this situation, the s.e. would be \$66.35 (where \$66.35 = \$663.46/$(100)^{.5}$). By doubling our sample size, we have reduced our statistical uncertainty by about 29% (where 29% = [(\$63.35 − \$93.83)/\$93.83]*100) by taking a sample of 100 instead of a sample of 50. If we had increased our sample by tenfold to 500, the s.e. would be \$29.67, which is about a 58% reduction in uncertainty.

What would happen if we held sample size constant and the standard deviation increased? As before, we know that the statistical uncertainty in the mean monthly family expenditures on food is s.e. = \$93.83 (where \$93.83 = \$663.46/$(50)^{.5}$). If the standard deviation had been twice this in a sample of 50, then s.e. would have been \$187.66 (where \$187.66 = (\$663.46*2)/$(50)^{.5}$). This is an increase of 100% in statistical uncertainty (where 99.99% = ((\$187.66 − \$93.83)/\$93.83)*100). What if the standard deviation was 10 times larger, at \$6,634.60? Here, we would have an s.e. of \$938.27 (where \$938.27 = (\$663.46*10)/$(50)^{.5}$). If the standard deviation had been ten times larger with a sample of 50, our statistical uncertainty would have been approximately 900 times larger (where 899.97% = ((\$938.27 − \$93.83)/\$93.83)*100).

D. Linking a Sample with Theory: The Standard Error Is the Key

Does the term "standard error" seem a bit strange? It stems from the fact it is used to measure "statistical error," which as you know is the difference between a sample mean and the mean of the population from which the sample was selected. It also stems from the fact it is used to produce a "sampling distribution," which is based on statistical theory. By making certain assumptions (which generally are valid as long as the sample is random and meets other criteria that I will discuss later), the standard error allows us to measure statistical error.

So, what is it that the standard error does? As you can see, it is calculated solely from information in the sample, but it represents an estimate of the standard deviation of the sampling distribution associated with an infinite number of samples of the same size of the sample in question. How does it work? Think of our sample of 50 families and the mean monthly expenditures on food. Our sample and its mean monthly expenditures on food is one of a very, very large number of samples of size 50 that could have been potentially selected, and for which we could have calculated the mean monthly expenditures on food. For example, if we took 10,000 samples of size 50 and calculated mean monthly expenditures on food, we would have a distribution of 10,000 means. Of course, we would not take 10,000 samples—if we had that much money, we could have probably done a census of all families and not have had to bother with statistical inference.

Let's continue with the idea that we actually had taken 10,000 samples of size 50 and had the 10,000 means of monthly food expenditures from them. I could take the mean of these 10,000 means and then find the standard deviation. It is this theoretical standard deviation that is being estimated by the standard error we calculated from our sample. Thus, the standard error can be viewed as an estimate of the standard deviation of all of the sample means in our theoretical sampling distribution. Since the standard error of mean monthly family expenditures on food is $93.83, we can say that this is our estimate of the standard deviation of the theoretical sampling distribution associated with sample of size 50. This brings us to the concept of a sampling distribution.

E. The Concept of a Sampling Distribution

A sampling distribution has two very, very useful features. First, it is "normal" in shape, and second, the mean of the sampling distribution is equal to the mean of the population from which our sample is drawn. Statisticians have proved that a sampling distribution is normal via the "Central Limit Theorem" (Hald, 2011). This remarkable theorem tells us that the distribution of a large number of (sample) means tends to be normal, even when the distribution from which the average is computed is not normal.[1]

Yep! You learn to drive by driving and you learn statistics by doing. Can I do it?

Furthermore, this normal distribution will have the same mean as the mean of the population that the sampling distribution represents, and its standard deviation is equal to the standard deviation of the population divided by the square root of the size of the sample represented in the sampling distribution. As such, the Central Limit Theorem is an important part of the theoretical foundation of statistical inference.

So, a sampling distribution is theoretical, and for means it is "normal" in shape (mound shaped and symmetrical). The mean of the sampling distribution (of sample means hypothetically taken from a very, very large number of samples, all of the same size, e.g., 10,000 samples of size 50) is equal to the mean of the population from which the sample was taken, and its standard deviation is equal to the standard deviation of the population divided by the square root of the size (e.g., 50) of the particular sample we have taken. Exhibit 9.1 provides an illustration of a sampling distribution, mound shaped, symmetrical, and with a mean equal to the mean of the population. This is an example of a "normal" distribution.

Exhibit 9.1. An Illustration of a Sampling Distribution

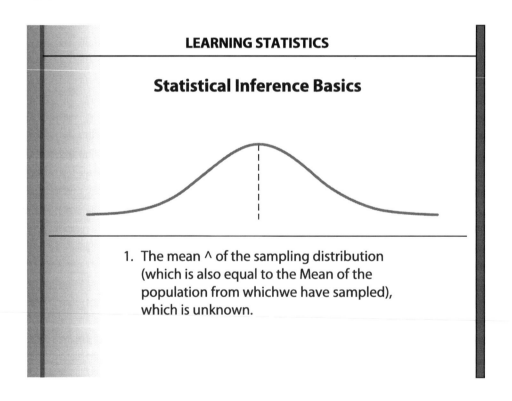

Exhibit 9.2. An Illustration of Sampling Distributions Generated by Different Standard Errors

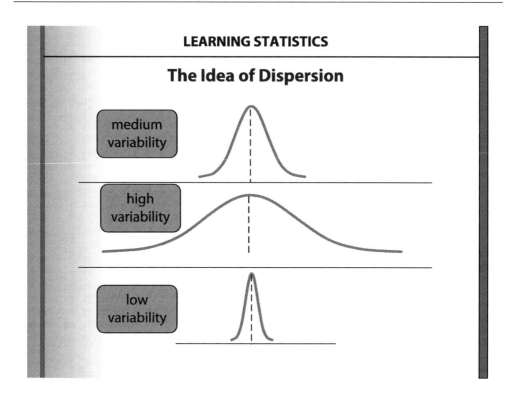

The normal distribution is a direct result of the Central Limit Theorem, and because of its properties, it serves as a fundamental distribution in inferential statistics. It has been studied and used under various names for nearly 300 years, with Abraham de Moivre usually being credited as its originator (Stigler, 1986).

While sampling distributions associated with the mean are all normal—symmetrical and mound shaped—their spread is not always the same. Exhibit 9.2 illustrates this. The bottom distribution in Exhibit 9.2 illustrates a sampling distribution with a standard error much lower than the middle one, which, in turn, has a higher standard error than the top one. So, If your sample has a small standard error, you would, relatively speaking, have a sampling distribution like the one at the bottom of Exhibit 9.2; if it had a large standard error, your sampling distribution would be like the middle one, while a medium standard deviation in a sample would generate a sampling distribution like the one in the middle of Exhibit 9.2. Again, these are all "normal" distributions, but they have different degrees of variation in them. The variation in each of them reflects statistical uncertainty. The less there is in variation in the sampling distribution, the less uncertainty in inferring to the population. The more variation there is in the sampling distribution, the more uncertainty in inferring to the population. The variation in each sampling distribution is a function of the two elements of statistical uncertainty: (1)

Sample size; and (2) the variation inherent in the population, which is reflected in the sample's variation.

To give you a concrete example of a sampling distribution being normal (per the Central Limit Theorem) and having an expected mean equal to the mean of the population from which the sample was drawn (per the Law of Large Numbers), I turn to the 50-family sample, and treating it as a population for purposes of the example, take samples from it. To do this, I am going to draw samples of size 25 a number of times from the 50-family data set, and calculate the mean monthly expenditures on food each time I draw a sample. Then, I will look at the mean of these means and their distribution at the point where I have 10 samples, 100 samples, 500 samples, 1,000 samples, and 10,000 samples.

At the start when I am drawing only ten samples, I will use Excel's "Sampling" function, which is part of the "Data Analysis" toolkit you "Added in." After that, I will turn to a "resampling" program I installed on my version of Excel (at a cost of $100 per year as a license fee), since taking more than ten samples via Excel's "sampling" function would be a slow process, especially in terms of 10,000 samples. The resampling program can take 10,000 samples of size 25 from the 50-family data set and record the mean food expenditure for each of them all in less than 50 seconds.[2]

Table 9.1 shows the results of my set of ten samples (n=25). As you can see, each of the ten means is different from one another and from the mean in the 50-family data set, which is $1,841.65. The mean of the ten sample means is $1,825.28, and as you can see in Figure 9.1, the distribution of these ten sample means is not very normal.

TABLE 9.1. EXCEL SAMPLING FUNCTION USED TO OBTAIN 10 SAMPLES (N=25) OF FOOD EXPENDITURES FROM THE 50 FAMILY DATA SET

	Sample 1	Sample 2	Sample 3	Sample 4	Sample 5	Sample 6	Sample 7	Sample 8	Sample 9	Sample 10
	$2,534.66	$2,328.96	$1,904.66	$2,308.16	$1,666.90	$1,638.26	$2,125.30	$2,122.52	$1,666.90	$2,665.78
	$3,211.64	$2,003.44	$780.70	$2,534.66	$1,638.26	$2,111.50	$1,792.18	$2,819.06	$1,273.34	$2,125.30
	$2,372.00	$2,328.96	$1,666.90	$2,477.34	$1,284.00	$1,502.94	$1,634.98	$2,122.52	$1,328.00	$1,295.64
	$2,477.34	$2,308.16	$990.74	$1,328.00	$2,477.34	$2,372.00	$1,810.96	$780.70	$1,295.64	$1,810.96
	$1,638.26	$780.70	$2,111.50	$975.10	$1,328.00	$780.06	$990.74	$1,939.00	$975.10	$2,328.96
	$2,122.52	$2,819.06	$3,103.54	$1,336.14	$1,666.90	$1,792.18	$877.52	$866.62	$2,108.14	$2,003.44
	$1,810.96	$877.52	$2,612.00	$2,950.72	$780.70	$1,284.00	$2,819.06	$2,328.96	$1,336.14	$780.06
	$975.10	$1,273.34	$877.52	$2,372.00	$2,122.52	$1,776.58	$2,534.66	$1,634.98	$1,148.24	$1,148.24
	$1,148.24	$1,472.44	$3,211.64	$1,502.94	$1,792.18	$3,103.54	$2,477.34	$2,253.46	$975.10	$1,953.58
	$1,638.26	$3,211.64	$877.52	$2,560.22	$2,763.40	$2,372.00	$1,273.34	$1,776.58	$1,939.00	$1,810.96
	$2,372.00	$1,472.44	$2,111.50	$1,904.66	$1,634.98	$1,068.38	$1,068.38	$2,295.04	$1,336.14	$1,810.96
	$2,295.04	$1,148.24	$2,003.44	$3,103.54	$1,189.40	$780.06	$1,284.00	$2,122.52	$990.74	$2,612.00
	$2,819.06	$1,284.00	$1,666.90	$1,776.58	$3,211.64	$2,534.66	$1,682.36	$1,295.64	$1,148.24	$2,560.22
	$2,612.00	$1,634.98	$866.62	$1,273.34	$2,560.22	$1,634.98	$2,125.30	$866.62	$2,950.72	$2,328.96
	$2,477.34	$2,295.04	$1,189.40	$866.62	$2,308.16	$780.06	$1,295.64	$877.52	$1,502.94	$2,111.50
	$2,372.00	$2,253.46	$2,665.78	$1,666.90	$1,792.18	$1,295.64	$877.52	$1,472.44	$2,763.40	$1,638.26
	$1,634.98	$2,328.96	$1,284.00	$2,560.22	$1,638.26	$1,472.44	$2,253.46	$2,125.30	$780.70
	$1,634.98	$2,665.78	$2,295.04	$1,472.44	$2,003.44	$2,612.00	$1,810.96	$1,472.44	$3,211.64	$2,328.96
	$2,477.34	$2,763.40	$866.62	$1,336.14	$1,336.14	$1,273.34	$780.70	$1,273.34	$1,273.34	$2,111.50
	$1,953.58	$2,612.00	$975.10	$990.74	$2,125.30	$1,273.34	$990.74	$1,792.18	$877.52	$1,284.00
	$1,295.64	$1,666.90	$2,295.04	$2,560.22	$2,328.96	$1,025.52	$2,108.14	$1,284.00	$1,682.36	$1,472.44
	$1,810.96	$2,443.06	$1,273.34	$1,792.18	$1,638.26	$2,295.04	$1,295.64	$1,666.90	$1,638.26	$780.06
	$866.62	$866.62	$1,638.26	$2,194.76	$1,189.40	$2,194.76	$2,560.22	$1,025.52	$2,612.00	$3,211.64
	$1,638.26	$2,372.00	$2,295.04	$877.52	$990.74	$3,103.54	$2,950.72	$723.52	$2,612.00	$1,904.66
	$2,819.06	$1,939.00	$2,560.22	$2,295.04	$1,284.00	$2,122.52	$1,295.64	$2,763.40	$2,253.46	$2,950.72
Mean	$2,040.31	$1,966.00	$1,764.92	$1,880.65	$1,790.05	$1,767.97	$1,708.62	$1,700.02	$1,721.84	$1,912.38

Figure 9.1. Distribution of Mean Food Expenditures in 10 Samples (n=25)

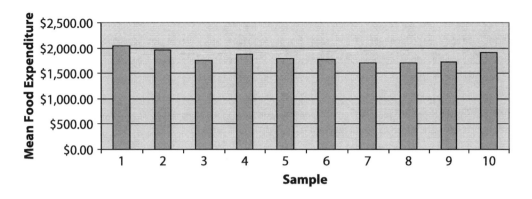

Now, let's look at the results of the means for 100 samples of size 25. Here, the mean of the 100 sample means is $1,845.27. The distribution of these 100 sample means is shown in Figure 9.2. The mean is a bit closer to the population mean ($1,841.65) than was the case for the mean of ten samples; the distribution of the 100 sample means, while not normal, is closer to it than is the distribution of the ten sample means.

Figure 9.2. Distribution of Mean Food Expenditures in 100 Samples (n=25)

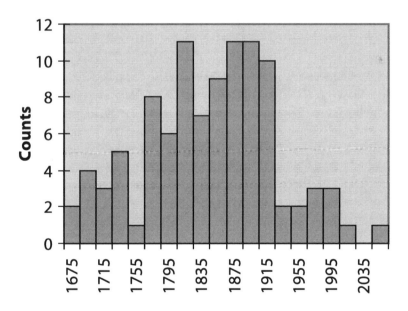

Continuing on this path, let's now look at the results of the means of 1,000 samples of size 25. Here, the mean of the 1,000 sample means is $1,841.62. The distribution of these 1,000 sample means is shown in Figure 9.3. The mean is closer to the population mean ($1,841.65) than was the case for the mean of 100 samples, and the distribution of the 1,000 sample means, while not normal, is much closer to it than is the distribution of the 100 sample means.

Figure 9.3. Distribution of Mean Food Expenditures in 1,000 Samples (n=25)

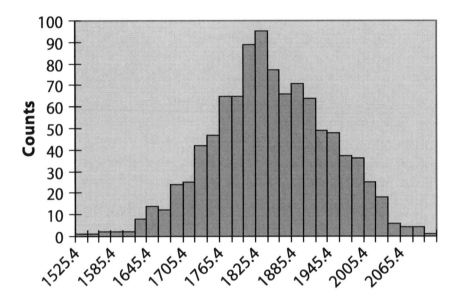

What do the results of the means of 5,000 samples of size 25 look like? The mean of the 5,000 sample means is $1,842.97. The distribution of these 5,000 sample means is shown in Figure 9.4. The mean is closer to the population mean ($1,841.65) than was the case for the mean of 1,000 samples, but the distribution of the 5,000 sample means, while not normal, is closer to it than is the distribution of the 1,000 sample means and starting to look like a normal distribution.

Figure 9.4. Distribution of Mean Food Expenditures in 5,000 Samples (n=25)

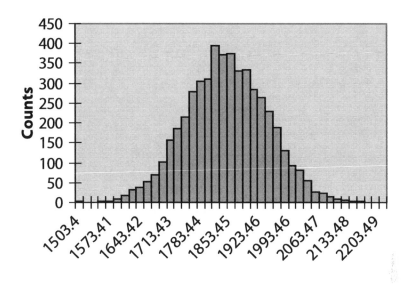

How about 10,000 samples of size 25? What does the distribution of means for these 10,000 samples look like? The mean of the 10,000 sample means is $1,842.11. The distribution of these 10,000 sample means is found in Figure 9.5. The mean is very close to the population mean ($1,841.65), and now looks very much like a normal distribution.

Figure 9.5. Distribution of Mean Food Expenditures in 10,000 Samples (n=25)

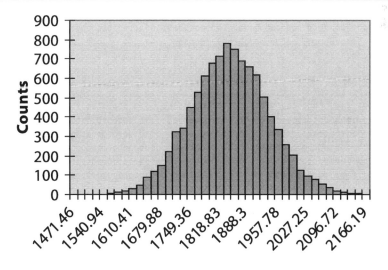

Finally, Figure 9.6 gives the results for the means of 25,000 samples of size 25. The mean of the 25,000 sample means is $1,841.63 and virtually the same as that of the population mean ($1,841.65). As you can see in Figure 9.6, the distribution of these 25,000 sample means is very, very close to being a normal distribution.

Figure 9.6. Distribution of Mean Food Expenditures in 25,000 Samples (n=25)

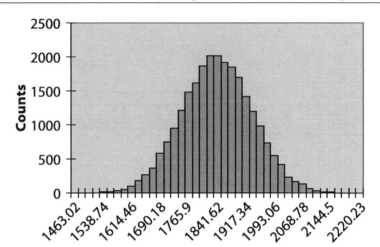

You should have a good idea of where this process would go, if we continued by taking 50,000 samples of size 25, then 100,000, 1,000,000, and so on to an "infinite" number of samples of size 25. As the Central Limit Theorem predicts (with some assistance from the Law of Large Numbers), the sampling distribution of the means becomes normal as the number of samples (of the same size) becomes larger (to the point of infinity) and the mean of the sample means approaches the (unknown) population mean. This is an example of the "theory" that forms the foundation of inferential statistics.

What is amazing about the sampling distribution is that it is normal regardless of the shape of the distribution in the population and in the sample that was drawn from it. This is illustrated very clearly by the distribution of monthly family food expenditures in the sample of 50, which we know is not symmetrical since it is "skewed right," as evidenced by the fact that the mean is larger than the median. Moreover, a normal distribution has a skewness score of zero, and this sample has a skewness score of 0.0794.

You should select ten samples of size 25 yourself using the "sampling" function in Excel's data analysis "Add-in," and see what the mean monthly family expenditures on food is for your ten sample means.

F. Sampling Distribution of the Mean

You now know that sampling distributions are important for inferential statistics. In practice, you will collect sample data, and from these data you estimate the "parameters" (i.e., the mean and standard deviation) of the sampling distribution. Using this theory in conjunction with a given sample will give you a sense of how close your particular sample mean is likely to be to the population mean. More specifically, as you will see in the next chapter, you can estimate the range of likely values for the population mean by using this theory in conjunction with the information in your (random) sample summarized in the form of the standard error. This standard deviation is called the standard error of the mean. If all the sample means were very close to the population mean (per the bottom distribution shown in Exhibit 9.2) , then the standard error of the mean will be small; if the sample means varied considerably (per the middle distribution shown in Exhibit 9.2), then the standard error of the mean will be large. Keep in mind that all statistics have sampling distributions, not just the mean. In Chapter 11, for example, I will discuss the sampling distribution of the difference between means, and in Chapter 13, the sampling distribution of a "regression coefficient."

We can take advantage of the fact that these sampling distributions are normal. Specifically, we can take advantage of the fact that the area under the "normal curve" is equal to 1.00, and we interpret this area as a probability. Since we also know that relative to the mean of the normal curve, we can quickly determine the area associated with standard errors and give them probability interpretations.

As a preview of the next chapter, look at Exhibit 9.3. In Exhibit 9.3, you can see that approximately 66% of the area in a normal curve is within one standard deviation (plus or minus) of the mean, approximately 95% of the area is within two standard deviations (plus or minus) of the mean, and approximately 99% is within three standard deviations (plus or minus) of the mean. You now know that (1) The standard error of a sample is an estimate of the standard deviation for a sampling distribution associated with your sample; (2) this sampling distribution has a normal distribution; (3) the mean of this sampling distribution is equal to the (unknown) mean of the population from which your sample was drawn; and (4) you can measure areas relative to the mean using the standard error; and (5) these areas can be interpreted as probabilities.

ASSIGNMENT FOR CHAPTER 9

Continue to pretend you are a research analyst working for a food retailer and that your management wants to know the financial impact of gardens on how much people spend monthly on food. For purposes of this assignment, pretend that you want to advise your management that it should take a sample of your clients as a cost-effective way to get an idea of the impact of gardens on food expenditures. Write a one- or two-page memo that is aimed at convincing management why taking a sample is a good idea. Save your MS-Word file (e.g., swanson.assign9.docx).

Exhibit 9.3. Areas Under the Normal Curve Given by the Standard Error Relative to the Mean

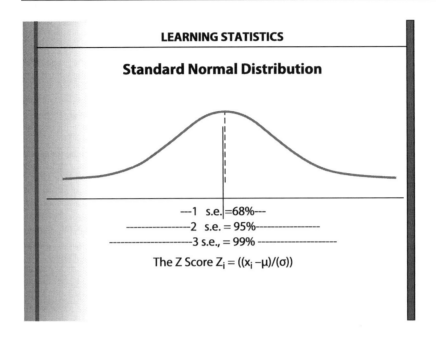

LEARNING STATISTICS

Standard Normal Distribution

---1 s.e. = 68%---
------------2 s.e. = 95%----------------
------------------3 s.e., = 99% --------------------
The Z Score $Z_i = ((x_i - \mu)/(\sigma))$

Endnotes

1. The Central Limit Theorem was postulated by Abraham de Moivre in an article published in 1733, in which he used the normal distribution to approximate the distribution of the number of heads resulting from many tosses of a fair coin. His idea was picked up 80 years later by Pierre-Simon Laplace, who used it in his book, *Théorie Analytique des Probabilités*, which was published in 1812. However, it took nearly 90 more years for the full impact of the Central Limit Theorem to be understood when, in 1901, a Russian mathematician named Aleksandr Lyapunov provided a general proof of it and showed how it worked (Hald, 2003, 2011; Stigler, 1986). Today, it is not an overstatement to say that the Central Limit Theorem is at the core of statistical inference and probability theory (Stigler, 1986). The Central Limit Theorem is closely linked with another remarkable idea called "the Law of Large Numbers," which is a theorem that states the average of the results obtained from a large number of "trials" should be close to the expected value, and will tend to become closer as more trials are performed (Stigler, 1986). The easy way to explain this is to look at a six-sided die with the numbers 1, 2, 3, 4, 5, and 6, each of which can appear with equal probability (1/6) on a given roll of the die. The expected value of a single die roll is the mean of the values, which is found by multiplying the value by its probability and summing up the products (mathematically, this is the same

as summing up the six numbers and dividing the sum by six). The "expected value" on any given roll is, therefore, 3.5 (where $3.5 = 21/6 = (1+2+3+4+5+6)/6$). As we know, this die will never actually produce a roll of 3.5, just like, we will not have a family of size of 3.26 (the mean of the size of families in our 50-family sample). However, as we roll the die and keep track of the outcomes, over time, the average of those outcomes will get closer to 3.5 and eventually settle at 3.5. Similarly, if we kept drawing a family from our 50-family sample (and putting it back so that it could be potentially drawn again), over time, the average family size will get closer to 3.26 and eventually settle at 3.26.

2. Information on the resampling program Add-in for Excel's data analysis pack can be found at http://www.resample.com/. This is a "computer-intensive" approach to inferential statistics that uses simulations in place of formulas and tables. As such, it represents a third approach to statistics beyond those offered by the frequentists and Bayesians, and extends what can be done in that you can do inference for statistics such as the median, which cannot be done with the other approaches.

References

Hald, A. (2003). *History of Probability and Statistics and Their Applications before 1790*. New York: Wiley-Interscience.

Hald, A. (2011). *A History of Parametric Statistical Inference from Bernoulli to Fisher, 1713 to 1935*. Dordrecht, The Netherlands: Springer.

Stigler, S. (1986). *The History of Statistics: The Measurement of Uncertainty before 1900*. Cambridge: Belknap Press of Harvard University Press.

Yule, G. U. (1897). "On the Theory of Correlation," *Journal of the Royal Statistical Society*, 60: 812–54.

Yule, G. U. (1919). *Introduction to the Theory of Statistics, 5th ed*. London, England: Charles Griffin and Company, Limited.

10. Making Decisions from Samples: Confidence Intervals

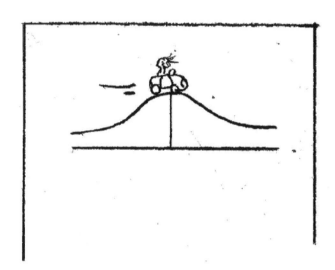

YES, I CAN!!

A. Introduction

What do you know so far? You know that a sampling distribution is needed to do statistical inference and that the standard error is the key to getting a sampling distribution for your sample. You also know that the sampling distribution is theoretical and for means it is "normal" in shape (that is, it is mound shaped and symmetrical). In addition, you know that the mean of the sampling distribution is equal to the mean of the population from which the sample was taken. Since sampling distributions are normal, you know that we can take advantage of the fact that the area under the "normal curve" is equal to 1.00, and we interpret this area as a probability. Thus, you know that relative to the mean of the normal curve, areas under the normal curve associated with standard errors can be determined, and these areas can be interpreted as probabilities. What you do not yet know is *how* to do this. However, you soon will, since this chapter shows you how to do all of this in terms of using statistical inference to generating "confidence intervals" around your sample mean. When you do this, you will obtain the probable range of the (unknown) mean in the population from which your sample was selected. To get you started, here is an example of how confidence intervals are used to guide decision making.

B. An Example of Confidence Intervals and Decision Making

This example is taken from a project on which I provided pro bono advice about 20 years ago. It involved a group of people in Kitsap County, Washington, who were concerned about rapid population growth and wanted to preserve "green space" before it was all gone. The group wanted to put a bond measure on a forthcoming local election to raise property taxes so that green space could be purchased by Kitsap County (and the cities in Kitsap County, such as Bremerton and Poulsbo) and set aside for parks and other green spaces. What they needed to know was how much the voters would be willing to pay in property taxes to preserve green space in Kitsap County. They needed to know this in advance of the election so that they could choose the additional amount of property tax to put on the ballot that voters would approve, with the idea of maximizing the amount of green space. As a result, the decision they needed to make with the assistance of statistical inference was how much additional tax to put on the forthcoming ballot. They wanted to make sure that the amount they put on the ballot would pass (it needed a simple majority, more than 50% to pass), but they also wanted to maximize the amount of green space they would preserve.

The forthcoming election was less than six months away as we started this project and if the measure failed to pass, it would be two more years before the next election, by which time a lot of current green space would have been developed. You can see what this group was dealing with: On the one hand, they wanted to be able to preserve as much green space as possible per the forthcoming election; but on the other hand, they were worried about asking voters for too much, thereby causing the measure to fail and then having to wait two more years to try again, by which time a lot of the available green space would be gone.

Before they asked me to assist them with designing a survey of voters to get this information, they decided that the maximum amount of additional property tax voters would approve would be $100 that would be in effect for five years. After assisting them with the survey design (the population was defined as all registered voters in Kitsap County, using a sample frame of all voters who voted in the last two elections plus current registered voters who had not voted in either of the last two elections. This was supplemented by a random sample of listed and unlisted telephone numbers. At the beginning of calls, respondents were screened to determine if they were registered voters in Kitsap County). Our target was a total of 400 completed interviews with registered voters.

We developed the questionnaire using Dillman's (1978) "Total Design Method," a predecessor to his "Tailored Design Method" (Dillman, 2000). I then trained the interviewers in using the questionnaire and the basics of telephone interviewing and then supervised them as they conducted the survey. Everything was aimed at minimizing measurement, coverage, non-response, and coding/transcription errors. I also knew that a sample size of 400 would provide us with a "precision of plus/minus 5 percent at a 95% level of confidence."

In the questionnaire, we jointly decided to put five levels of additional tax on the questionnaire for the survey respondents to answer either "yes, I would be willing to tax myself this additional amount per year for five years" or "no, I would not be willing to tax myself this additional amount per year for five years." The five amounts were $10, $25, $50, $75, and $100. We did, in fact, collect 400 completed interviews. I then assembled the information on the five amounts, calculated means for each of the five amounts (the proportion of voters who would say yes to a given amount of additional tax), standard errors for mean of each of the five amounts, and 95% confidence intervals around each of the means, by which we could say we were 95% certain where the (unknown) population (all registered voters in Kitsap County) mean was for each of the five amounts with a precision of plus or minus five percent. These results are shown in Exhibit 10.1.

Exhibit 10.1. Results of the Kitsap County Survey of Registered Voters

Doing Statistics

Confidence Interval Example: Kitsap County Voter Poll

95 % C.I. For Percent "yes" to Open-Space Bond by How Much Tax One Would Pay

Tax	Confidence Interval	Sample Mean	Std. Error
$10	78.7–86.7	82.7	2.00
$25	77.2–85.6	81.5	2.05
$50	72.5–81.7	77.1	2.30
$75	57.1–68.3	62.7	2.80
$100	52.7–64.3	58.5	2.90

What are you looking at in Exhibit 10.1? First, you can see the five amounts that were on the ballot—$10, $25, $50, $75, and $100. Reading across to the right from each amount is the "95% confidence interval for the percent that would vote yes at that amount for all registered voters in Kitsap County," which is followed by the percent that would vote yes to that amount in the survey. Continuing to the right, we next see the standard error for each of the five amounts. It is the standard error that was used to generate the confidence interval for each amount. You already know that the standard error is equal to the standard deviation in the sample divided by the square root of the sample size.

The approximate 95% confidence interval is constructed as follows: 95 % CI = sample mean − 2se and sample mean + 2se. So, we are 95% certain that, of all registered voters in Kitsap County:

(1) between 78.7% and 86.7% would vote yes for $10 in additional tax;

(2) between 77.2% and 85.6% would vote yes for $25 in additional tax;

(3) between 72.5% and 81.7% would vote yes for $50 in additional tax;

(4) between 57.1% and 68.3% would vote yes for $75 in additional tax; and

(5) between 52.72% and 64.3% would vote yes for $100 in additional tax.

The preceding information was discussed by the group at length in consultation with me in order to come to a decision about what amount to put on the forthcoming ballot. What amount would you choose, and why? If you send me your answer, I will tell you what the group chose (and why) and what the result of the election was. You also can look in Chapter 11 for a clue.

You now have seen a real-life example of using inferential statistics to make a decision, and you are probably asking yourself how it works. You know that it involves: (1) A theoretical sampling distribution, "normal" in shape; (2) that it is associated with a standard error; (3) that the areas under the normal shape of the sampling distribution can be found via the standard error; and (4) that these areas can be interpreted as probabilities. Here is how these items are put together to do statistical inference in the form of confidence intervals.

C. Constructing a Confidence Interval

Let's start by looking at Exhibit 10.2 (a reproduction of Exhibit 9.3), where you can see that approximately 66% of the area in a normal curve is within one standard deviation (plus or minus) from the mean, approximately 95% of the area is within two standard deviations (plus or minus) from the mean, and approximately 99% is within three standard deviations (plus or minus) from the mean. As you might be starting to suspect, the "95% area" was the basis for constructing the 95% confidence intervals around the percent saying that they would vote yes to a given additional amount of tax. In fact, you are right. You also may be thinking that the confidence interval was constructed around a given mean (percent saying "yes" for a given additional amount of tax) from the sample of Kitsap County voters, whereas we do not know where that given mean is in the sampling distribution. Again, you are right, and moreover, you are on track for how to construct confidence intervals.

Exhibit 10.2. Areas Under the Normal Curve Given by the Standard Error Relative to the Mean

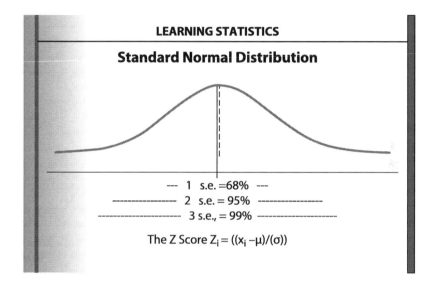

LEARNING STATISTICS

Standard Normal Distribution

--- 1 s.e. =68% ---
2 s.e. = 95%
3 s.e., = 99%

The Z Score $Z_i = ((x_i - \mu)/(\sigma))$

As an example of how this works, think back to the Kitsap County Survey (Exhibit 10.1), where 77.1% of the sample said that they would vote yes for $50 in additional tax. Suppose that this is less than the actual percent of Kitsap County voters who would in fact vote yes. Further, suppose that the actual percent is 79%. Now, look at Exhibit 10.3, which shows how the confidence interval would work in this case.

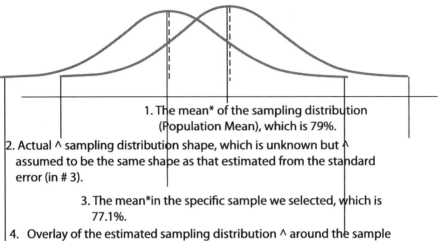

1. The mean* of the sampling distribution (Population Mean), which is 79%.

2. Actual ^ sampling distribution shape, which is unknown but ^ assumed to be the same shape as that estimated from the standard error (in # 3).

3. The mean*in the specific sample we selected, which is 77.1%.

4. Overlay of the estimated sampling distribution ^ around the sample ^ mean from the standard error of 2.3.

In Exhibit 10.3, you see two identical distributions. They both represent the sampling distribution generated from the standard error of 2.3 for the percent saying yes to $50 in additional tax. The one to the right represents the sampling distribution centered on the (hypothetical) 79% saying yes in the entire population of Kitsap County voters. Its mean (79%) is identified by the vertical line ending at the asterisk (*) in sentence # 1 and its boundaries are identified by the vertical line at each end of this distribution ending at the chevrons (^) in sentence # 2. The sampling distribution to the left is centered on the mean (77.1%) found in the sample, which is identified by the vertical line ending at the asterisk (*) in sentence # 3; its boundaries are identified by the vertical line at each end of this distribution ending at the chevrons (^) in sentence # 4. Now, multiply the standard error of 2.3 by 2, and add and subtract this amount to the sample mean of 77.1%, which represents the 95% confidence interval for the location of the (hypothetical) population mean of 79%. Recall from Exhibit 10.3 that the 95% confidence interval is from 72.5 to 81.7%. Note that this confidence interval encompasses the (hypothetical) population mean of 79%.

The 95% confidence interval is illustrated in Exhibit 10.4, which is the same as Exhibit 10.3 except for the addition of the horizontal line centered on the sample mean of 77.1% that represents the 95% confidence interval. As you can see, this interval covers 95% of the area under the sampling distribution centered on the sample mean—and importantly, as noted in the previous paragraph—it also "encompasses" the (hypothetical) mean.

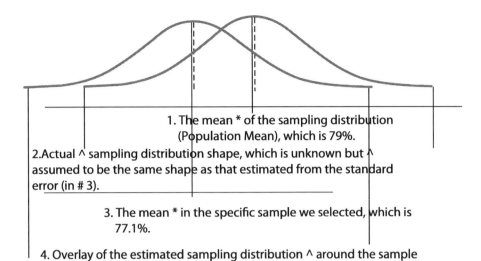

1. The mean * of the sampling distribution (Population Mean), which is 79%.

2. Actual ^ sampling distribution shape, which is unknown but ^ assumed to be the same shape as that estimated from the standard error (in # 3).

3. The mean * in the specific sample we selected, which is 77.1%.

4. Overlay of the estimated sampling distribution ^ around the sample ^mean from the standard error of 2.3.

The example in Exhibit 10.4 provides an illustration of how statistical inference essentially works in terms of confidence intervals. The sampling distribution generated by the standard error is centered on the sample mean. We know that the true, but unknown, population mean is somewhere in this distribution. However, even though we do not know where it is, by constructing a 95% confidence interval around our sample mean, we have a 95% chance of encompassing the unknown population mean.

D. More on Confidence Intervals

We can use the area under the "normal curve" represented by the sampling distribution in conjunction with the standard error that generated it to find all sorts of confidence intervals. While we cannot generate either a zero or 100% confidence interval, we can, in principle, generate anything in between. In addition to a 95% confidence interval, for example, we can generate a 10% confidence interval, a 30% confidence interval, 50%, 67%, 80%, 96%, and a 99% confidence interval, for example. As you can guess, it is not very useful to generate a confidence interval where we are only 10% certain that the population mean is contained in it and some of the other many possibilities seem odd (e.g., a 51% confidence interval).

In regard to which levels of confidence to use, we have tradition to guide us. In this regard, it has become traditional in statistics to generally use only certain confidence intervals unless some special reason exists for using something else. These traditional intervals are 67%, 95%, 99%, and 99.99%. The reason for this tradition is twofold: These intervals tend to be useful and they can be quickly approximated. An approximation for the 67% confidence interval is to simply add the standard error to the mean and subtract it from the sample mean. For the 95% confidence interval, we can approximate it by multiplying the standard error by two and then adding this product to and subtracting it from the sample mean, respectively. For the 99% confidence interval, we can approximate it by multiplying the standard error by three and adding and subtracting this product to and from the sample mean, respectively. We can approximate the 99.99% confidence interval by multiplying the standard error by four and adding this product to the sample mean and subtracting it from the sample mean.

As you can see from the preceding discussion, if we wish to be more confident about where the true, but unknown, population mean is located, the confidence interval gets wider (e.g., a 99.99% confidence interval is approximated by four standard errors above and below the sample mean). If we wish to be less confident, the interval shortens (e.g., a 67% confidence interval is only one standard error above and below the sample mean). This makes sense in that to be more certain, the confidence interval must be wider. As these examples suggest, a confidence interval is an example of an "interval estimate." That is, we can only estimate the range in which the true, but unknown, population mean can be found—not its exact value.

The confidence interval can be used to provide a probability of a sample mean outside of it. For example, since we know that there is 95% chance that the true percent of voters who would say yes is between 72.5% and 81.7%, then there is only a 5% change that the true percent is outside of the range of 72.5 to 81.7%. Since we know that the distribution is symmetrical, we can extend this to say that there is a 2.5% chance that the true percent is less than 72.5%, and a 2.5% change that it is greater than 81.7%. As you can see, we divided the "5%" chance in half, and said that there is less than a 2.5% chance that the percent who would say less is under 72.5% and less than a 2.5% chance that the percent is more than 81.7%.

There are many subtleties to confidence intervals than is feasible to discuss at this point. If you continue to take statistics courses, you will learn more about them and see more precisely what is going on with confidence intervals beyond the approximations I am discussing here. However, not so subtle is the relationship of confidence intervals to the topic we take up in the next chapter, which is statistical testing. While these two forms of statistical inference are distinct, they are related, and to some extent complementary. The essential distinction is that statistical testing is used to make comparisons, while confidence intervals are used to make estimates. However, the latter can be used to make comparisons. It is a bit awkward, but valid. Remember that the comparison is between two (potentially) different populations. That is, the decision we might want to make is whether or not the mean in one population is higher than the mean in another population. How do we proceed? Here are two examples.

Comparison Example 1—Food Expenditures. Suppose that we have a random sample from each of two populations in terms of the average amount spent monthly on food for a single-person household. Suppose in Population A we have a sample of 400 and find that the mean is $430, with a standard deviation of $80. In Population B, suppose that we have a sample of 900, a mean of $450, and a standard deviation of $90. The first step is to compute the standard error for each sample. For Population A, we have a standard error of $80/(sqrt(400)) = $80/20 =$4. For Population B, we have a standard error of $90/(\text{sqrt}(900)) = \$90/30 = \$3$. The second step is to determine a confidence interval for each sample mean. Let's use 95%. For Population A, we have an approximate 95% CI from \$422 to \$438 ($430 - 2*$4) to ($430 + 2*$4). For Population B, we have an approximate 95% CI from \$444 to \$456 ($450 - 2*$3) to ($450 + 2*$3). The decision I would make is that the average monthly expenditure on food by a single-person household is not the same in Populations A and B. How did I come to this decision? Notice that: (1) The upper boundary of Population A's 95% CI does not encompass the 95% CI's lower boundary of B's population mean, where for sample A, the mean = \$430, with a 95% confidence level that the mean of Population A is between \$422 and \$438; and (2) the lower boundary of Population B's 95% CI does not encompass the 95% CI's upper boundary of A's population mean, here B's sample mean = \$450, with a 95% confidence level that the population mean of B is between \$444 and \$456. Exhibit 10.5 provides a graphic illustration of what we have.

Exhibit 10.5. Samples Means for A and B Food Expenditures and Their Sampling Distributions

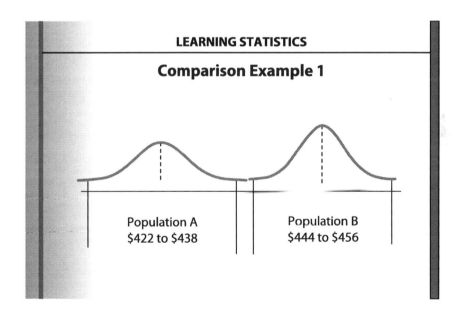

When we get to hypothesis testing in the next chapter you will see that this result can be more precisely stated as being "statistically significant" at the .05 level. That is, we would expect to find sample means this different only 5% or less of the time (in taking an infinite number of samples of size 400 from A and size 900 from B), if, in fact, A and B actually had the same population means.

Comparison Example 2—Wine Expenditures. Suppose now we are looking at wine expenditures from our two samples of single-person households in populations A and B. (Another question in the same survey as the question on food expenditures.) As was the case earlier for Population A, we have a sample of 400, but we find that the mean monthly wine expenditure is $130, with a standard deviation of $80. And in Population B, we also again have a sample of 900, but with a mean monthly wine expenditure of $140 and a standard deviation of $90. Again, the first step is to compute the standard error for each sample. For Population A, we have a standard error of $80/(sqrt(400)) = $80/20 =$4. For Population B, we have a standard error of $90/(sqrt(900)) = $90/30 =$3. As in the first comparison example, the second step is to compute the confidence interval for each sample. For Population A, we have an approximate 95% CI from $122 to $138 ($130 – 2*$4) to ($130 + 2*$4). For Population B, we have an approximate 95% CI from $134 to $146 ($140 – 2*$3) to ($140 + 2*$3). The third step is to compare the boundaries of the two confidence intervals for each of the sample means. For Population A, the 95% CI is from $122 to $138. For Population B, the 95% CI is from $134 to $146. The decision I would make in this comparison is that average monthly expenditure on food by a single-person household is not different in populations A and B. How did I come to this decision? Notice that: (1) The upper boundary of Population A's 95% CI encompasses the 95% CI's lower boundary of Population B's mean, where for sample A, the mean = $430, with a 95% level of confidence that the mean for Population A is between $422 and $438; and (2) the lower boundary of Population B's 95% CI encompasses both the 95% CI's upper boundary of Population A's mean, where for sample B, the mean = $450, with 95% level of confidence that the mean for Population B is between $444 and $456. Exhibit 10.6 provides a graphic illustration of what we have.

Exhibit 10.6. Sample Means for A and B Wine Expenditures and Their Sampling Distributions

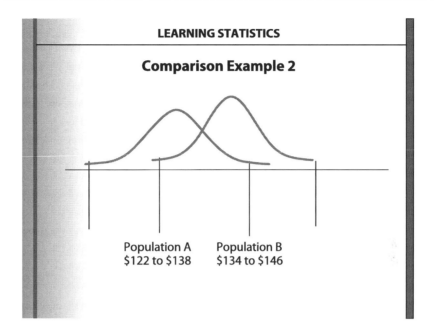

So, from the two questions in our two samples from populations A and B, we will act as if monthly food expenditures by single-person households are different, while monthly wine expenditures are not.

As was the case with the first comparison example, when we get to hypothesis testing in the next chapter, you will see that this result can be more precisely stated as being "Not Statistically Significant" at the .05 level. That is, we would expect to find sample means this different more than 5% of the time (in taking an infinite number of samples of size 400 from A and size 900 from B), if, in fact, A and B actually had the same population means.

ASSIGNMENT FOR CHAPTER 10

Open any of the MS-Word files you have created in earlier assignments and the Excel file that you created in Assignment 8. Continue to pretend you are a research analyst working for a food retailer and that your management wants to know the financial impact of gardens on how much people spend monthly on food. For purposes of this assignment, treat the 50-family data set as a random sample and write something in MS-Word about the impact of gardens on food expenditures, taking into account statistical uncertainty from the standpoint of confidence intervals. Include in your two- to three-page essay what the likely range of the financial impact is. Whatever new work is not in your previous files, save in your updated files (e.g., swanson.assign10.xls and e.g., swanson.assign10.docx).

References

Dillman, D. (1978). *Mail and Telephone Surveys: The Total Design Method.* New York: Wiley-Interscience.

Dillman, D. (2000). *Mail and Internet Surveys: The Tailored Design Method, 2nd ed.* New York: John Wiley & Sons.

11. Making Decisions from Samples: Hypothesis Testing

Hey Data, Stu and Stella want me to pick out a wine to take with us on our road trip. One that goes good with salmon. Would you sample them, then give me your opinion?

A

B

OH, DATA! That is not a choice! It's not even wine!

A. Hypothesis Testing in Action: Two Examples

Hypothesis testing is used to make comparisons. It is composed of six rigidly prescribed steps. The result of a hypothesis test is used to guide decision making under the condition of statistical uncertainty (Henkel, 1976; Mohr, 1990). The comparisons can be made using samples from different populations, a sample of the same population at different points in time, or using a sample and some criterion (i.e., a "standard"). The comparisons also may be made among three or more populations. In this chapter, however, I will not cover the methods, such as the Analysis of Variance, used to make comparisons involving more than two populations. Instead, I will describe in some detail two types of comparisons: (1) Those made using samples from two different populations; and (2) those made using a sample and a "standard."

Let's pick up with the comparison examples at the end of the preceding chapter, which were made using samples from two different populations. Suppose again that we have a random sample from each of two populations in terms of the average amount spent monthly on food for a single-person household. Suppose in Population A we have a sample of 400 and find that the mean is $430, with a standard deviation of $80. In Population B, suppose that we have a sample of 900, a mean of $450, and a standard deviation of $90. (This is "Comparison Example 1" from the end of the last chapter.) As was the case when we used confidence intervals to make the comparison, we would again compute the standard error for each sample. From the sample of Population A, recall that the standard error is $4, while from the sample of Population B, it is $3. However, instead of determining a confidence interval for each sample mean, we would conduct a hypothesis test, which yields a probability that we use to make a decision on whether or not two populations have the same mean.

I will describe the six steps making up a hypothesis test in detail a bit later and what they represent, but for now, I will just go through them. The first step is to specify a research question. Here, my research question is whether or not there is a difference in mean food expenditures between Population A and Population B. That is, I suspect that the two means may be different. Second, I set up something called a "Null Hypothesis," which in the case of our comparison is that the mean expenditure on food in Population A is the same as the mean in Population B. The third step is to specify what is called the "Alternative Hypothesis," for which I am going to say that the mean in Population A is not the same as in Population B. This is a restatement of my research question. The fourth step is to specify an "alpha level" (α), for which I will use 0.05. The alpha level specifies a level of probability, for which I will "reject the Null Hypothesis." That is, if I get a probability when I actually calculate my test that is less than 0.05, then I reject the "Null Hypothesis" and by default go with the "Alternative Hypothesis."

The fifth step is do the hypothesis test, which in this case involves subtracting the sample mean for A ($430) from the sample mean for B ($450), and then dividing this difference by the sum of the two standard errors ($7 = $4 + $3), which yields 2.86 = [($450 – $430)/$7]. This turns out to be a "Z" score, which I can use to see how much of the area under the normal curve is associated with a score of 2.86. I find this score associated with a probability of 0.002 that the "Null Hypothesis" is true. This probability of 0.002 is considerably less than the "alpha level" of .05 that I preset before I did the actual test. Because it is lower than my alpha level probability, I "reject the Null Hypothesis" that the means in populations A and B are equal, which leads me by default to the alternative hypothesis—that the means of A and B are not equal. My sixth and final step is the decision that the mean expenditure by single-person households in Population A is different from the mean by single-person households in Population B. I make this decision with about a 0.2% chance (where 0.2% = 0.002*100) of having rejected a "true Null Hypothesis." Thus, I am pretty sure that the means (which, remember, are unknown) in A and B are different in that I have about a 0.2% chance of being wrong.

You can see that the hypothesis test led me to the same decision I made using the confidence interval approach described at the end of the last chapter. However, unlike the confidence interval approach, the hypothesis test has provided me with a specific probability that the two populations have the same mean, 0.002. Since this probability is much lower than my "alpha level" of 0.05, I have rejected the null hypothesis that the two populations have the same mean, and by rejecting it, I can interpret 0.002 as the probability that I am wrong in having decided that the two populations have different means.

What about the second comparison example from the last chapter, the one where the confidence interval approach indicated that the two population means were not different? In terms of expenditures on wine by single-person households, in Population A, we still have a sample of 400, but in looking at wine expenditures we find that the mean is $130, with a standard deviation of $80. And in Population B we again have a sample of 900, but in terms of wine expenditures we have a mean of $140 and a standard deviation of $90. Again, the first step is to compute the standard error for each sample. For Population A, we have a standard error of $80/(sqrt(400)) = $80/20 =$4. For Population B, we have a standard error of $90/(sqrt(900)) = $90/30 =$3.

Let's now go through the hypothesis test steps with the wine expenditure data and see what decision we come to. Here, recall that from our sample of 400 single-person households in Population A, we found that the mean monthly expenditure on wine was $130 and a standard deviation of $80. And from our sample of 900 single-person households in Population B, the mean monthly wine expenditure was $140 and a standard deviation of $90.

Again, the first step is to state a research question, which in this case is simply that the two means are different. The second step is to specify the "Null Hypothesis," which in the case of our comparison is that the mean expenditure on food in Population A is the same as the mean in Population B. The third step is to specify what is called the "Alternative Hypothesis," for which I am going to say that the mean in Population A is not the same as in Population B. Again, this is a restatement of my research question. The fourth step is to specify an "alpha level," for which I will again use 0.05. The fifth step is to do the hypothesis test, which in this case involves subtracting the sample mean for A ($130) from the sample mean for B ($140) and then dividing this difference by the sum of the two standard errors ($7 = $4 + $3), which yields 1.43 = [($140 − $130)/$7].

This also turns out to be a "Z" score, which I can use to see how much of the area under the normal curve is associated with a score of 1.43. I find this score associated with a probability of 0.076 that the "Null Hypothesis" is true. This is not less than the "alpha level" of 0.05. Because the probability yielded by the test (0.076) is not less than the probability of 0.05 specified by my alpha level, I "do not reject the Null Hypothesis" that the means in populations A and B are equal. Thus, my decision is that the mean expenditure by single-person households in Population A is not different from the mean by single-person households in Population B. This is the sixth and final step. Although the probability that the Null Hypothesis is true is pretty low at 0.076, I follow the convention of hypothesis testing and do not reject it, since it is larger than the 0.05 probability specified by the alpha level I selected.

You can see that the hypothesis tests led me to the same decision I made using the confidence interval approach described at the end of the last chapter. In the case of mean monthly food expenditures by single-person households I decided that they were different in the two populations, A and B, while in the case of mean monthly wine expenditures by single-person households, I decided that they were not different in the two populations, A and B. However, unlike the confidence interval approach, the hypothesis tests have provided me with a specific probability that the two populations have the same mean: 0.002 in the case of monthly food expenditures, and 0.076 in the case of monthly wine expenditures.

Now that you have seen hypothesis testing in action, let's go through its concepts and details.

B. Hypothesis Testing: Some Basics

In each of the examples, I conducted what is known as a "two-tailed" hypothesis test with two "large, independent samples." There are other variants of the hypothesis test, which I will discuss later in this chapter. While there are variants, they all share a common set of six steps, each of which was done in the two examples. Here are the six steps described in terms of deciding if the mean of a given variable is different between two populations, A and B.

Step 1. Formulate a research question in terms of comparing the mean of a given variable in two populations. The research question can take any one of three forms: (1) The two means are different; (2) the mean of Population A is larger than the mean of Population B; and (3) the mean of Population A is smaller than the mean of Population B.

Step 2. Specify the null hypothesis. The null hypothesis is always that there is no difference in the means of Population A and Population B.

Step 3. Specify the alternative hypothesis. The alternative hypothesis is a restatement of your research question, and as such, can take one—and only one—of the three following forms: (1) The mean of Population A is larger than the mean of Population B; (2) the mean of Population A is smaller than the mean of Population B; and (3) the two means are different. By default, if your test leads you to reject the null hypothesis, then you default to acting like the alternative hypothesis is true. Using either of the first two alternatives (either that A is larger than B or that A is smaller than B) leads to a "one-tailed hypothesis test," while using the third alternative (A and B have different means) leads to a "two-tailed hypothesis test."

Step 4. Specify the alpha (α) level, which is also known as the significance level. It is customary in nonexperimental research to use 0.05 and 0.01. This is the level that determines the decision you make in regard to rejecting or not rejecting the Null

Hypothesis. If the probability from your test comes back lower than your preset alpha level probability, then you reject the null hypothesis (and by default go with the alternative hypothesis); if the probability from your test comes back higher than your preset alpha level, then you do not reject the Null Hypothesis.

Step 5. Compute the probability value (also known as the "p" value) for your test. Basically, you are dividing the difference in the sample means by the statistical uncertainty present in the two samples. Thus, the numerator consists of the difference between the two sample means and the denominator consists of the sum of the standard errors of the two samples. This calculation will yield the probability of obtaining the difference actually observed in the two sample means, given that the samples were drawn from two populations with different means, taking into account the statistical uncertainty (the standard deviation and sample size, as summarized in the standard error) in each sample. This step can be done in Excel.

Step 6. Compare the probability value with the alpha level. If the probability value yielded by the test is lower than your preset alpha level, then you reject the null hypothesis and by default go with one of the three possible alternative hypotheses you selected in Step 3. **If the probability value returned by the test is not lower than your preset alpha level, then you do not reject the null hypothesis**.

To summarize, the six steps in every hypothesis test are

1. Formulate the Research Question;
2. Set the Null Hypothesis (H_o) That There Is No Difference;
3. Your Research Question Is the Alternative Hypothesis (H_a);
4. Set Your Alpha Level (α);
5. Run the Appropriate Test; and
6. Decide Whether or Not to Reject the Null Hypothesis (H_o).

Now let's look at each of these steps in detail:

1. Formulate the Research Question. In thinking about the mean food expenditures of single-person households in populations A and B, you may have reason to believe that the mean in one of the populations is higher (or lower) than the mean in the other population. What often forms this belief is prior research, but it could also simply represent a belief. So, you could have two distinct research questions based on this: (1) The mean of Population A is larger than the mean of Population B (equivalent to the mean of Population B is lower than the mean of Population A); and (2) the mean of Population A is lower than the mean of Population B (equivalent to the mean of Population B is higher than the mean of Population A). It also may be the case that you have no reason to believe the mean in one is higher (or lower) than the mean in the other population. In this case, your research question is simply whether or not the two means are different. So, in making a comparison using a sample from two different populations, you have three possible research questions: (1) The mean of A is higher than B; (2) the mean of A is lower than B; and (3) the mean of A is different from B. For reasons I will discuss shortly, the first two research questions lead to what is known as a "one-tailed hypothesis test," while the third one leads to what is known as a "two-tailed hypothesis test."

2. Set the Null Hypothesis (H$_0$) that There Is No Difference. Here, it is that the mean food expenditures of single person households in Population A is not different from the mean food expenditures of single person households in Population B.

3. Your Research Question Is the Alternative Hypothesis (H$_a$). This is a restatement of the choice you made among the three possible research questions in comparing the food expenditures of single-person households in Population A with the mean of Population B. If your research question is that the mean of A is larger than B, then this becomes your alternative hypothesis. If your research question is that the mean of A is smaller than B, then this is your alternative hypothesis. If your research question is the third and most general possibility, namely that the means are different, then this is your alternative hypothesis. As I mentioned earlier, the logic of a hypothesis test is such that if you "reject the Null Hypothesis" test, then by default you have support for the alternative hypothesis you have selected.

4. Set Your Alpha Level (α). This is also known as the "level of (statistical) significance." It is customary to use either 0.05 or 0.01 as the alpha level, although there are occasions where other levels could be used (e.g., 0.001). It is set in advance of doing your test. If your test returns a low probability value, then it suggests you should reject the null hypothesis because it is not likely to be true. The issue is how low must the probability value be in order to decide to reject the null hypothesis. There is no simple answer to this question, since it involves subjective judgment. However, it is customary to reject the null hypothesis if the probability value returned by the test is less than the alpha level. Whichever alpha level you set in advance of the actual test, the result of your test is described as being "statistically significant" if the null hypothesis is rejected. For example, in the case of comparing mean food expenditures between the single-person households in Population A and Population B, the probability value yielded by the test was 0.002, which is far less than the preset alpha level of 0.05. As such, we would call the results of this test "statistically significant." In the case of mean expenditures on wine by the single-person households in populations A and B, the probability value yielded by the test was 0.076, which is above the preset alpha level of 0.05. As such, we would call the results of this test as "statistically not significant." It is very important to keep in mind that "statistical significance" indicates only that the null hypothesis is rejected; it does not mean that the difference is important in a substantive sense. Similarly, "statistically not significant" only indicates that that the null hypothesis was not rejected. It does not indicate that there is no important difference in a substantive sense.

5. Run the Appropriate Test. I have described the formula underlying a comparison of means between two populations. In actual practice, you would use Excel to run the appropriate test, which also will return the probability of the null hypothesis being true associated with the test.

6. Decide Whether or Not to Reject the Null Hypothesis. If the test yields a probability value (e.g., $p = 0.002$) that is less than the preset alpha level (e.g., $\alpha = 0.05$), you reject the null hypothesis, which by default leaves you with your alternative hypothesis. If the test yields a probability value (e.g., $p = 0.076$) that is not less than your preset alpha level (e.g., $\alpha = 0.05$), then you do not reject the null hypothesis.

A hypothesis test is often described in symbolic terms, which, like many symbols in mathematics and statistics, is used in favor of long descriptions in text form. The test of monthly food expenditure means in Populations A and B would appear in symbolic terms as follows:

$$H_0: \mu_A = \mu_B$$
$$H_a: \mu_A \neq \mu_B$$
$$\alpha = 0.05$$
$$p = 0.002$$

where

H_0 = Null Hypothesis (the two means are equal);

H_a = Alternative Hypothesis (which in this case is that the two means are not equal);

μ_A = mean food expenditures of single-person households in Population A;

μ_B = mean food expenditures of single-person households in Population B;

α = the preset alpha level, which in this case is 0.05;

p = the probability of H_0 being true that was returned by the test. Since $p < \alpha$, we reject H_0 and by default go with H_a, which is that the two means are not equal.

Now let's look at different types of two-tailed and one-tailed tests, then at the types of hypothesis tests. After that, we will look at the concepts underlying hypothesis testing.

C. How Many Tails Does Your Test Have?

What is a "two-tailed" test and what is a "one-tailed" test? These two procedures can be used with any of the three hypothesis tests involving means that I describe in the next section of this chapter. They are associated with your choice of one of the three possibilities for an alternative hypothesis. If you select the alternative hypothesis that states that the two means are different, then your test will be two-tailed. If you select either of the other two alternative hypotheses (e.g., the mean of Population A is higher than the mean of B or the mean of Population A is lower than the mean of B), then your test will be one-tailed. In other words, a two-tailed test computes the probability of the two means simply being different, while a one-tailed test computes the probability that one mean is higher (lower) than the other mean. Exhibit 11.1 shows the areas in the sampling distribution associated with the two-tailed test, while Exhibit 11.2 shows the area in the sampling distribution associated with a one-tailed test, in which the alternative hypothesis is that the mean of A is higher than the mean of B. Exhibit 11.3 shows the area in the sampling distribution associated with a one-tailed test, in which the alternative hypothesis is that the mean of A is lower than the mean of B.

Exhibit 11.1. The Areas in the Sampling Distribution Associated with a Two-Tailed Test Ha: $\mu A \uparrow \mu B$

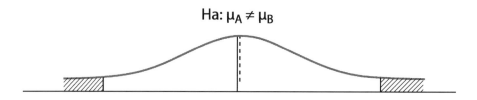

Exhibit 11.2. The Area in the Sampling Distribution Associated with a One-Tailed Test

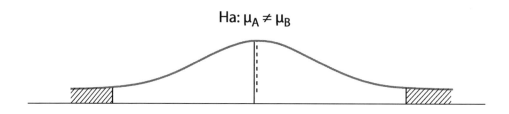

Exhibit 11.3. The Area in the Sampling Distribution Associated with a One-Tailed Test

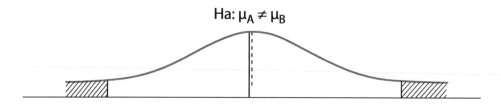

Recall that we can interpret the area under the "curve" in terms of probability. In Exhibit 11.1, you can see a shaded area in both of the "tails" of the sampling distribution's "curve." If you are using an alpha level of 0.05, then each shaded area would represent half of 0.05 (0.025) of the area in the distribution. In the example I gave earlier of the test for a difference in the two means for food consumption between single-person households in Population A and single-person households in Population

B, the alternative hypothesis was that the two means were different. This resulted in a two-tailed test. Using my alpha level of 0.05, the test resulted in a score of 2.86 (where $2.86 = [(\$450 - \$430)/(\$3 + \$4)]$), which was well beyond the score associated with the 0.025 area on the "positive" side of the curve, such that the area associated with 2.86 was 0.002. The point in the middle of the curve shown in Exhibit 11.1 (as well as in Exhibits 11.2 and 11.3) is associated with a score of zero, with 50% of the area of the curve to the right of this point and 50% to the left of it. How would a score of zero result from the test? The answer is if the two sample means were the same. Had we had a mean of $430 in both Population A and Population B, then the score in the test would have been 0.00 $= [(\$430 - \$430)/(\$3 + \$4)]$, and a score of zero in the two-tailed test would result in a probability of 0.5, which is well above the 0.025 to the right of the curve and the 0.025 to the left of the curve.

Note also that if I had reversed the order of the two sample means when I calculated the test and subtracted the mean for B from the mean for A, the test would have yielded -2.86, where $-2.86 = [(\$430 - \$450)/(\$3 + \$4)]$. A score of -2.86 would have been well beyond the score at the left of the curve associated with the "0.025" area, since the area associated with a score of -2.86 is 0.002. Again, I would have rejected the null hypothesis that the means in the two populations were equal, which leads to the alternative hypothesis (in my two-tailed test) that they are not equal. I make this decision because the probability of the null hypothesis being true is 0.002, which is well below my preset alpha level of 0.05.

As you know already, a one-tailed test is associated with either of the remaining two alternative hypotheses, where one of the means is hypothesized to be either larger or smaller than the other. You are getting an idea of how this works, since you now know how a two-tailed test works. Returning to the example of the two means for food expenditures of single-person households in Populations A and B, suppose I would have used the alternative hypothesis that the mean of A is smaller than the mean of B and had set the alpha level at 0.05. In this test, I would have ended up with the score we just saw ($-2.86 = [(\$430 - \$450)/(\$3 + \$4)]$), which again is associated with a probability of 0.002. This would have led to the decision to reject the null hypothesis, and by default go with the alternative that the mean of Population A is smaller than the mean of Population B. However, instead of comparing it to the area of 0.025 as is the case with the two-tailed test when $\alpha = 0.05$, I would have compared it directly to the area of 0.05. Similarly, had my alternative hypothesis been that the mean of Population B is larger than the mean of Population A, the score would have been $2.86 = [(\$450 - \$430)/(\$3 + \$4)]$), which is associated with an area of 0.002, far smaller than the area of 0.05. This would have led me to reject the null hypothesis, and by default go with the alternative that the mean of Population B is larger than the mean of Population A.

You may be asking yourself by now where I got the probabilities associated with the test scores I have discussed. The answer is that I got them from a "Probability Table for the Standard Normal Curve," which you have seen in Chapter 6 (Exhibit 6.8) and can again see in the appendix to this chapter. This table, known as the "Z-Test Probability

Table," gives the area from zero to my score (which, by the way, as I wrote earlier is a "Z" score), so when I found the area associated with 2.86 to be 0.4979, I had to subtract it from 0.5 (the area associated with a Z score of zero), which resulted in 0.5 − 0.4979 ≈ 0.002. See if you can figure out where the probability of 0.076 came from in this table using a Z score of 1.43 (the result of the test for the equality of the two means for wine expenditures among single-person households in Populations A and B). I knew I could use this table, because my sample size was above 25 in both Population A (where it was 400) and in Population B (where it was 900). If my sample size was around 25 or so, I would have used the "T-Test Probability Table," which is designed specifically for small samples.[1]

Keep in mind that I am showing the probability table for the Z scores with the idea of helping you understand what is going on in a hypothesis test. In actual practice, you will be using Excel to do all of these calculations, including finding the probability that the null hypothesis is true. I will do so taking into account the size of your sample, thus using the appropriate table (Z or T).

D. Types of Hypothesis Tests

There are many types of hypothesis tests. In this chapter, I will describe two at some length and then briefly describe a third. All three of the tests I describe in this chapter involve comparisons of means. In addition, there are two other hypothesis tests not involving means that you will see in Chapter 13. The three tests I will describe in this chapter are for: (1) Determining if there is a difference between the means of two "independent" populations; (2) determining if a single mean is different from some standard; and (3) determining if there is a difference between the means of two "related" populations—that is, two populations that are "not independent." You have already seen examples of the first type, testing for a difference between the means of two independent populations so you have an idea of how they operate.

Underlying all of these tests are assumptions (as is the case in virtually all of statistical inference). Since in most research these assumptions are treated as being true, I will describe only one of them here, which is whether or not the samples are from populations that have the same variance. You will learn more about the other assumptions and the consequences of violating them if you continue with more statistical classes. Basically, the assumptions are always violated to some extent, but the tests are sufficiently "robust" to handle most of the violations. It is only when the assumptions are horribly violated that the test results can be rendered invalid.

Two Independent Populations. In terms of the assumption about whether or not the variable whose mean you are comparing has the same variance in the two populations being compared, Excel can handle either situation, but you are never making an "incorrect" assumption if you simply assume that the two variances are not equal. This leads you to the more general form of the hypothesis test, which in Excel is called the "T-Test: Two-Sample Assuming Unequal Variances." As an example of using this test, I used monthly family expenditures on food by the presence of a garden from our 50-family sample. There are 30 families without gardens and 20 with gardens. I can assume that these two groups are selected from "different" populations, because information from one group is not correlated with the information in the other group. I also can use the "unequal variances" assumption, since this is the most general.

The structure of my hypothesis test is as follows. First, my research question is that I believe families without gardens spend more on food than families with gardens (which leads to a one-tailed test). The null hypothesis is that the mean expenditures on food for the two populations (with and without gardens) are equal. The alternative hypothesis is that the mean expenditures on food for families without gardens is higher than the mean expenditures on food for families with gardens, and I select 0.05 as my alpha level. To run the test in Excel, I sorted the 50-family sample by garden (0 = no garden; 1 = garden) as shown in Table 11.1.

I then opened the Data Analysis package under the "Tools" tab, scrolled through the items available in the Data Analysis package until I found "T-Test: Two-Sample Assuming Unequal Variances," and selected it. This brought up the pop-up menu shown in Exhibit 11.4.

Because the food consumption values for families without gardens were in cells D21 to D50, I placed them into the "Variable 1 Range" shown in the pop-up in Exhibit 11.4; since the food consumption values for families with gardens were in cells D51 to D70, I placed them in the "variable 2 range" of the same pop-up. I then entered "0" in the "hypothesized mean difference" area as the "null hypothesis," and entered cell "J23" as the location for the results of the test. Exhibit 11.5 shows how the input values look in the pop-up. Exhibit 11.6 shows the results of the T-Test.

The results show that for the one-tailed test, the "p value" is 0.000013, which is far lower than my alpha level of 0.05. Thus, I reject the null hypothesis, and by default go with my alternative hypothesis that the mean food expenditures for families without gardens is higher than the mean for families with gardens. If I had used the alternative hypothesis that the two means were different, what decision would I have made?

Testing a Mean Against a Standard. In testing a single mean against a standard, we only have one sample. From this sample, we are testing to see if the mean of the population from which the sample was taken is the same as a mean selected on the basis of belief, prior experience, or because it is used to make decisions. That is, we are comparing the mean of the population from which our sample was drawn against a mean being used as a standard, one that is not from another population. Referring to the mean expenditures on food in Population B, which was $450, it might be the case that from prior experience we were pretty sure that the mean was $440. Thus, we could use $440 as the standard. In this situation, it is highly likely that our research question is if the mean of Population B is, in fact, above $440. This would lead to the alternative hypothesis that the mean of Population B is more than $440. If we selected α = 0.05, then our test would look as follows:

	Table 11.1 Food Income Family Size and Garden Data Set			
Case	Monthly Family Food Expenditures	Annual Family Income	Family Size	Garden (1=yes; 0 = no)
4	$1,148.24	$81,420.00	1	0
6	$2,560.22	$127,110.00	1	0
7	$2,122.52	$134,260.00	1	0
8	$3,211.64	$148,120.00	1	0
11	$1,792.18	$62,660.00	2	0
14	$1,953.58	$71,030.00	2	0
15	$2,372.00	$75,160.00	2	0
16	$1,810.96	$85,620.00	2	0
17	$1,776.58	$86,510.00	2	0
18	$1,284.00	$94,610.00	2	0
20	$1,682.36	$110,600.00	2	0
21	$1,472.44	$116,440.00	2	0
22	$2,194.76	$117,940.00	2	0
23	$2,328.96	$119,540.00	2	0
25	$2,108.14	$83,320.00	3	0
26	$2,295.04	$91,270.00	3	0
27	$1,939.00	$100,540.00	3	0
28	$2,443.06	$103,000.00	3	0
32	$1,904.66	$144,370.00	3	0
34	$2,125.30	$73,110.00	4	0
35	$2,003.44	$106,190.00	4	0
36	$2,534.66	$116,580.00	4	0
37	$2,111.50	$147,250.00	4	0
38	$2,665.78	$148,450.00	4	0
40	$2,477.34	$75,860.00	5	0
41	$2,819.06	$131,430.00	5	0
42	$2,763.40	$142,780.00	5	0
45	$2,612.00	$119,150.00	6	0
46	$2,253.46	$139,680.00	6	0
48	$2,308.16	$112,260.00	7	0
1	$723.52	$41,230.00	1	1
2	$1,025.52	$59,110.00	1	1
3	$866.62	$71,940.00	1	1
5	$877.52	$94,540.00	1	1
9	$1,189.40	$53,130.00	2	1
10	$1,295.64	$54,920.00	2	1
12	$780.06	$66,100.00	2	1
13	$1,273.34	$69,730.00	2	1
19	$1,502.94	$96,650.00	2	1
24	$975.10	$132,950.00	2	1
29	$1,638.26	$118,540.00	3	1
30	$1,666.90	$121,080.00	3	1
31	$1,068.38	$135,730.00	3	1
33	$780.70	$43,710.00	4	1
39	$1,328.00	$64,760.00	5	1
43	$990.74	$45,240.00	6	1
44	$1,336.14	$66,930.00	6	1
47	$1,634.98	$52,920.00	7	1
49	$2,950.72	$68,730.00	8	1
50	$3,103.54	$127,520.00	9	1

Exhibit 11.4. The Pop-up Menu for "T-Test: Two-Sample Assuming Unequal Variances"

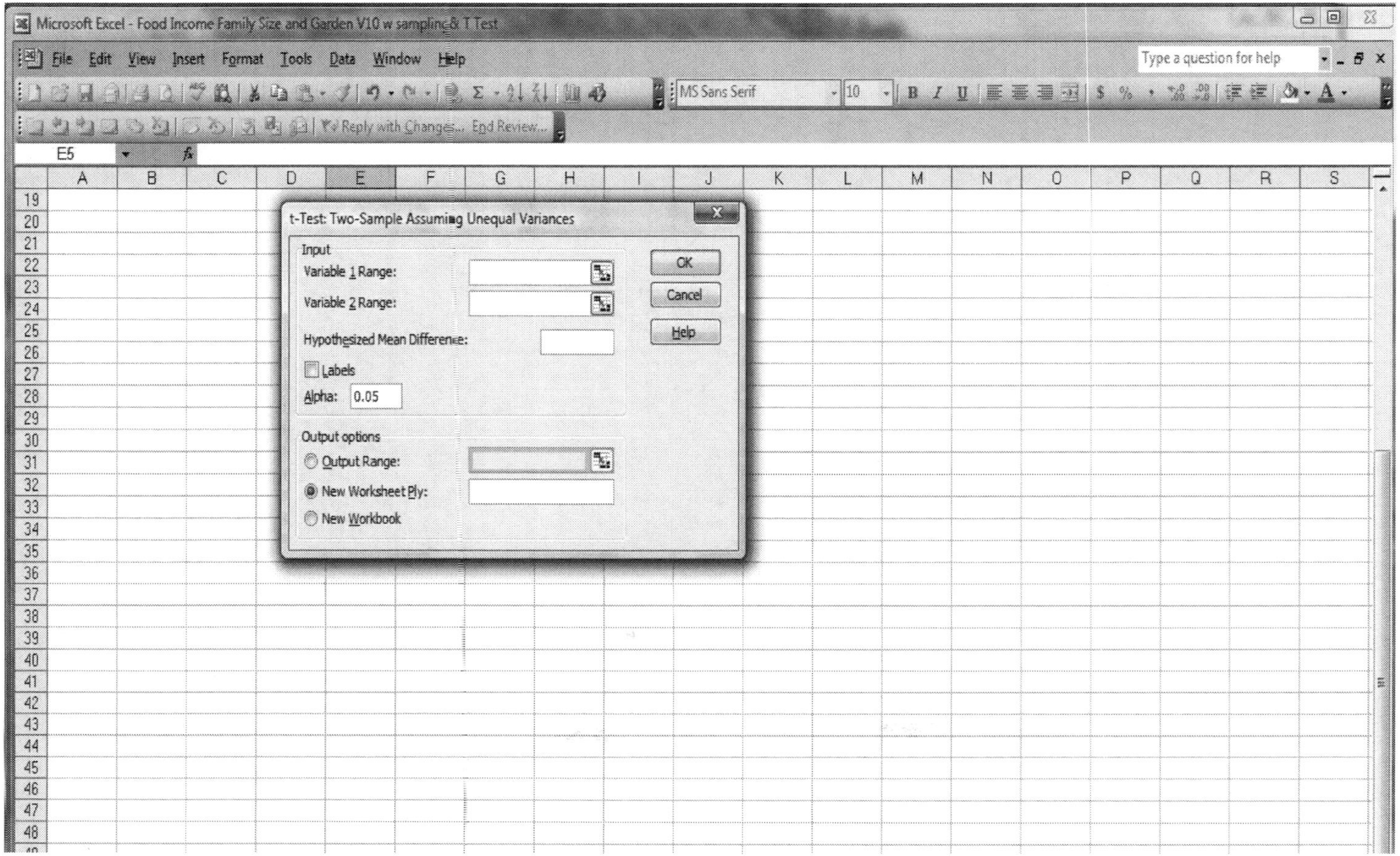

Exhibit 11.5. Input Values for the T-Test (Two Populations with Unequal Variances) of the Equivalence of Mean Family Food Expenditures between Families without Gardens and Families with Gardens

	C	D	E	F	G
21	4	$1,148.24	$81,420.00	1	0
22	6	$2,560.22	$127,110.00	1	0
23	7	$2,122.52	$134,260.00	1	0
24	8	$3,211.64	$148,120.00	1	0
25	11	$1,792.18	$62,660.00	2	0
26	14	$1,953.58	$71,030.00	2	0
27	15	$2,372.00	$75,160.00	2	0
28	16	$1,810.96	$85,620.00	2	0
29	17	$1,776.58	$86,510.00	2	0
30	18	$1,284.00	$94,610.00	2	0
31	20	$1,682.36	$110,600.00	2	0
32	21	$1,472.44	$116,440.00	2	0
33	22	$2,194.76	$117,940.00	2	0
34	23	$2,328.96	$119,540.00	2	0
35	25	$2,108.14	$83,320.00	3	0
36	26	$2,295.04	$91,270.00	3	0
37	27	$1,939.00	$100,540.00	3	0
38	28	$2,443.06	$103,000.00	3	0
39	32	$1,904.66	$144,370.00	3	0
40	34	$2,125.30	$73,110.00	4	0
41	35	$2,003.44	$106,190.00	4	0
42	36	$2,534.66	$116,580.00	4	0
43	37	$2,111.50	$147,250.00	4	0
44	38	$2,665.78	$148,450.00	4	0
45	40	$2,477.34	$75,860.00	5	0
46	41	$2,819.06	$131,430.00	5	0

t-Test: Two-Sample Assuming Unequal Variances

Input
Variable 1 Range: $D$21:$D$50
Variable 2 Range: $D$52:$D$70
Hypothesized Mean Difference: 0
Labels
Alpha: 0.05

Output options
Output Range: $I$21
New Worksheet Ply:
New Workbook

OK   Cancel   Help

Exhibit 11.6. Results of the T-Test (Two Populations with Unequal Variances) of the Equivalence of Mean Family Food Expenditures between Families without Gardens and Families with Gardens

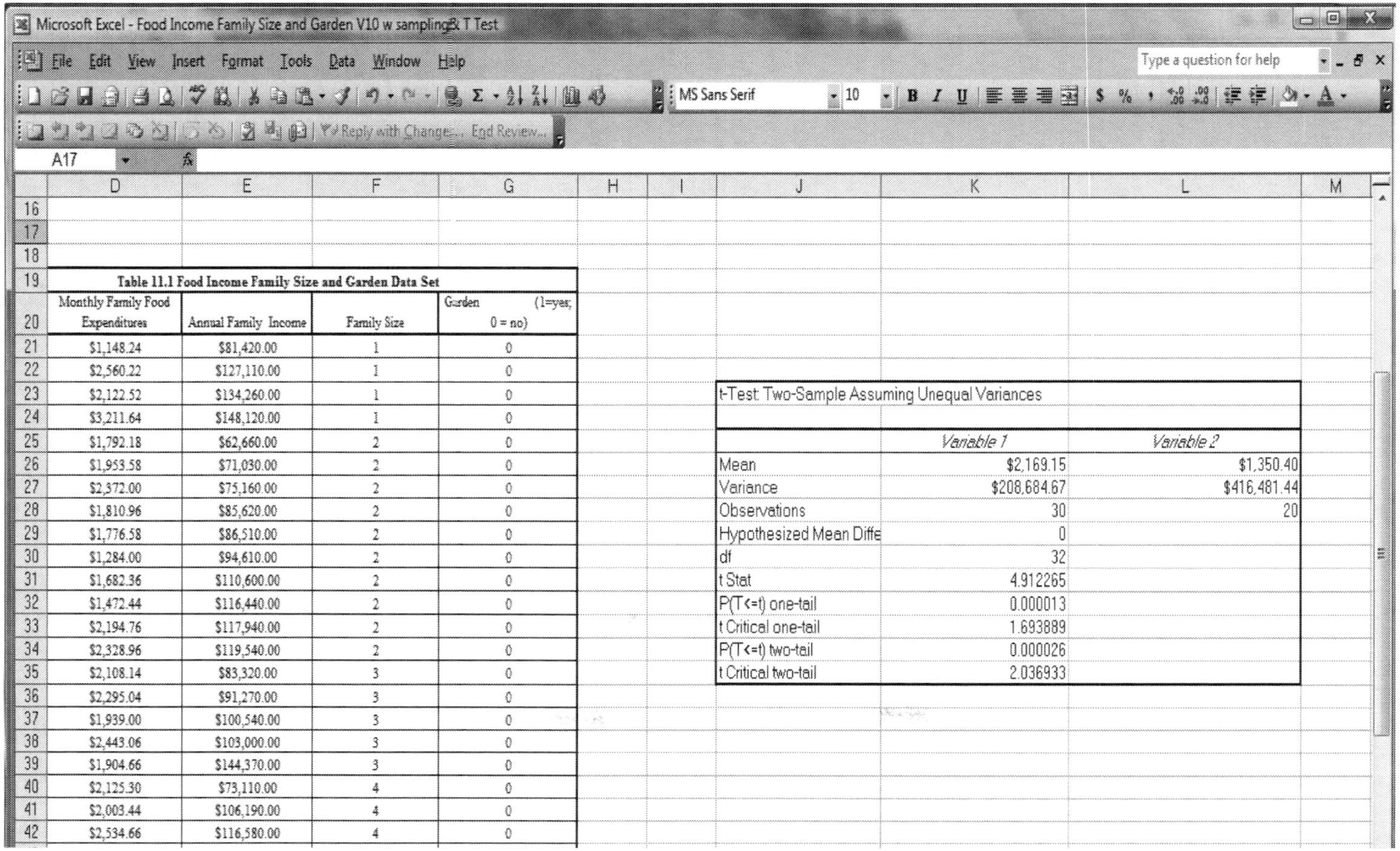

Screenshot: Microsoft Excel - Food Income Family Size and Garden V10 w sampling & T Test

Cell reference: A17

Table 11.1 Food Income Family Size and Garden Data Set

	Monthly Family Food Expenditures	Annual Family Income	Family Size	Garden (1=yes; 0 = no)
20				
21	$1,148.24	$81,420.00	1	0
22	$2,560.22	$127,110.00	1	0
23	$2,122.52	$134,260.00	1	0
24	$3,211.64	$148,120.00	1	0
25	$1,792.18	$62,660.00	2	0
26	$1,953.58	$71,050.00	2	0
27	$2,372.00	$75,160.00	2	0
28	$1,810.96	$85,620.00	2	0
29	$1,776.58	$86,510.00	2	0
30	$1,284.00	$94,610.00	2	0
31	$1,682.36	$110,600.00	2	0
32	$1,472.44	$116,440.00	2	0
33	$2,194.76	$117,940.00	2	0
34	$2,328.96	$119,540.00	2	0
35	$2,108.14	$83,320.00	3	0
36	$2,295.04	$91,270.00	3	0
37	$1,939.00	$100,540.00	3	0
38	$2,443.06	$103,000.00	3	0
39	$1,904.66	$144,370.00	3	0
40	$2,125.30	$73,110.00	4	0
41	$2,003.44	$106,190.00	4	0
42	$2,534.66	$116,580.00	4	0

t-Test Two-Sample Assuming Unequal Variances

	Variable 1	Variable 2
Mean	$2,169.15	$1,350.40
Variance	$208,684.67	$416,481.44
Observations	30	20
Hypothesized Mean Diffe	0	
df	32	
t Stat	4.912265	
P(T<=t) one-tail	0.000013	
t Critical one-tail	1.693889	
P(T<=t) two-tail	0.000026	
t Critical two-tail	2.036933	

$H_o: \mu_B = \$440;$
$H_a: \mu_B > \$440;$
$\alpha = 0.05.$

To obtain the Z score, we would subtract the standard from our sample mean (the numerator), and then we would divide this difference by the standard error (the denominator). Hence, our Z score would be calculated as 3.33 = ($450–$440/$3). Is this result "statistically significant?" Let's look up 3.33 in the Z score table in the appendix to see. In doing this, I find that a Z score of 3.33 is associated with a probability of 0.0004 (where 0.0004 = 0.5 – .4996). This is well below the alpha level of 0.05 in our one-tailed test, and therefore, I would reject the null hypothesis that the mean of Population B is $440 and by default go with the alternative I selected, which is that the mean is higher than $440.

The difference between this test and the preceding one I described for testing means from two different populations is in the denominator. In the test of means from two different populations, the denominator consists of the sum of the standard errors from both samples. In the test of a single mean against a standard, the denominator consists of the single standard error from the single sample. There is no Excel procedure specifically set up to do this type of hypothesis test. I suspect this is because it can be done easily enough by getting Excel to calculate the mean of the sample in question and its standard error, from which you can finish the test using some simple Excel calculations. The only issue you would have to deal with is if your sample size is around 25, which means you would have to locate a "T-Test Probability Table" and learn how to use it.

The Paired T-Test. The third type of hypothesis test is one in which the two means are from populations that are not independent. This often called the "Paired T-Test." Typically, this is found in semi-experimental or fully experimental research, where the subjects are examined twice. For example, an elementary school teacher may administer a reading examination at the start of the school year to students in his or her class and then administer the same reading examination at the end of the school year to see what, if any, average improvement took place in terms of the class as a whole. Our hypothesis test would involve comparing the two means, but the populations are not independent since the same students are in both of the two populations (or nearly so). This is why the hypothesis test for this situation is often called the "Paired T-Test." That is, we can pair up the scores of each student in the two examinations. In so doing, we are likely to find that students who scored above the average in the first examination are likely to score above the average in the second examination. Similarly, we are likely to find that the students who scored below the average in the first examination are likely to score below the average in the second examination. That is, the scores in the two examinations are "correlated" (a topic we pick up in the next chapter). If it is not removed, this "correlation effect" would render our hypothesis test invalid. So, to do a valid hypothesis test the correlation effect, is, in fact removed. It is a rather complicated process, but Excel has a hypothesis test that is set up to do this. It is called the "T-Test: Paired Sample for Two Means."

E. Conceptual Issues

Some History. Although there were earlier pioneers, the hypothesis testing described in this chapter is what has become known as the "classical approach" to statistical testing. This approach is largely a hybrid of ideas developed by Ronald A. Fisher on the one hand, and Jerzy Neyman and Egon Pearson (Hubbard and Bayarri, 2003) on the other. Fisher was responsible for the idea of setting up a null hypothesis and then rejecting it if the researcher sets up a null hypothesis that a sample comes from a "hypothetical infinite population" with a known sampling distribution (essentially, this is the approach found in the "single-sample test of a mean against a standard" described in the preceding section). Fisher went on to advise that if the p-value of the test is lower than a standard "level of significance," then the null hypothesis was to be rejected. Fisher advised that "it is useful and convenient for experimenters to take 5% (e.g., $\alpha = 0.05$) as the standard level of significance (Fisher, 1966: 13). Fisher's reasoning is basically inductive, an approach to logic that does not sit well with many mathematicians, who are accustomed to using deductive logic. Both Neyman and Pearson wanted to improve on Fisher's idea of significance testing by recasting it in deductive form. In so doing, they developed the idea of the alternative hypothesis and called their approach "hypothesis testing" (Hubbard and Bayarri, 2003). They were successful in this endeavor, in that the structure of hypothesis tests uses a form of deductive logic called a syllogism.[2] In addition, Neyman and Pearson extended the implicit "single-sample test of a mean against a standard" approach used by Fisher to an approach that could compare means of real populations by using samples selected from these real populations.

In their extension of Fisher's ideas, Neyman and Pearson recognized that in Fisher's system, there was only one type of possible error—namely, that one could "reject a true null hypothesis." However, with the addition of an alternative, they recognized that there were two types of possible errors, "rejecting a true null hypothesis" and "failing to reject a false null hypothesis" (because by default, if one rejected the null hypothesis, one went with the alternative hypothesis). In fact, Neyman and Pearson (1933) named these errors: (1) Type I error, which is the rejection of a true null hypothesis; and (2) Type II error, which is the failure to reject a false null hypothesis. We will look at these two types of errors in some depth. However, first we will look at the idea of statistical significance, which occurs in both the formulation of "significance testing" by Fisher and the formulation of "hypothesis testing" by Neyman and Pearson.

Statistical Significance. In the classical approach to hypothesis testing described here, statistical significance means simply that you decided to reject the null hypothesis. It is important to keep in mind that statistical significance is not the same as an "important difference." Whereas statistical significance simply means that the null hypothesis was rejected, an important difference is more judgmental and has to do with the actual difference between two means. For example, if you took a sample of 10,000 single-person households in San Jose, California, and found that the average monthly expenditure on wine was $139.75 while a sample of 10,000 single-person households in San Francisco showed that it was $139.50, the difference is inconsequential. Moreover, given that the standard deviations were small, with sample sizes this large, it is likely that a T-Test would return a p-value that would lead you to reject the null hypothesis that the means were equal in the two populations from which the two samples were drawn. However, the finding of "statistical significance" would lead to a big-time "so what" for a marketing company or public health organization interested in wine consumption in the two cities, given the nearness of the two means. However, differences on the order of $100 or more would likely get the attention of both the marketing company and the public health organization.

In the test just conducted that compared the difference in monthly family food expenditures between those without a garden and those with a garden, the result was statistically significant (p =0.00001). In addition, the difference is substantial. The families without gardens spend on average $2,169.15 monthly on food, while those with gardens spend on average $1,350.40. The difference is $818.75, which is not trivial. This is an example of what I would call an important difference.

In fact, the developer of the T-Test, W. S. Gosset, was acutely aware of the difference between statistical significance and an important difference since he was trying to brew high-quality beer for the Guinness Brewery at reasonable prices (Ziliak and McCloskey, 2008). However, this important distinction was late to come both to R. A. Fisher and to J. Neyman and E. Pearson, whose ideas became widespread and literally "ritualized" into the practice of statistical testing without conveying the idea of taking into account whether or not there was an "important difference." Unfortunately, the ritualized nature of statistical testing exacerbated this by placing "statistical significance" as the only result worth reporting in scientific research (Ziliak and McCloskey, 2008).

At the other end of the important difference dimension, in a simple majority election, the difference between 50.1% of the vote and 49.9% means a win on the one hand, and a loss on the other. Thus, a statistically significant finding in a sample of voters that shows even a very small difference could be quite an important difference when the election is very close. As an example of this, shortly you will see the Kitsap County voter sample in terms of a hypothesis test.

When a hypothesis test results in a high probability value, it means that the data provide little or no evidence that the null hypothesis is false. However, the high probability value is not conclusive evidence that the null hypothesis is true. The problem is that it is impossible to distinguish no difference from a very small difference, especially when small samples are involved. So, how should you interpret a non-significant result? Essentially, is that you withhold judgment, which is why you use the phrase "the null hypothesis was not rejected" instead of the phrase that the "null hypothesis is accepted." This may sound like a silly difference, but if you say that you accepted the null hypothesis, you are literally saying that it is true, and, in fact, even if you decided not to reject it, the null hypothesis may not be true.

The situation is similar in using the phrase that the "null hypothesis is rejected" instead of the phrase "the alternative hypothesis was accepted." If we make the decision to reject the null hypothesis, we have strong statistical evidence that it is not true, but there is no guarantee that the alternative is true. What we have is that "we go with the alternative" via the "drop-through" logic of the syllogistic structure of the hypothesis test. That is, we act as if the alternative is true, but we know (via the p-value) the probability that it may not be, and this probability is always greater than zero.

The Results of a Hypothesis Test. So, you know that you can have a false null hypothesis or a true null hypothesis. Associated with these two possibilities are four possible decisions, two of which are correct and two of which are not correct. If the null hypothesis is true and you decide not to reject it, you have made the correct decision; however, if the null hypothesis is true and you decide to reject it, you have made a "Type I error." If the null hypothesis is false and you decide to reject it, you have made the correct decision; however, if the null hypothesis is false and you decide not to reject it, you have made a "Type II error." You also know that the p-value you get back from a given hypothesis test gives you the probability that the null hypothesis is true. Hence, if you decide to reject the null hypothesis, this same p-value gives you the probability that you have made a Type I error.

At this point, you may be wondering if one can see the probability of making a Type II error? In fact, there is, but unfortunately, it is not simply found by subtracting your p-value from 1.00. While the probability of making a Type II error goes up as the p-value goes higher (and decreases as the p-value gets lower), there are several factors that go into its computation; Excel is not set up to use them and do the calculations. The factors include the alpha level, sample size(s), and the magnitude of the difference between the means being compared.

Even though Excel is not set up to calculate the probability of making a Type II error, we can decrease the probability of making a Type II error by setting alpha at a higher level that the conventional level of 0.05. For example, if alpha is set at 0.10, we are decreasing the probability of making a Type II error. The trade-off, of course, is that if we increase the alpha level, we increase the probability of making a Type I error. But we can always see this probability. Moreover, there are many situations where the "cost" of making a Type I error versus the cost of making a Type II error can be assessed, at least to some degree. That is, the consequence of making a Type I error as opposed to making a Type II error can be used in setting up a hypothesis test to reflect these costs. The following two hypothetical examples illustrate how this can be done.

In the first example, suppose you work for a major, well-established, and profitable pharmaceutical company that is developing a new drug to fight a specific type of cancer, and that evidence to date shows that the new drug is much less expensive than the existing drug on the market used to fight this type of cancer. In addition, current research suggests that the new drug is equally effective (in terms of average survival time after the drug is administered to patients with the cancer at the same stage of about the same age, sex, and so on). You are now responsible for setting up final clinical trials for comparing the effectiveness of this new drug to the existing drug before your company applies to the U.S. Food and Drug Administration for approval to bring the new drug to market. Suppose further that your company is fiscally conservative, which in the case of bringing an experimental drug to market means that it is highly averse to bringing a new drug to market that will not return a profit. In terms of the testing you are about to set up, this means that the company absolutely does not want to bear any additional costs of bringing the new drug to market if it is not equally as effective as the existing drug. Given the information you have and assuming the sample size is set along with all the testing protocols, there are three questions you have to answer: (1) What is the null hypothesis? (2) What is the alternative hypothesis? and (3) Where should you set the alpha level? Think about this, come up with your answers to these three questions, and then look at my suggested answers in Exhibit 11.7.

Exhibit 11.7. Pharmaceutical Company Example 1

$$H_0: \mu_n = \mu_o$$
$$H_a: \mu_n < \mu_o$$
$$\alpha = 0.20$$

where
n = new drug
o = old drug

What did you select for H_o, H_a, and α? If it was different from my suggestions, consider my reasons for giving them. First, we know that H_o has to be that the mean survival time of the new drug is the same as that for the old drug. The real question is what should H_a be. I chose $H_a: \mu_n < \mu_o$ to deal with the company's conservative fiscal nature. That is, what is of real concern is that the new drug might be less effective than the old drug. If, in fact, the new drug turns out to be more effective than the old drug, then that will be the icing on the cake. The fiscal nature of the company is what led me to select $\alpha = 0.20$. This is clearly much higher than the standard of $\alpha = 0.05$. Choosing 0.20, I have made it much easier to reject H_o, which is in line with the company aversion to losing money. It may be the case that the new drug is much less expensive than the old drug, but if it is not at least as effective, doctors would have trouble justifying using it even though it is much less expensive. Since your company is well established and profitable, it would rather run the risk of not hitting a home run with the new drug than striking out with it by taking it to market.

In the second example, suppose you are still working for the same major, well-established, and profitable pharmaceutical company. However, now it is developing a new drug to fight a specific type of cancer, and that evidence to date shows the new drug is much more expensive than the existing drug on the market used to fight this type of cancer. In addition, current research suggests that the new drug is much more effective (in terms of average survival time after the drug is administered to patients with the cancer at the same stage who are about the same age, sex, and so on). You again are responsible for setting up final clinical trials for comparing the effectiveness of this new drug to the existing drug before your company applies to the U.S. Food and Drug Administration for approval to bring this new drug to market. Given the information you have and assuming the sample size is set along with all the testing protocols, there are three questions you again have to answer: (1) What is the null hypothesis? (2) What is the alternative hypothesis? and (3) Where should you set the alpha level? Think about this, come up with your answers to these three questions, and then look at my suggested answers in Exhibit 11.8.

Exhibit 11.8. Pharmaceutical Company Example 2

$$H_o: \mu_n = \mu_o$$
$$H_a: \mu_n < \mu_o$$
$$\alpha = 0.001$$

where
n = new drug
o = old drug

What did you select for H_o, H_a, and α in this second example? If it was different from my suggestions, consider my reasons for giving them. First, we again know that H_o has to be that the mean survival time of the new drug is the same as that for the old drug. Second, the major question is what we should use for H_a. I chose $H_a: \mu_n > \mu_o$ to deal with the company's conservative fiscal nature. That is, what is of real concern is to be very sure that the new drug is more effective than the old drug before taking it to the market. Third, the fiscal nature of the company is what led me to select $\alpha = 0.001$. This is clearly much lower than the standard of $\alpha = 0.05$. By choosing 0.001, I have made it much more difficult to reject Ho, which is in line with the company aversion to losing money. If the new drug is not more effective than the old drug, then doctors would have trouble justifying its use, especially given its higher cost. Since your company is well established and profitable, it once again would rather run the risk of not hitting a home run with the new drug than striking out with it by taking it to market.

In both of the examples, the structuring of the hypothesis tests and the setting of alpha reflects a conservative approach, which would likely be the case with a major, well-established, profitable company. A new company (not well established) might be more aggressive, hoping for a home run in the market. In the case of a new company hoping for a home run, I would set alpha lower (e.g., α = 0.10 or even 0.05) in example 1 and in example 2, I would set it much higher (e.g., α = 0.01 or even 0.05).

The approach to the hypothesis tests and their respective alpha levels might be quite different if it was a public health entity conducting the tests. The overriding concern for it is not likely to be profitability and patient health, but cost effectiveness relative to patient health. As you can see from these examples, there is a lot of good judgment needed, not just in the interpretation of hypothesis tests, but their design. And critical to the design is the understanding of the trade-off between Type I and Type II errors. As stated by Hubbard and Bayarri, 2003), the trade-offs between Type I and Type II errors has "… nothing to do with statistical theory, but are based instead on context-dependent pragmatic considerations where informed personal judgment plays a vital role."

As a practical example of the judgment involved in hypothesis testing, recall the situation of the Kitsap County Survey in Chapter 10, where in advance of the election voters were asked how much they were willing to tax themselves so that bonds could be purchased in order to preserve green space. In a sample of 400, 58.5% of the respondents stated that they would be willing to tax themselves $100 more per year for five years to preserve green space. The standard error was 2.90. We can do a hypothesis test to see if the percent saying yes is above 50 (majority rules). Here, the issue of "important difference" boils down to 1% (or less) in that more than 50% of the voters must vote in favor of taxing themselves an additional $100 in order to pass the bond issue. I would set up the test structure as follows:

H_o: μ_y = 50.00%
H_a: μ_y > 50.00%
α = 0.01
where
μ_y = percent of voters saying yes (remember that a percentage is in fact a mean).

In running the "single sample" test, we find that Z = 2.93 (58.5–50.00)/2.90, and the probability of getting Z = 2.93 if H_o is true is p = 0.0067, which is far less than 0.01, which leads us to reject H_o and by default go with H_a. That is, we would act as if more than 50% of the voters would vote to tax themselves $100 to preserve green space in Kitsap County, Washington, and we would be inclined to put the bond issue on the ballot, resulting in the $100 additional property taxes per year. However, this decision must be tempered with the possibility that non-sampling errors also exist in the data. The major concern is that there is measurement error in that some respondents figured out that they were being polled by the people who wanted to preserve green space and reported that they would vote for $100 in additional tax when in fact they would not.

The Sampling Distribution. You suspect, I am sure, that the sampling distribution for a comparison of means is normal, but you are probably asking yourself how this could be when there are two different means and two sampling distributions involved in a test comparing the means from two samples representing two different populations (or even two related populations). Good question. The answer is that if two sampling distributions are normal then the sampling distribution of the differences between the two means also is normal. The reason this is so is that we are essentially taking the differences between the two means in every set of samples, and if the null hypothesis is true, then the mean of these differences is zero, which becomes the mean of the sampling distribution of two means. By extension, the differences of all other sets of means are also normally distributed.

F. Confidence Intervals and Hypothesis Tests: Two Sides of the Same Coin

As you could see in the first section of this chapter, there is a close relationship between confidence intervals and significance tests. Specifically, if a statistic is significantly different from 0 at the 0.05 level, then the 95% confidence interval will not contain the mean of the comparison group. There is a similar relationship between the 99% confidence interval and statistical significance at the 0.01 level. On the one hand, a major advantage held by the confidence interval approach is that you can see the likely range of values for the two means being compared, which cannot be done with the hypothesis test approach; on the other hand, a major advantage of the hypothesis test approach is that it provides the probability that the null hypothesis is true, which also is the probability of making a Type I error if you decide to reject the null hypothesis.

You can see that the standard error enters into both confidence interval construction and hypothesis testing. This is as it should be, since the standard error incorporates both the elements making up statistical uncertainty, sample size and variation. In constructing a confidence interval, the standard error provides the range of uncertainty directly around a mean found in a sample. Because the hypothesis test is a comparison, however, the standard error is divided into the difference between the two means (or the single sample mean and a standard). That is, in a hypothesis test involving means, the magnitude of the difference in means found in the sample(s) is divided by the degree of statistical uncertainty as measured by the standard error(s). If the magnitude of difference becomes large while the degree of statistical uncertainty remains constant, then the probability that the null hypothesis is true gets smaller, as is the case when the magnitude of difference remains constant while the degree of statistical uncertainty decreases. If the degree of statistical uncertainty increases while the magnitude of difference remains constant, then the probability of the null hypothesis being true increases, as is the case when the magnitude of difference decreases when the degree of statistical uncertainty remains constant.

Exhibit 11.9 shows the formula for calculating the score (T or Z) in a hypothesis test involving means from two independent samples. Think about the numerator (the magnitude of the difference in means) and the denominator (the degree of statistical uncertainty) as you look at it.

Exhibit 11.9. The Internal Workings of a Hypothesis Test Involving a Comparison of Means

---

LEARNING STATISTICS

How the two sample t-test works

$$\frac{\text{difference}}{\text{uncertainty}} = \frac{\text{difference between group means}}{\text{Variation \& sample size}}$$

$$= \frac{\bar{X}_s - \bar{X}_r}{SE(\bar{X}s - \bar{X}r)}$$

$$= \text{t-value}$$

G. Comparisons

Implied in all of the comparisons described in this chapter is the idea that there is some relationship between the variable in question (e.g., monthly family expenditures on food) and the basis of the comparison (e.g., presence of a garden). This leads naturally to a question about the nature of the relationship. Clearly, there is an association between monthly family food expenditures and the presence of a garden, in that our hypothesis test led us to reject the null hypothesis that there was no difference and go with the alternative hypothesis that families without gardens have on average higher monthly food expenditure than those who do not. Moreover, the difference was substantial, in that the families without gardens spent on average $818.75 monthly on food than the families with gardens. That is, the test indicates that there is a relationship between two variables, family food expenditures and the presence of a garden. Moreover, the difference of $818.75 suggests that the relationship is "strong." In the next chapter, we look at methods that are explicitly designed to look at whether or not there is a relationship between two variables, and if so, the nature and strength of the relationship.

Open any or all of the MS-Word files you have created in earlier assignments and the Excel file you created for Assignment 10. Continue to pretend you are a research analyst working for a food retailer and that your management wants to know the relationship between monthly family food expenditures and several variables. Right now, the management is interested in seeing if there is a financial impact of gardens on how much families spend on food per month. For purposes of this assignment, treat the 50-family data set as a random sample and write something in MS-Word about the impact of gardens on food expenditures, taking into account statistical uncertainty from the standpoint of a hypothesis test. Include in your two- to three-page essay what the likely range of the financial impact is. Whatever new work is not in your previous files, save it in your updated files (e.g., swanson.assign11.xls and e.g., swanson.assign11.docx).

Appendix. The Z-Test Probability Table*

Areas under the Standard Normal curve from 0 to Z

z	0	1	2	3	4	5	6	7	8	9
0.0	0.0000	0.0040	0.0080	0.0120	0.0160	0.0199	0.0239	0.0279	0.0319	0.0359
0.1	0.0398	0.0438	0.0478	0.0517	0.0557	0.0596	0.0636	0.0675	0.0714	0.0754
0.2	0.0793	0.0832	0.0871	0.0910	0.0948	0.0987	0.1026	0.1064	0.1103	0.1141
0.3	0.1179	0.1217	0.1255	0.1293	0.1331	0.1368	0.1406	0.1443	0.1480	0.1517
0.4	0.1554	0.1591	0.1628	0.1664	0.1700	0.1736	0.1772	0.1808	0.1844	0.1879
0.5	0.1915	0.1950	0.1985	0.2019	0.2054	0.2088	0.2123	0.2157	0.2190	0.2224
0.6	0.2258	0.2291	0.2324	0.2357	0.2389	0.2422	0.2454	0.2486	0.2518	0.2549
0.7	0.2580	0.2612	0.2642	0.2673	0.2704	0.2734	0.2764	0.2794	0.2823	0.2852
0.8	0.2881	0.2910	0.2939	0.2967	0.2996	0.3023	0.3051	0.3078	0.3106	0.3133
0.9	0.3159	0.3186	0.3212	0.3238	0.3264	0.3289	0.3315	0.3340	0.3365	0.3389
1.0	0.3413	0.3438	0.3461	0.3485	0.3508	0.3531	0.3554	0.3577	0.3599	0.3621
1.1	0.3643	0.3665	0.3686	0.3708	0.3729	0.3749	0.3770	0.3790	0.3810	0.3830
1.2	0.3849	0.3869	0.3888	0.3907	0.3925	0.3944	0.3962	0.3980	0.3997	0.4015
1.3	0.4032	0.4049	0.4066	0.4082	0.4099	0.4115	0.4131	0.4147	0.4162	0.4177
1.4	0.4192	0.4207	0.4222	0.4236	0.4251	0.4265	0.4279	0.4292	0.4306	0.4319
1.5	0.4332	0.4345	0.4357	0.4370	0.4382	0.4394	0.4406	0.4418	0.4429	0.4441
1.6	0.4452	0.4463	0.4474	0.4484	0.4495	0.4505	0.4515	0.4525	0.4535	0.4545
1.7	0.4554	0.4564	0.4573	0.4582	0.4591	0.4599	0.4608	0.4616	0.4625	0.4633
1.8	0.4641	0.4649	0.4656	0.4664	0.4671	0.4678	0.4686	0.4693	0.4699	0.4706
1.9	0.4713	0.4719	0.4726	0.4732	0.4738	0.4744	0.4750	0.4756	0.4761	0.4767
2.0	0.4772	0.4778	0.4783	0.4788	0.4793	0.4798	0.4803	0.4808	0.4812	0.4817
2.1	0.4821	0.4826	0.4830	0.4834	0.4838	0.4842	0.4846	0.4850	0.4854	0.4857
2.2	0.4861	0.4864	0.4868	0.4871	0.4875	0.4878	0.4881	0.4884	0.4887	0.4890
2.3	0.4893	0.4896	0.4898	0.4901	0.4904	0.4906	0.4909	0.4911	0.4913	0.4916
2.4	0.4918	0.4920	0.4922	0.4925	0.4927	0.4929	0.4931	0.4932	0.4934	0.4936
2.5	0.4938	0.4940	0.4941	0.4943	0.4945	0.4946	0.4948	0.4949	0.4951	0.4952
2.6	0.4953	0.4955	0.4956	0.4957	0.4959	0.4960	0.4961	0.4962	0.4963	0.4964
2.7	0.4965	0.4966	0.4967	0.4968	0.4969	0.4970	0.4971	0.4972	0.4973	0.4974
2.8	0.4974	0.4975	0.4976	0.4977	0.4977	0.4978	0.4979	0.4979	0.4980	0.4981
2.9	0.4981	0.4982	0.4982	0.4983	0.4984	0.4984	0.4985	0.4985	0.4986	0.4986
3.0	0.4987	0.4987	0.4987	0.4988	0.4988	0.4989	0.4989	0.4989	0.4990	0.4990
3.1	0.4990	0.4991	0.4991	0.4991	0.4992	0.4992	0.4992	0.4992	0.4993	0.4993
3.2	0.4993	0.4993	0.4994	0.4994	0.4994	0.4994	0.4994	0.4995	0.4995	0.4995
3.3	0.4995	0.4995	0.4995	0.4996	0.4996	0.4996	0.4996	0.4996	0.4996	0.4997
3.4	0.4997	0.4997	0.4997	0.4997	0.4997	0.4997	0.4997	0.4997	0.4997	0.4998
3.5	0.4998	0.4998	0.4998	0.4998	0.4998	0.4998	0.4998	0.4998	0.4998	0.4998
3.6	0.4998	0.4998	0.4999	0.4999	0.4999	0.4999	0.4999	0.4999	0.4999	0.4999
3.7	0.4999	0.4999	0.4999	0.4999	0.4999	0.4999	0.4999	0.4999	0.4999	0.4999
3.8	0.4999	0.4999	0.4999	0.4999	0.4999	0.4999	0.4999	0.4999	0.4999	0.4999
3.9	0.5000	0.5000	0.5000	0.5000	0.5000	0.5000	0.5000	0.5000	0.5000	0.5000

*Adapted from Appendix Table 2 in Zelditch (1959)

Endnotes

1. The T distribution is very similar to the normal distribution when the estimate of variance is based on many degrees of freedom but the normal distribution has relatively more scores in the center of the distribution and the T distribution has relatively more in the tails, thus making it "leptokurtic." William Sealy Gosset developed the T distribution and statistical tests associated with it while working for the Guinness brewery in Ireland. He had to deal with very small sample sizes (e.g., assessing the quality of barley and hops being used), and statisticians of the day were only dealing with large samples. Gosset developed the T distribution and the T-Test specifically for small samples (ca $n = 25$ or less). Because of a contractual agreement with the brewery, he published the article under the pseudonym of "Student." That is why the T-Test is often called "Student's T" (see, e.g., Ziliak and McCloskey, 2008: 214–37).

2. There are variations, but the basic syllogism consists of three parts: the major premise, the minor premise, and the conclusion. Here are two examples of syllogistic logic. In the first, the correct conclusion is made; in the second it is not.

Major premise: All Alfa Romeo automobiles are fast.

Minor premise: This automobile is an Alfa Romeo.

Conclusion: This automobile is fast (correct, since the major premise states that all Alfa Romeos are fast).

Major premise: All Alfa Romeo automobiles are fast.

Minor premise: This automobile is fast.

Conclusion: This automobile is an Alfa Romeo (incorrect, since the major premise does not say that only Alfa Romeos are fast).

The structure of hypothesis testing developed by Neyman and Pearson also conforms to the principle of falsification (Popper, 1959), whereby one cannot conclusively affirm a hypothesis, but one can conclusively negate it. Since the null hypothesis is always there is no difference between the means being compared, it translates into a difference of zero. In principle, this condition can be "falsified" by finding that there is a difference (given that the probability of the null hypothesis is sufficiently low to enable rejecting it). There is no comparable condition if the null hypothesis was anything other than no difference.

References

Fisher, R. A. (1966). *The Design of Experiments, 8th ed.* Edinburgh, Scotland: Oliver and Boyd.

Hald, A. (2010). *A History of Parametric Statistical Inference from Bernoulli to Fisher, 1713–1935.* Dordrecht, The Netherlands: Springer.

Henkel, R. (1976). *Tests of Significance.* Quantitative Applications in the Social Sciences No. 4. Newbury Park, CA: Sage Publications.

Hubbard, R., and M. J. Bayarri (2003). "P Values Are Not Error Probabilities." Technical Report 14–03. Department of Statistics and Operations Research. University of Valencia, Valencia, Spain (http://www.uv.es/sestio/TechRep/tr14-03.pdf).

Mohr, L. (1990). *Understanding Significance Testing*. Quantitative Applications in the Social Sciences No. 73. Newbury Park, CA: Sage Publications.

Neyman, J., and E. S. Pearson (1933). "The Testing of Statistical Hypotheses in Relation to Probabilities A Priori." *Proceedings of Cambridge Philosophical Society* 20: 492–510.

Popper, K. (1959). *Logic of Scientific Discovery*. London, England: Hutchinson.

Zelditch, M. (1959). *A Basic Course in Social Statistics*. New York: Henry Holt and Company.

Ziliak, S., and D. McCloskey (2008). *The Cult of Statistical Significance: How the Standard Error Costs Us Jobs, Justice and Lives*. Ann Arbor: The University of Michigan Press.

12. Relationships Between Variables

Hmmmm. We are going on a road trip to the desert at the end of March. I wonder what the weather will be like? I wonder which outfit I should take? A or B?

A. or B.

A. Introduction

At the conclusion of Chapter 11, I mentioned that within the comparisons used as examples, the idea was implied that there may be a relationship between the variable being tested (e.g., monthly family expenditures on food) and how the populations were identified (e.g., by the presence or absence of a garden). I also noted that in fact we were looking at the relationship between two variables in these comparisons (e.g., the relationship between monthly family food expenditures and the presence of a garden). In this chapter, we will continue on this path and also cover some ground that the last chapter did not cover. You may have noticed in the last chapter that all of the examples and discussion concerning hypothesis testing used variables measured at the ratio level. This is ground that needs to be covered. In this chapter, I will start to cover it by looking at "comparisons" for variables measured at the nominal and ordinal levels via the "relationship" approach, a topic that will be expanded to include hypothesis testing regarding relationships in the next chapter. Let's start looking at relationships in terms of nominal and ordinal variables.

B. Nominal and Ordinal Level Variables

The starting point for investigating the possibility of a relationship between two variables measured at the nominal level (or between two variables measured at the ordinal level, or between a variable measured at the nominal level and a variable measured at any other higher level) is the construction of a "cross-tabulation table" (also known as a "contingency table"). An example of this type of table was found in Chapter 3 (Table 3.3). Exhibit 12.1 provides another example of a cross-tabulation table. In this case, it represents a cross-tabulation of two variables in a sample survey I did in the mid-1980s on the penetration of VCRs (Video Cassette Recorders) within households in Toledo, Ohio. The two variables that are cross-tabulated are (1) Presence of a VCR in a household; and (2) the sex of the Principal Income Earner (PIE).

Exhibit 12.1. Cross-Tabulation of Sex of Principal Income Earner and VCR Presence

Learning Statistics

Cross-Tabulated Data

VCR BY SEX OF PRINCIPAL INCOME EARNER IN HOUSEHOLD*

PIE SEX

VCR	Male	Female	Total
Yes	112	20	132
	(.53)	(.30)	(.48)
No	98	46	144
	(.47)	(.70)	(.52)
Total	210	66	276
	(1.00)	(1.00)	(1.00)

* Percentages are expressed in terms of column totals.

As shown in the rightmost column of the cross-tabulation table in Exhibit 12.1, about 48% of the households in the sample (n = 276) reported that a VCR was present, while 52% reported that there was no VCR present. Now let's look at the relationship between VCR presence and the sex of the PIE. Let's start with the column for males. Here we can see that of the 210 households that reported a male as the PIE, 53% reported the presence of a VCR, while 47% reported that there was no VCR present. Looking at the column for females, we see that of the 66 households that reported a female PIE, only 30% reported the presence of a VCR, while 70% reported no VCR present. The fact that 53% of households with male PIEs report a VCR as being present compared to only 30% of the households with female PIEs suggests that there is a relationship between VCR presence and the sex of the PIE. Since the data are from a sample, we will need to do a hypothesis test to be able to infer to the entire set of households in Toledo, Ohio, but that will come in the next chapter. In the meantime, we can look at a way to measure the "strength of the relationship" between PIE gender and VCR presence. To do this, I am going to use the "Proportionate Reduction in Error" (PRE) framework.

C. Measuring Association with the "PRE" Framework

The PRE framework is a way of looking at the possibility of a relationship between two (or more) variables that first looks at how one accurately one can "predict" the values of a given variable from information found in the data for the variable itself. After finding the accuracy of this way of predicting, it then considers if the relationship between the given variable and some other variable improves the accuracy of the prediction (Costner, 1966; Swanson and Tayman, 1995). For example, in Exhibit 12.1, we saw that 48% of the households reported that a VCR was present and 52% reported that it was not. If I randomly drew a household from the same population as the sample of 276 households (and if it was 1985) and asked you to guess whether or not it had a VCR, what would you guess? I would always guess that it did not, since the majority (52%) of households report no VCR. In using this strategy, I could expect to be wrong about 48% of the time, but my strategy would be more accurate than any other given the information at hand. Now, suppose I provide you with the other information in Exhibit 12.1, which is the distribution of VCR presence by sex of the PIE, and when I draw a household I am going to tell you the sex of the PIE before you guess if a VCR is present. Now, if you know that the PIE is male, you would always guess that a VCR is present. In so doing, you could expect to be correct about 53% of the time and wrong about 47% of the time. If you know that the PIE is female, you would always guess that there is no VCR present. In so doing, you could expect to be right about 70% of the time and wrong about 30% of the time. By knowing the sex of the PIE, it looks like the accuracy of our guesses would be more accurate than by not knowing the sex of the PIE. Let's calculate the proportionate reduction in error for this and see how much more accurate we can expect to be with the additional information of PIE gender available in guessing if a VCR is present.

First, I will calculate how many households I would misclassify without knowledge of the sex of the PIE. In this case, I would misclassify 132 of the 276 households as not having a VCR that, in fact, did have a VCR. We will call this the number of errors made using "Rule 1" to predict VCR presence in a household.

Second, we need to know how many households I would expect to misclassify using the additional information available, which is the sex of the PIE. For households with a male PIE, I would misclassify 98 of the male PIE 210 households as having a VCR when, in fact, they did not; for households with a female PIE, I would misclassify 20 of the 66 female PIE households as not having a VCR when, in fact, they did. Thus, my total error using the PIE gender information is 118 = 98+20. This is the number of errors made using "Rule 2" to predict VCR presence in a household.

Third, my Proportionate Reduction in Error (PRE) using the PIE gender information is 0.1061 = (132–118)/132. In other words, by knowing the sex of the PIE, I can expect to reduce my misclassifications by 10.61% over the long run. The basic PRE framework is that you subtract the number of errors made using Rule 2 (e.g., PIE gender) from the number of errors made using Rule 1, and then divide this difference by the number of errors made under Rule 1:

$$PRE = \frac{\text{(Prediction errors using Rule 1)} - \text{(Prediction errors using rule 2)}}{\text{(Prediction errors using Rule 1)}}$$

A PRE measure is always between zero and 1.00. If a PRE measure has a score is zero, it says that the additional information associated with using "Rule 2" provides no improvement in accuracy over and above using "Rule 1." If a PRE measure has a score is 1.00, it says that the additional information associated with Rule 2 provides a 100% reduction in error. In other words, by using Rule 2, we can predict values of the variable in question perfectly.

In the next chapter, we will not only look at a hypothesis test to see if a relationship does (or does not) exist between two variables measured at the nominal or ordinal level, but also at ways to measure how strong it is, using the PRE framework. Specifically, we will look at the "chi-squared" ($\chi2$) hypothesis test to see how likely it is that a relationship exists in the population from which a sample was drawn, and if this test indicates that there is a relationship we will look at the "lambda" (λ) measure to see how strong it is.[1] Now let's turn to looking at the relationship between two variables measured at either the ratio or interval level. In so doing, we will again use the PRE framework.

D. Ratio and Interval Level Variables

In the preceding section, you saw that the way to look at relationships between variables measured at the nominal or ordinal level was to use cross-tabulation tables in conjunction with the PRE framework. The cross-tabulation of variables measured at the ratio or interval level is cumbersome unless the variables have been "collapsed" to an ordinal or nominal level of measurement (e.g., we use the median to partition monthly food expenditures into "high" (above the median) and "low" (below the median). However, we have a very effective way to look at the relationship of ratio and interval level variables without resorting to collapsing them (and thereby losing information). The way forward is to use the mean.

To start, consider the example of monthly family food expenditures from our sample of 50 families. We know that the mean of this variable in our sample is $1.841.65. If I were to randomly draw a family from the population from which our 50-family sample was taken and ask you to guess its monthly food expenditures, your best guess would be the mean of $1,841.65. Why? Because in the long run, guessing the mean in every case would lead a lower average error than any other strategy, given that no additional information is available beyond knowing the mean and standard deviation of the variable for which I am trying to predict values. In fact, by using the mean, we know what our average error would be. It is given by the standard deviation, which in this case is $663.46, which represents the "prediction errors using Rule 1" in the PRE framework.

Now, suppose that we thought the additional information available from one of the other variables in our data set might improve the accuracy of our guessing. We could take any of the others, but suppose you decide to use family size. How can we use family size to do this? The answer is that we use "regression."

E. Regression Analysis

"Regression" is, in fact, a way to measure the association of two (or more) variables measured at the ratio or interval level, but it is a strange name. The reason for the name is that while the ideas underlying this method had been around, the name came from Francis Galton, who, like his cousin, Charles Darwin, was interested in genetics. In the late 19th century, Galton was doing research on the association between the average height of parents and the average height of their children. He noticed that, on average, the children of tall parents tended to be shorter than their parents and that, on average, the children of short parents, tended to be taller than their parents. He called this phenomenon "regression" (toward the mean), and started investigating ways to measure it. Although his understanding of "regression" is not the same as modern-day statisticians, the name he gave the method stuck (Hald, 2010; Stigler, 1986).

So, how does regression work and how does it lead to "prediction errors using Rule 2" in the PRE framework? Let me start with a really small data set (n = 11), and then return to show you a regression between monthly family food expenditures and family size. The data set I am using is one of four developed by Francis Anscombe (1973) to illustrate the importance of graphing the relationship between two variables measured at the ratio or interval level. This data set is displayed in Exhibit 12.2, in the form of a table showing values of X and Y. Keep in mind that there are 11 cases, and that each set of X and Y values in a given row represents the values of X and Y for that case. For example, in case # 1, the value of X is 10 and the corresponding value of Y is 8.04.

Exhibit 12.2. Variables X and Y, from the First of Anscombe's Four Data Sets

Learning Statistics

Anscombe Data Set 1

Case	Variable	
	X1	Y1
1.	10.00	8.04
2.	8.00	6.95
3.	13.00	7.58
4.	19.00	8.81
5.	11.00	8.33
6.	14.00	9.96
7.	6.00	7.24
8.	4.00	4.26
9.	12.00	10.84
10.	7.00	4.82
11.	5.00	5.68

In regression analysis, it is customary to label an interval or ratio variable whose values we are trying to guess (estimate) as "Y" and the interval or ratio variable whose values might be useful in estimating Y as "X." It also is customary to call "Y" the "dependent variable" and "X" the "independent variable." The idea underlying these two terms is that the values of the dependent variable vary in response to changes in the independent variable. In trying to estimate values of Y without any additional information from X or any other variable, I would use, as before, the mean of Y, which is 7.50. In using this as my strategy for guessing values of Y if you randomly drew one of the 11 values of Y, my average error over the long run would be 2.03, which is Y's standard deviation.

Now, let's take a look at the nature of the relationship between X and Y. The starting point of any regression analysis is to use a "scatter" plot to show how, if at all, Y might be related to X. Exhibit 12.3 shows a "scatter plot," which shows the relationship of variable Y to variable X. I generated the graph using the scatter graph procedure in Excel's chart wizard. Values of Y are ordered on the vertical (Y) axis and values of X are ordered on the horizontal (X) axis. Each of the 11 points in the scatter plot represents the value of X and Y for a given case. For example, case # 1, for which X = 12 and Y = 10.84, is found by following the arrow in Exhibit 12.3 that starts approximately at 12.0 on the X axis to its end at approximately 10.84 on the Y axis.

Exhibit 12.3. The Relationship Between Two Variables, X and Y

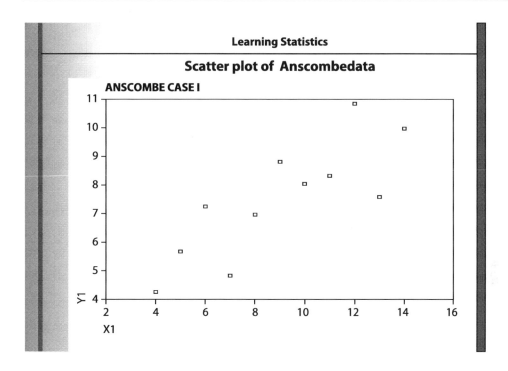

The scatter plot in Exhibit 12.3 shows that as X goes from its smallest value (4) at the far left to its largest value (14) to the right of the X axis, the values of Y also tend to become larger. That is, they tend to vary in a positive manner relative to changes in X. This "positive linear" relationship between X and Y is, however, not perfect. That is, as values of X become larger. it is not the case that each of the associated value of Y does so. For example, when X is at its maximum value of 14, the corresponding value of Y (9.96) is the second largest of the Y values. If the linear relationship between X and Y was "perfect," all of the plotted points would be on a line, as is shown on the scatter plot in Exhibit 12.4.

Exhibit 12.4. The Relationship Between Two Variables, X and Y, with a Line Showing Where the Plotted Points Would Be if the Relationship between X and Y Were "Perfect"

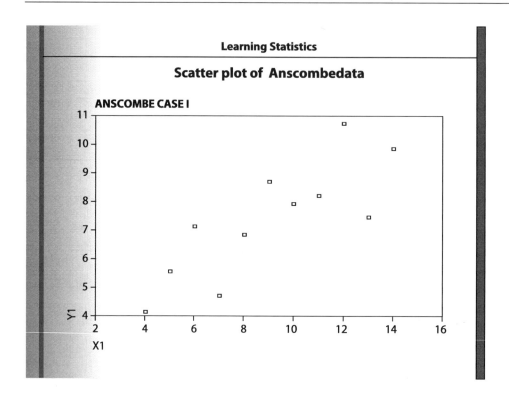

The line shown in Exhibit 12.4 is a "regression" line. It was generated using the regression procedure in Excel's data analysis pack (which I will show you how to use shortly). The procedure found that the "best fitting" line to the X and Y is to multiply X by 0.5 and then add that product to 3 as an estimate of Y based on values of X. As an equation this is $\hat{y}_i = 3 + .5*X_i$. Since X_1 is 10, then the regression estimate of Y_1 is $Y_1 = 3 + .5*10 = 8.0$. The actual value of Y_1 is 8.04, so the estimate is not bad. The estimate of Y_9 using the value of X_9 (12) is $Y_9 = 3 + .5*12 = 9$. The actual value of Y_9 is 10.84, so the difference between our estimate and the actual value of Y_9 is 1.84 (where 1.84 = 10.84 −9). We could continue on and find the difference between each of the estimated values of Y generated from our regression model and the actual value. This notion leads us back to the idea of "Least Squared Error," which, as I mentioned in Chapter 5, would be a topic we take up in discussing regression in this chapter. The concept of "least squared error" is closely related to the concept of "average error" associated with the standard deviation.

The idea of least squared error is essentially the idea of variance (the square of the standard deviation). We can calculate both the average squared error of Y using the mean of Y as a predictor and the average squared error of Y using the regression estimates of Y in conjunction with each value of X. The average squared error for the regression approach follows the same form as found in using the mean, the only difference is that for each value of X we substitute in the equation the estimated value of Y from the regression equation for the mean of Y. First, recall that if we calculated the variance of Y using the mean, it would look as follows:

Variance (using the mean) = $\{[\Sigma(X_i - mean)^2]/(n-1)\}$

When we substitute the mean of Y with the estimated value of Y using the regression equation for each given value of X, the equation looks as follows:

$$\text{Variance (using the regression)} = \{(\Sigma(Y_i - (a + bX_i))^2)/(n-1)\}\backslash$$

Since we know that the variance (using the mean) provides the average "squared" error in estimating values of Y using the mean of Y (prediction errors using Rule 1), you can probably see that we can find the average "squared" error in estimating values of Y using the standard deviation found by substituting the regression equation's estimate of Y_i given X_i for the mean of Y. In other words, we can use this form of the standard deviation to find the "prediction errors using Rule 2." This suggests that we can use the PRE framework to assess the relationship between X and Y, if any. You can probably see that we can use the variance associated with using the regression in terms of the errors using rule 2. In using the PRE framework, recall:

PRE = $\dfrac{\text{(Prediction errors using Rule 1)} - \text{(Prediction errors using rule 2)}}{\text{(Prediction errors using Rule 1)}}$

The variance calculated from the mean of Y is 4.12 (where 4.12 = $(2.03)^2$) and the variance calculated from the regression is 1.38. Using these two numbers in the PRE framework suggests that by using the regression model to estimate values of Y instead of the mean value of Y to estimate values of Y, we have reduced the error by about 67%:

0.67 = $\dfrac{(4.12) - (1.38)}{(4.12)}$

The value "0.67" tells us that the regression model provides a substantial improvement in estimating values of Y over the accuracy obtained by using the mean of Y. An alternative way to state this is that there is a relationship between X and Y. From the scatter plot, we also know that the relationship is positive. That is, as values of X tend to get larger, so do values of Y. What would a "negative" relationship look like in a scatter plot? The answer is that as values of X become larger, values of Y would tend to become smaller. Sometimes the term "direction" is used in conjunction with positive and negative. So, a relationship in a positive direction is one in which values of Y tend to become larger if values of X are becoming larger. A relationship in a negative direction is one in which values of Y tend to become smaller as values of X become larger.

F. Some Regression Basics

How does regression work? Essentially it is set of mathematical equations that finds the "best fitting" straight line through the points of a scatter plot (where each point is the intersection of the ordered values of the X and Y variables for a given case). It does so in such a manner that the sum of the squared differences between each Y value represented by the actual data and the Y value estimated by the regression equation is at a minimum. In this sense, it is very similar to the mean, in that the mean is the single number that minimizes the sum of the squared differences between each value of Y and the Y value "estimated" by using the mean of Y.

Thus, the "least squares" procedure essentially yields the "optimal" linear regression equation: $\hat{y}_i = a + b^*x_i$. The set of equations underlying the "least squares" approach is straightforward, but it is best expressed in mathematical symbols rather than a textual description. The derivation of the equations that provides the least squares solution is found in the appendix.

The type of regression described in the equation $\hat{y}_i = a + b^*x_i$ is known as "simple" or "bivariate" linear regression, because there is only one "predictor" variable (e.g., using x to predict values of y; using family size to predict monthly family food expenditures). It is, of course, possible to use a range of predictor variables (e.g., use family size, income, presence of a garden to predict monthly family food expenditures). Not surprisingly, it is called "multiple regression," since more than one predictor variable is used. This is something you can learn in your next statistics class.

You may have heard the term "correlation." It is a concept that is intimately tied to regression and is a measure of both the strength and the "direction" of the relationship between two variables measured at the ratio or interval level. In fact, if we have a correlation "coefficient" between two variables, we can square it to see how much proportionate reduction in error we would get by using a regression model to predict values of one of them from the other instead of the mean of the given variable. That is, the square of the correlation coefficient is a PRE measure. Since we know that all PRE measures have a range from zero to 1.00, we know that the range of the squared value of the correlation coefficient also is from zero to 1.00. This value is known as the "coefficient of determination" and shown symbolically as "r^2." Not surprisingly, the correlation coefficient is usually shown symbolically as "r." Because we know that $0 \leq r^2 \leq 1$ represents the range of values that r^2 can take on, we can quickly see that the range of r is from -1 to +1. That is, $-1 \leq r \leq +1$. As you also suspect, if r is less than zero, then the direction of the relationship between X and Y is negative; if r is greater than zero, then the direction of the relationship between X and Y is positive. As an illustration of these ideas, let's look again at the regression that was shown in Exhibit 12.4. The regression function in Excel's data analysis pack found that the "best fitting" line to the X and Y is to multiply X by .5 and then add that product to 3 as an estimate of Y based on values of X. As an equation recall that this is expressed as: $\hat{y}_i = 3 + .5^*X_i$. In addition to the preceding equation, Excel's regression function provided both r and r^2, which were +0.816 and .67, respectively. (Does "0.67" look familiar?)

Are you ready to use the regression function to look at the nature of the relationship between monthly food expenditures and family size?

G. Doing Regression in Excel

In looking at the use of the regression function using as an example monthly food expenditures as the "dependent variable" (Y) and family size as the "independent variable (X), recall Table 3.1 and Exhibit 3.1 from Chapter 3, which showed the values of the 50-family data set. Although you could not see the entire data set in Exhibit 3.1 (whereas you could see it in Table 3.1), the values of monthly family expenditures on food were in column B from row 3 to row 52 (B3:B52) and the values of family size were in column D from row 3 to row 52 (D3: D52). Before I use the regression function, I want to make a scatter plot of X and Y so that I get a visual picture of the relationship, if any, between X and Y. You can see this scatter plot in Figure 12.1.

Figure 12.1. Scatter Plot of Food Expenditure by Family Size

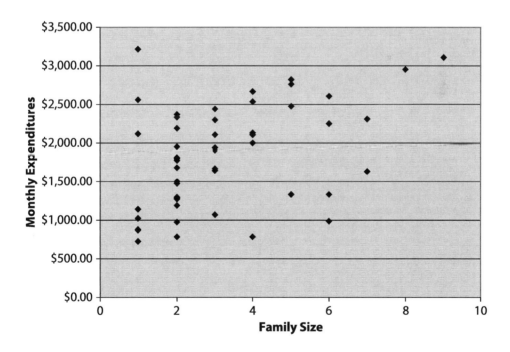

The scatter plot shows that there is a lot of variation in food expenditures (Y) by single-person families and that the variation decreases on average as family size (X)

Exhibit 12.5. The Regression Function in the Data Analysis Pack

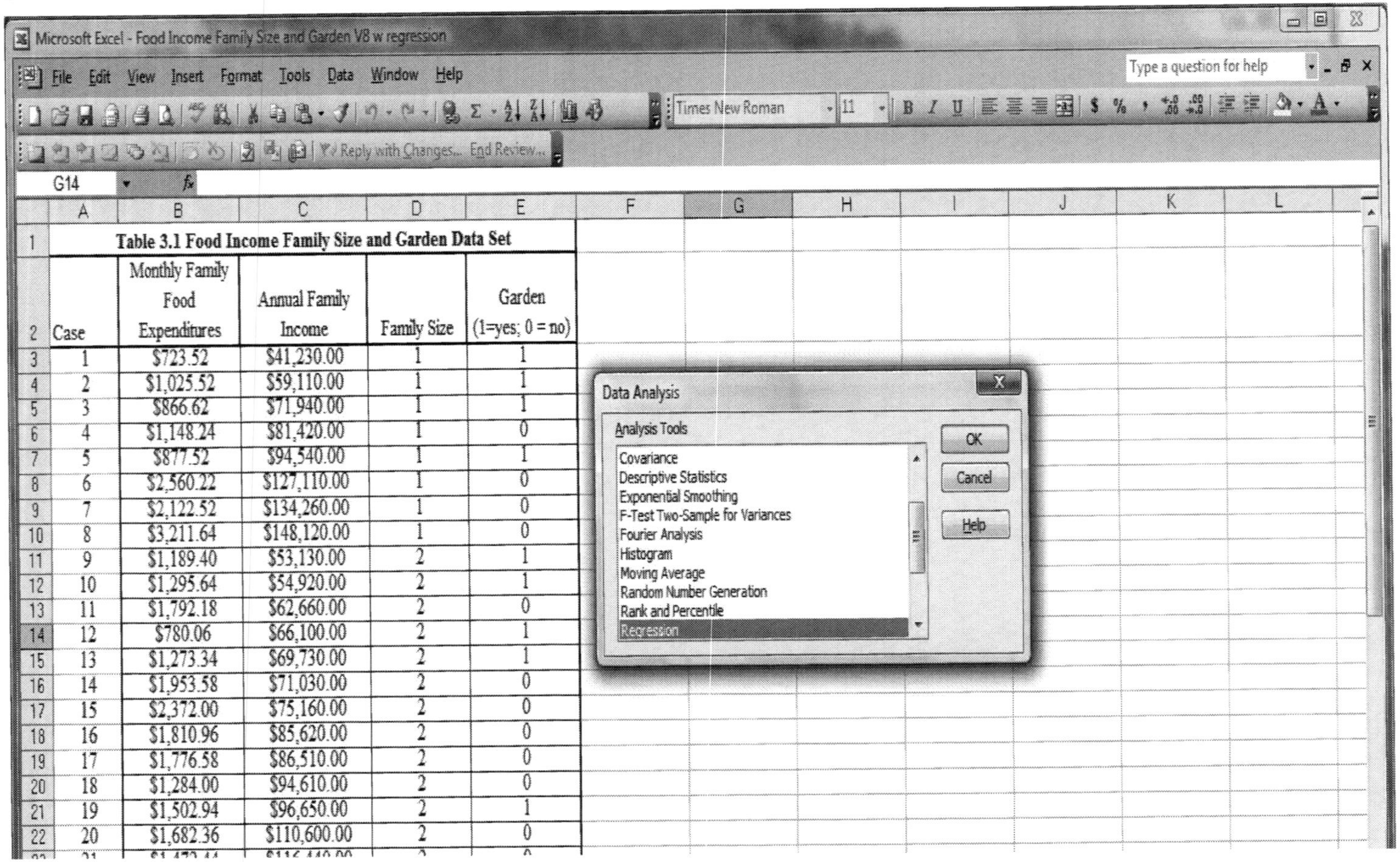
Microsoft Excel - Food Income Family Size and Garden V8 w regression
File Edit View Insert Format Tools Data Window Help
Type a question for help
Times New Roman
11
Reply with Changes... End Review...
G14
A B C D E F G H I J K L
Table 3.1 Food Income Family Size and Garden Data Set
Case
Monthly Family Food Expenditures
Annual Family Income
Family Size
Garden (1=yes; 0 = no)
1 $723.52 $41,230.00 1 1
2 $1,025.52 $59,110.00 1 1
3 $866.62 $71,940.00 1 1
4 $1,148.24 $81,420.00 1 0
5 $877.52 $94,540.00 1 1
6 $2,560.22 $127,110.00 1 0
7 $2,122.52 $134,260.00 1 0
8 $3,211.64 $148,120.00 1 0
9 $1,189.40 $53,130.00 2 1
10 $1,295.64 $54,920.00 2 1
11 $1,792.18 $62,660.00 2 0
12 $780.06 $66,100.00 2 1
13 $1,273.34 $69,730.00 2 1
14 $1,953.58 $71,030.00 2 0
15 $2,372.00 $75,160.00 2 0
16 $1,810.96 $85,620.00 2 0
17 $1,776.58 $86,510.00 2 0
18 $1,284.00 $94,610.00 2 0
19 $1,502.94 $96,650.00 2 1
20 $1,682.36 $110,600.00 2 0
Data Analysis
Analysis Tools
Covariance
Descriptive Statistics
Exponential Smoothing
F-Test Two-Sample for Variances
Fourier Analysis
Histogram
Moving Average
Random Number Generation
Rank and Percentile
Regression
OK
Cancel
Help

Exhibit 12.6. The Regression Function Open and Ready to Use in Excel

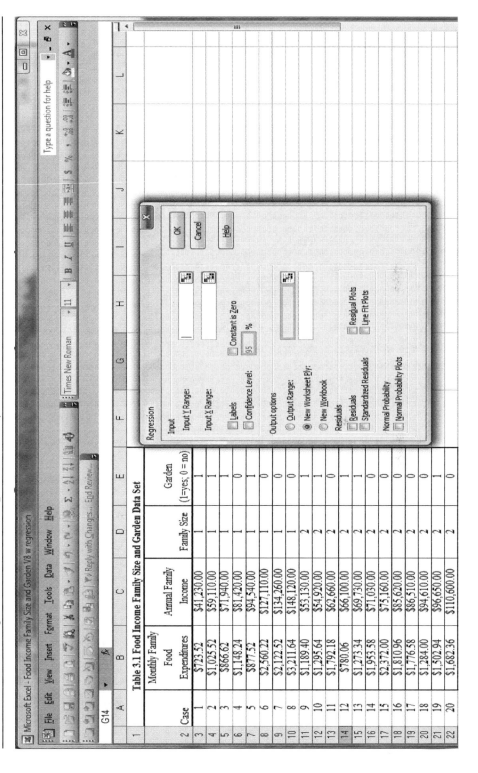

Table 3.1 Food Income Family Size and Garden Data Set

Case	Monthly Family Food Expenditures	Annual Family Income	Family Size	Garden (1=yes; 0 = no)
1	$723.52	$41,230.00	1	1
2	$1,025.52	$59,110.00	1	1
3	$866.62	$71,940.00	1	1
4	$1,148.24	$81,420.00	1	0
5	$877.52	$94,540.00	1	1
6	$2,560.22	$127,110.00	1	0
7	$2,122.52	$134,260.00	1	0
8	$3,211.64	$148,120.00	1	0
9	$1,189.40	$55,130.00	2	1
10	$1,295.64	$54,920.00	2	1
11	$1,792.18	$62,660.00	2	0
12	$780.06	$66,100.00	2	1
13	$1,273.34	$69,730.00	2	1
14	$1,953.58	$71,030.00	2	0
15	$2,372.00	$75,160.00	2	0
16	$1,810.96	$85,620.00	2	0
17	$1,776.58	$86,510.00	2	0
18	$1,284.00	$94,610.00	2	0
19	$1,502.94	$96,650.00	2	1
20	$1,682.36	$110,600.00	2	0

Regression dialog:

Input
Input Y Range:
Input X Range:
Labels
Confidence Level: 95 %
Constant is Zero

Output options
Output Range:
New Worksheet Ply:
New Workbook

Residuals
Residuals
Standardized Residuals
Residual Plots
Line Fit Plots

Normal Probability
Normal Probability Plots

OK
Cancel
Help

increases. It also shows that there is a "positive" linear relationship between X and Y, in that as X increases, Y tends also to increase.

The scatter plot is informative as it gives a visual picture of the nature of the relationship between X and Y. To get a more precise picture of it, I need to use the regression function to open the "Data Analysis" pack under the "Tools" tab and then locate "Regression" in the former, as is shown in Exhibit 12.5.

Once you have the "Regression" function highlighted as shown in Exhibit 12.5, click "OK" and you will see the screen shown in Exhibit 12.6. (If you are not using Excel 2003, then you may not see exactly what is shown, but it will be close.)

When you can see the preceding screen (or something similar in your version of Excel), the first thing is to identify where the values of the "Y" (dependent) and the "X" (independent) variables are located. My "Y" variable is monthly family food expenditures, for which the values are located in cells B3:B52; my "X" variable is family size, for which the values are located in cells D3:D52. This is what I enter in the "Input Y Range" area and the "Input X Range" area, respectively. One I have done this, I will also tell Excel to put the results of the regression for these two variables in the cells of Excel's choosing in a "New Worksheet," which is the default option for the output (note that the button to "New Worksheet Ply" is highlighted). For now, I will ignore the remaining boxes (some of which you will see being used in the next chapter when we use statistical inference in regard to these same variables from our 50-family sample data set). The results of these activities are shown in Exhibit 12.7.

I then will click on the "OK" tab so that Excel does the regression function as I specified. The results (output) will appear in a new worksheet. Since I have used this function a fair number of times, I know that the default column widths are too narrow. By the time you see the results in Exhibit 12.8 I will have already widened them to see the results more clearly.

What you see in Exhibit 12.8 is a whole lot of "output," which is typical of Excel and any other statistical program's regression function. Some of the output you can ignore for now because it has to do with statistical inference, which we will cover in the next chapter using this same regression. Other items in the output are used for general information and still others as part of the regression "diagnostics" to determine if a regression is valid. I did not ask Excel to provide the full range of its diagnostic information at this time, because the output would be overwhelming at this point in learning about regression.

So, what is relevant in the screen shot shown as Exhibit 12.8? First, we need to know the nature of the relationship between Y (monthly food expenditures) on X (family size) in terms of the regression equation, $\hat{y}_i = a + b^*x_i$. In our case, $a = 1391.294242$ and $b = 138.14567$. We can round these two numbers to 1,391.29 and 138.15, respectively.

Exhibit 12.7. Specification of the Regression Function for Monthly Food Expenditures (Y) and Family Size (X)

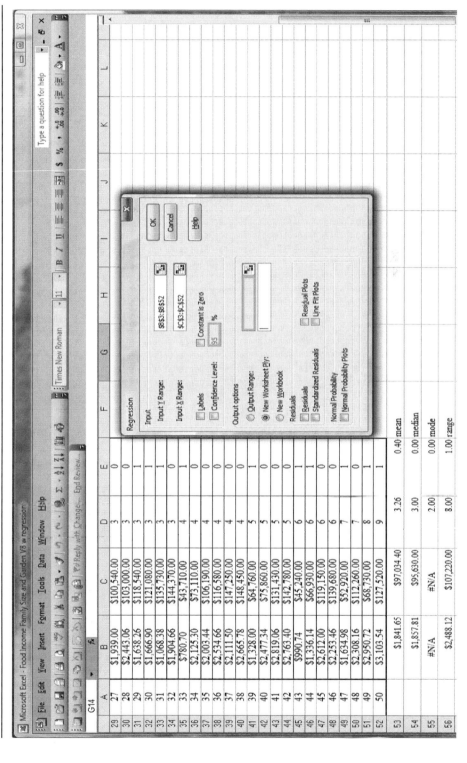

Exhibit 12.8. Specification of the Regression Function for Monthly Food Expenditures (Y) and Family Size (X)

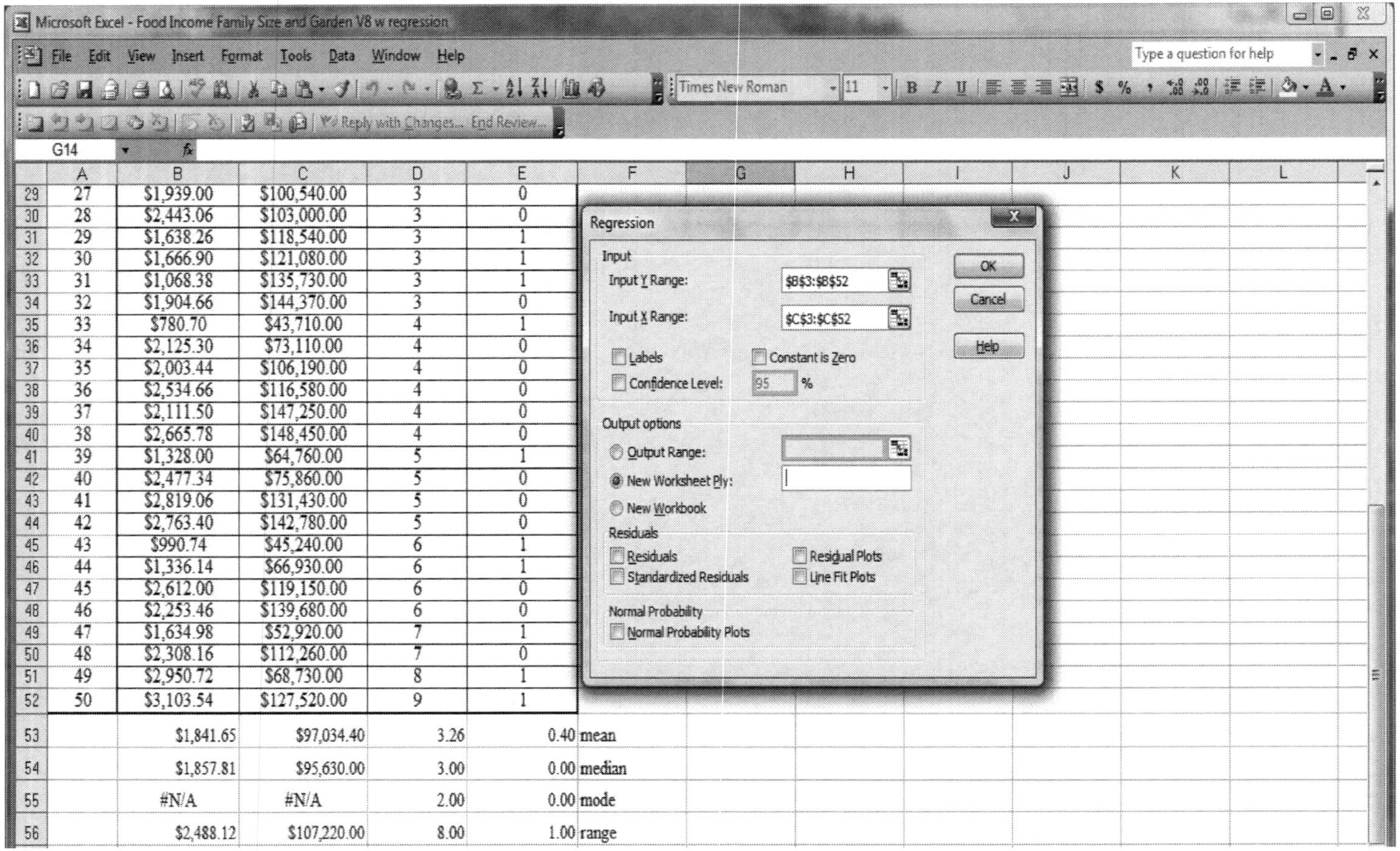

Microsoft Excel - Food Income Family Size and Garden V8 w regression
File Edit View Insert Format Tools Data Window Help
Type a question for help
Times New Roman
11
Reply with Changes... End Review...
G14
A B C D E F G H I J K L
29 27 $1,939.00 $100,540.00 3 0
30 28 $2,443.06 $103,000.00 3 0
31 29 $1,638.26 $118,540.00 3 1
32 30 $1,666.90 $121,080.00 3 1
33 31 $1,068.38 $135,730.00 3 1
34 32 $1,904.66 $144,370.00 3 0
35 33 $780.70 $43,710.00 4 1
36 34 $2,125.30 $73,110.00 4 0
37 35 $2,003.44 $106,190.00 4 0
38 36 $2,534.66 $116,580.00 4 0
39 37 $2,111.50 $147,250.00 4 0
40 38 $2,665.78 $148,450.00 4 0
41 39 $1,328.00 $64,760.00 5 1
42 40 $2,477.34 $75,860.00 5 0
43 41 $2,819.06 $131,430.00 5 0
44 42 $2,763.40 $142,780.00 5 0
45 43 $990.74 $45,240.00 6 1
46 44 $1,336.14 $66,930.00 6 1
47 45 $2,612.00 $119,150.00 6 0
48 46 $2,253.46 $139,680.00 6 0
49 47 $1,634.98 $52,920.00 7 1
50 48 $2,308.16 $112,260.00 7 0
51 49 $2,950.72 $68,730.00 8 1
52 50 $3,103.54 $127,520.00 9 1
53 $1,841.65 $97,034.40 3.26 0.40 mean
54 $1,857.81 $95,630.00 3.00 0.00 median
55 #N/A #N/A 2.00 0.00 mode
56 $2,488.12 $107,220.00 8.00 1.00 range
Regression
Input
Input Y Range: $B$3:$B$52
Input X Range: $C$3:$C$52
Labels
Constant is Zero
Confidence Level: 95 %
OK
Cancel
Help
Output options
Output Range:
New Worksheet Ply:
New Workbook
Residuals
Residuals
Residual Plots
Standardized Residuals
Line Fit Plots
Normal Probability
Normal Probability Plots

As you can see from where I found "1,391.29" in the regression output shown in Exhibit 12.8, it is labeled as the "Intercept" by Excel. Similarly, from where I found "138.15" in the regression output shown in Exhibit 12.8, it is labeled as the "X Variable 1." Since monthly family food expenditures are given in dollars, we can refine these two numbers even further: $1,391.29 and $138.15. We also can interpret these two numbers. The first, $a = \$1,391.29$, forms the starting point for the straight line identified by the regression function; the second, $b = \$138.15$, tells us what is happening to monthly food expenditures as family size increases. Specifically, each additional person in a family adds, on average, $138.15 to monthly family food expenditures. This is known as the "slope" of our regression equation. That is, b shows the expected change in Y for each "unit" change in X, where a "unit" change follows the units in which X is measured. If X is measured in dollars, then a unit change is a dollar. If X is measured in family size, then a unit change is one family member. Since X is measured in terms of the number of family members, we can interpret $b = \$138.15$ as indicating that, on average, each additional family member increases monthly family food expenditures by $138.15.

To find the degree of association between X and Y, I can use r and r^2. In Exhibit 12.8, r is shown to the right of the label "Multiple R" and r^2 is shown to the right of the label "R Square." These two values (rounded to four significant digits) are $r = 0.4119$ and $r^2 = 0.1696$, respectively. The former confirms what we saw in Figure 18.1, namely the relationship between X and Y is positive. The latter tells us how much we proportionately reduce the error found in using the mean of monthly family food expenditures to estimate each family's monthly food expenditures by instead using the regression equation to estimate each family's monthly food expenditures. Thus, the regression equation reduces the error by 16.96%.

H. More Regression Basics

There are six major assumptions underlying bivariate regression (Berry and Feldman, 1985; Schroeder, Sjoquist, and Stephan, 1986). Violations of these assumptions can cause problems. The first major assumption is that both the dependent variable (Y) and the independent (X) variable are assumed to be measured at the interval level and without error. If this assumption is violated, the regression coefficient (b) may be biased (it may be too high or too low—you don't know).

The second major assumption is that the mean is zero for all of the differences between the actual values of Y and the regression-estimated values of Y. If this assumption is violated, you may get a biased (it may be too high or too low, you don't know) estimate of the intercept (a).

The third major assumption is that the variance of the differences between the actual values of Y and the estimates of Y made using the regression equation is assumed to be constant. If this assumption is violated, the standard error (remember this term?) for either the intercept (a) or the regression coefficient (b) or both, may be inflated, which may lead to a Type II error when using hypothesis tests to judge the statistical significance of *a* and *b*. We will cover this topic in some detail in the next chapter.

The fourth major assumption is that there is no relationship between X and the differences between the actual values of Y and the values estimated using the regression equation. An example of a violation of this assumption would be that as values of X become larger, the differences tend to increase. If this assumption is violated, the regression coefficient (*b*) may be biased (it may be too high or too low—you don't know).

The fifth major assumption is that the differences between the actual values of Y and the values of Y estimated using the regression equation are normally distributed. If this assumption is violated, the standard error (once again, remember this term?) for either the intercept (*a*) or the regression coefficient (*b*) or both, may be inflated, which may lead to a Type II error when using hypothesis tests to judge the statistical significance of *a* and *b*. We will cover this topic in some detail in the next chapter.

The sixth major assumption is that the relationship between X and Y is approximately linear. If this assumption is violated, you are likely to get a regression equation with a low coefficient of determination (r^2).

Here is a summary of these six assumptions and the consequences of violating them:

1. Violation of assumptions 3 and 5 generally affects statistical inference, because in each case the standard errors estimated for each parameter are artificially inflated (tendency to make type II errors). This is a topic we will cover in the next chapter.
2. Violation of assumptions 1, 2, 4 (and 6) affects the estimation of *a* and *b* and model validity.

There are several issues that may not represent violations of the major assumptions underlying regression, but they can affect the quality of a regression equation. These include the presence of "outliers" (a topic we covered in Chapter 4, and one we will return to examine in the next section), the use of theory (or experience or good judgment) to develop and evaluate a given regression "model" (i.e., the regression equation), and the presence of a "nonlinear" relationship between X and Y (a topic we will cover in the next section).

Fortunately, regression has a good set of tools for diagnosing and overcoming problems associated with violations of its major assumptions and the related issues, such as the presence of outliers and nonlinearity (Fox, 1991). We will not cover all of the tools (which you will see if you continue to take more statistics courses), but we will examine the basic ones you can use to diagnose problems in a given regression model, along with ways to overcome these problems.

I. Some Basic Diagnostic Tools for Regression

The most basic—and perhaps the most important—diagnostic tool you can employ is the use of scatter plot graphs to visually inspect the relationship between X and Y. These graphs will also reveal the presence of outliers, and at the same time offer clues about the validity of the assumptions underlying a regression model you are trying to construct. To do this, I will use the four data sets developed by Francis Anscombe (1973), which are known among statisticians as "Anscombe's Quartet." As a preview, here is what you will see in each of the four data sets of Anscombe's Quartet:

Data Set	Problem
I	None
II	Nonlinearity
III	Outlier/influential data
IV	Outlier/influential data

The four data sets are small, each with only 11 cases. The full quartet is shown in Exhibit 12.9. Under the columns labeled X1 and Y1 (the first two columns on the far left) are the X and Y values of Data Set I. To the immediate right of X1 and Y1 are columns labeled X2 and Y2, which contain the X and Y values for Data Set II. To the right of X2 and Y2 are two columns labeled X3 and Y3, which contain the X and Y values for Data Set III. Finally, the two rightmost columns, labeled as X4 and Y4, contain the X and Y values for Data Set IV.

Exhibit 12.9. Anscombe's Quartet

			Learning Statistics					
			Anscombe Data					
	X1	Y1	X2	Y2	X3	Y3	X4	Y4
1.	10.00	8.04	10.00	9.14	10.00	7.46	8.00	6.38
2.	8.00	6.95	8.00	8.14	8.00	6.77	8.00	5.76
3.	13.00	7.58	13.00	8.74	13.00	12.74	8.00	7.70
4.	19.00	8.81	9.00	8.77	9.00	7.11	8.00	8.84
5.	11.00	8.33	11.00	9.26	11.00	7.81	8.00	8.47
6.	14.00	9.96	14.00	8.10	14.00	8.84	8.00	7.04
7.	6.00	7.24	6.00	6.13	6.00	6.08	8.00	5.25
8.	4.00	4.26	4.00	3.10	4.00	5.39	19.00	12.50
9.	12.00	10.84	12.00	9.13	12.00	8.15	8.00	5.56
10.	7.00	4.82	7.00	7.26	7.00	6.42	8.00	7.91
11.	5.00	5.68	5.00	4.74	5.00	5.73	8.00	6.89

Anscombe Data Set I. Exhibit 12.10 shows Data Set I, which you saw earlier in this chapter. The graph indicates that the relationship between X and Y is approximately linear and without outliers, and that there are no major violations of assumptions. This graph suggests that we can proceed with constructing a regression model to predict values of Y from the values of X and not be overly concerned with problems.

Exhibit 12.10. Data Set I. No Major Problems Indicated

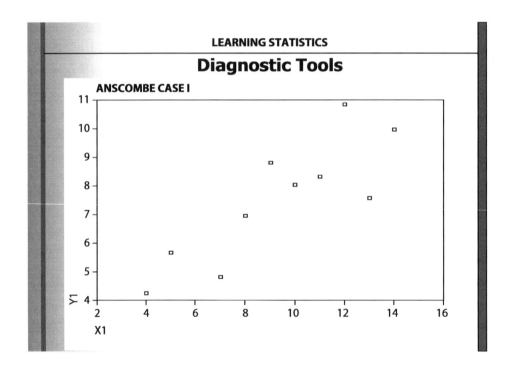

Anscombe Data Set II. Exhibit 12.11 shows Data Set II. The graph indicates that the relationship between X and Y is without outliers but decidedly nonlinear. This graph suggests that, while we can proceed with constructing a regression model to predict values of Y from the values of X, we would likely do better to either "transform" the data so that they have more of a linear relationship (e.g., by using logarithms) or turning to a more advanced regression technique, one that is set up to deal with nonlinear relationships between X and Y.

Exhibit 12.11. Data Set II. A Nonlinear Relationship Between X and Y

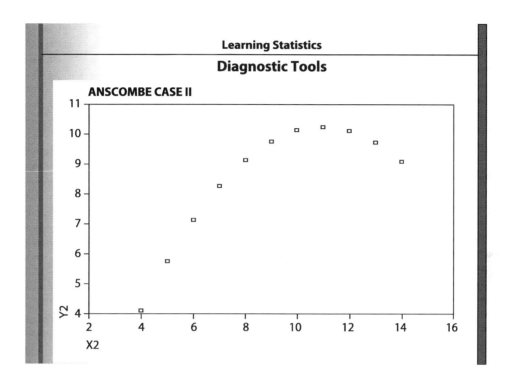

Anscombe Data Set III. Exhibit 12.12 shows Data Set III. The graph indicates that the relationship between X and Y is linear but there is an outlier present. This graph suggests that, while we can proceed with constructing a regression model to predict values of Y from the values of X, we would likely do better to deal with the outlier. The first thing to do is check the data set to make sure that there was no coding/transcription error that led to the outlier. If it is not the result of such an error, it may be the result of "measurement error." One common approach is to eliminate this case and re-run the regression without it. Another approach is to substitute the mean value of Y for the actual value of Y, or do the same for both X and Y and then re-run the regression.

Exhibit 12.12. Data Set III. The Presence of an Outlier

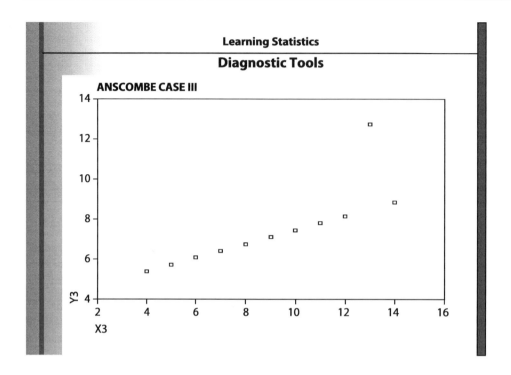

Learning Statistics

Diagnostic Tools

ANSCOMBE CASE III

Anscombe Data Set IV. Exhibit 12.13 shows Data Set IV. The graph indicates that the relationship between X and Y is nonexistent and that a regression model would be an artificial construction caused entirely by the presence of the outlier. This graph suggests that it might be worthwhile to go back and examine the data for coding or transcription errors—it would not be worthwhile to continue to attempt to construct a regression model or otherwise examine the relationship between X and Y.

Exhibit 12.13. Data Set IV. An "Artificial" Regression Caused by a Single Outlier

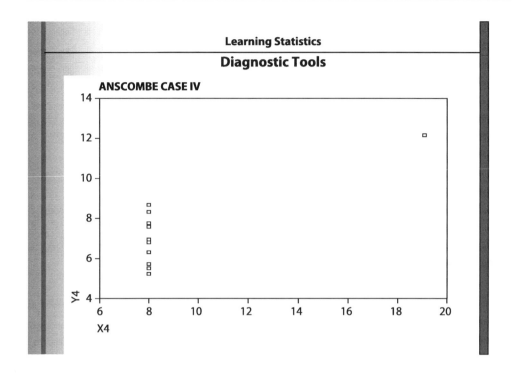

You should now have the idea of the importance of using scatter plots to visually examine the relationship between X and Y before proceeding to construct a regression model. One important feature of Anscombe's Quartet that serves to emphasize the importance of a visual inspection is that the same regression model "fits" all four data sets. In all four cases, we have the same regression model: $\hat{y}_i = 3 + 0.5^*x_i$. In addition, the means of X and Y are the same in each of the four data sets, with the mean of X equal to 9.0 and the mean of Y equal to 7.5.

In the next chapter we look at the relationship between monthly food expenditures and family size in the light of both hypothesis testing and the full range of diagnostic tools. Here, before concluding this chapter, it is worthwhile to reflect a bit on the issue of "causality" in terms of relationships between X and Y.

J. Does a Relationship Indicate That X "Causes" Y?

Even if we have a strong relationship between X and Y (e.g., $r^2 > .90$), it does not mean that X "causes" Y. The presence of a relationship ("correlation") simply shows that X and Y are related, while "causality" is the relationship between cause and effect. That is, for a given effect, you could find the cause. For example, we could find in a sample survey that there is a strong correlation between wealth and happiness. However, it may not be entirely out of line to say that wealth to some degree "causes" happiness. However, it would be more difficult to say that happiness "causes" wealth. If we pursue the idea that to some degree wealth "causes" happiness, we may find that there are variables between "wealth" and "happiness" that mediate the relationship. For example, it may be in the United States that "possessions" are more directly related to happiness than is actual wealth, but since possessions are enabled by wealth, we can easily confound the effects of wealth on happiness. Similarly, it may be that wealth leads to better health, which also is more directly related to happiness than is wealth, with again, health being enabled by the ability to buy the best health care available in the United States.

Another example is from a study done some years ago, in which it was found that there was a positive linear relationship between the amount of pesticide being used on cotton fields and the numbers of the pest. On the surface, the relationship suggests that more pesticides "causes" more pests—that is, rather than being killed by the pesticide, the pests are thriving on it. However, closer examination would reveal the presence of a timing issue in the data used to construct the regression model. More pests would lead to the application of more pesticides, which, in turn, would lead to fewer pests. To correctly get at the relationship, the measurement of the number of pests should both precede and follow the application of the pesticide.

These simple examples also suggest how to think about regression and the more general issue of constructing models. Regression models can be constructed, for example, that use more than one independent variable, and they can have "mediating" variables like "possessions" in between a primary independent variable such as wealth, and a dependent variable such as happiness (Tabachnick and Fidell, 2007). They also can be set up to be time ordered (Hauser, 1971).

K. A "Dummy Coded" Independent Variable

In the discussion of levels of measurement in Chapter 3, I briefly described "dummy coding" as a way to make a nominal level variable with two values into a ratio level variable. Although you are more limited in what can be done with dummy coded variables compared to regular ratio level variables, one important use is that they can be used as independent variables in a regression analysis (but not as "dependent variables," unless more sophisticated types of regression analyses are invoked than what I describe here). As an example of this use, consider the variable "presence of a garden." This is clearly a nominal level variable with two values. As you have seen, it is already dummy coded in that the presence of a garden is coded as "1" and the absence of a garden is coded as "0." Since it is a ratio level variable by virtue of this dummy coding, we can calculate a mean for it by summing its values and dividing by 50. Since there are 20 families with a garden and 30 without, we can see that the sum is 20. When this sum is divided by 50, we obtain the mean, which is 0.40. This mean represents the proportion of families with gardens.

In Chapter 11, your assignment was to use a hypothesis test to determine the impact of a garden on mean monthly family food expenditures. You should have done this using a two-sample test. You can perform this same analysis by using the presence of a garden as the independent variable (X) in a regression model used to predict monthly family food expenditures (Y).

Exhibit 12.14 shows the results of running this regression in Excel. From this output, we can see that the regression model is $\hat{y}_i = 2169.148 - 818.747^*x_i$. Let's start to look at this model by restating the intercept (a) and regression coefficient (b) in terms of dollars and only two significant digits: $\hat{y}_i = \$2,169.15 - \$818.75^*x_i$. This model shows that on average, families without gardens spend \$2,169.15 monthly on food; those families with gardens reduce this expenditure, on average, by \$818.74. As you can see, the intercept of \$2,169.15 is, in fact, the mean monthly expenditures for the 30 families without gardens. By algebraically adding the regression coefficient of -\$818.75 to the intercept, we obtain \$1,350.40 (where \$1,350.40 = \$2,169.15 - \$818.75), which is the mean monthly food expenditures for the 20 families with gardens. Moreover, the regression coefficient of \$818.75 is not a trivial difference, especially since the independent variable of "presence of a garden" has a moderately strong relationship with expenditures ($r^2 = 0.3655$). That is, the presence of a garden "explains" about 37% of the variation in monthly food expenditures. Because these data are from a sample, we will need to use statistical inference to see if the relationship found between X and Y in the sample holds for the population, but you are probably not surprised to hear that we will find in the next chapter where we do this, the results are "statistically significant."

ASSIGNMENT FOR CHAPTER 12

1. Create a cross-tabulation table using monthly food expenditures and the presence of a garden. To do this, collapse monthly family food expenditures into two categories, high and low, using the median as the dividing point; then cross-tabulate your collapsed categories with the presence of a garden. Treat the data as if they represent a population. Look at the table and decide if there is or is not a relationship and discuss the reasons for your decision. Write a one- to two-page essay on your work and include the cross-tabulation table in it. Save your Excel file with this work (e.g., swanson.assign12part1.xls) and the MS-Word file (e.g., swanson.assign12part1.docx).

2. Open any or all of the MS-Word files you have created in earlier assignments and the Excel file you created for Assignment 11. Continue to pretend you are a research analyst working for a food retailer, and that your management wants to know the relationship between how much families spend monthly on food and several variables. In this case, the interest is in the relationship between monthly family food expenditures and family income. For purposes of this assignment, treat the 50-family data set as the entire population (i.e., do not do any statistical inference) and write

Exhibit 12.14. Regression Results for Predicting Expenditures from Presence of a Garden

SUMMARY OUTPUT					
Regression Statistics					
Multiple R	0.604558853				
R Square	0.365491406				
Adjusted R Square	0.352272477				
Standard Error	539.3862798				
Observations	50				
	Coefficients	*Standard Error*	*t Stat*	*P-value*	
Intercept	2169.148	98.47801088	22.03	0.0000000000	
X Variable 1	-818.747	155.7074069	-5.26	0.0000033276	

something in MS-Word about the impact of income (X) on food expenditures (Y). Include in your three- to five-page essay: (1) A scatter plot graph of the relationship between X and Y along with a short discussion of what you see to include any possible assumption violations, the presence of outliers, and possible nonlinearity; (2) the actual regression model you constructed to estimate Y using X, along with its characteristics (a, b, r, and r^2); (3) an example of the estimated food expenditures for a family of one, a family of four, and a family of nine; and (4) a general discussion of how well the model estimates food expenditures and suggestions for improvement. Whatever new work is not in your previous files, save in your updated files (e.g., swanson.assign12part2.xls and, e.g., swanson.assign12part2.docx).

Appendix. Proof that $\hat{y}_i = a + b^*x_i$ Is the "Least Squares" Solution[2]
This is adapted from several sources, including Schroeder, Sjoquist, and Stephan (1986).
The bivariate regression model is given by

$$y_i = a + bx_i + e_i$$
where
$$y_i = \hat{y}_i - e_i$$
$$b = (r_{xy}) * (s_y/s_x)$$
$$a = \ddot{y} - (b^*\bar{X})$$

So, how are a and b found, such that the sum of the squared errors (SSE) is minimized? First, recall that SSE $= \Sigma(y_i - \hat{y}_i)^2$

$$= \Sigma(y_i - (a + bx_i))^2$$

The values of a and b that minimize SSE are found by taking the partial derivative of SSE with respect to a and b, then setting the resulting derivatives to zero, solving for a and b, and then checking to make certain that the locations are at a local minimum (not a maximum).
This yields

$$\eth SSE/\eth a = (-2) \Sigma(y_i - (a + bx_i)) = 0$$
$$\eth SSE/\eth b = (-2) \Sigma [(x_i)(y_i - (a + bx_i))] = 0$$

Dividing these equations through by -2 and rearranging terms yields the two "normal" equations:

$$\Sigma y_i = aN + b\Sigma x_i$$
$$\Sigma(x_i y_i) = a\Sigma x_i + b\Sigma(x_i)^2$$

These two "normal" equations can be solved for a and b, because all other terms are available from the data set. Thus, we can find the specific values for a and b, respectively, that minimize SSE, whereas before

$$\text{SSE} = (\Sigma(y_i - \hat{y}_i)^2 = \Sigma(y_i - (a + bx_i))^2$$

In solving the two "normal" equations, we can rearrange them as follows, since we know

$b = (\Sigma(x_i y_i) - a\Sigma x_i)/(\Sigma(x_i)^2)$, which can be expressed as
$b = [\Sigma (x_i - \bar{X}) (y_i - \ddot{y})]/((\Sigma x_i - \bar{X})^2$

and when b is found, then

$$a = \ddot{y} - (b^* \bar{X})$$

where the preceding equation is found by dividing $(\Sigma yi = aN + b\Sigma x_i)$ by N, it is worthwhile to express again

$$a = \ddot{y} - (b^* \bar{X})$$

as

$$\ddot{y} = a + b \bar{X}$$

because the latter form demonstrates that the regression line always passes through the point defined by the mean values of X and Y, $\bar{X}$ and $\ddot{y}$, respectively.

Thus, the line represented by $\hat{y}_i = a + b^* x_i$ minimizes the sum of squared differences between the estimated values of $\hat{y}_i$ (from the regression equation) and the actual values, y_i.

Endnotes

1. The measure, lambda (λ), is also known as "Goodman and Kruskal's Lambda" (Liebetrau, 1983: 17–24).

2. This is adapted largely from Schroeder, Sjoquist, and Stephan (1986).

References

Anscombe, F. (1973). "Graphs in Statistical Analysis." *The American Statistician* 27: 17–22.

Berry, W., and S. Feldman (1985). *Multiple Regression in Practice.* Quantitative Applications in the Social Sciences No. 50. Newbury Park, CA: Sage Publications.

Costner, H. (1966). "Criteria for Measures of Association." *American Sociological Review* 30: 341–53.

Fox, J. (1991). *Regression Diagnostics.* Quantitative Applications in the Social Sciences No. 79. Newbury Park, CA: Sage Publications.

Hald, A. (2010). *A History of Parametric Statistical Inference from Bernoulli to Fisher, 1713 to 1935.* Dordrecht, The Netherlands: Springer.

Hauser, R. M. (1971). *Socioeconomic Background and Educational Performance.* Rose Monograph Series. Washington, DC: American Sociological Association.

Liebetrau, A. (1983). *Measures of Association.* Quantitative Applications in the Social Sciences No. 32. Newbury Park, CA: Sage Publications.

Schroeder, L., D. Sjoquist, and P. Stephan (1986). *Understanding Regression Analysis: An Introductory Guide.* Quantitative Applications in the Social Sciences No. 57. Newbury Park, CA: Sage Publications.

Stigler, S. (1986). *The History of Statistics: The Measurement of Uncertainty before 1900.* Cambridge: The Belknap Press of Harvard University Press.

Swanson, D., and J. Tayman (1995). "Between a Rock and a Hard Place: The Evaluation of Demographic Forecasts." *Population Research and Policy Review* 14 (233–49).

Tabachnick, B. G., and L. Fidell (2007). *Using Multivariate Statistics, 5th ed.* Boston: Allyn and Bacon.

13. Relationships Between Variables in Samples

OK, Statcat said they chose the red wine to take with us. Now I need to know if it goes better with olives or with cheese ... well, I'll just have to sample them!

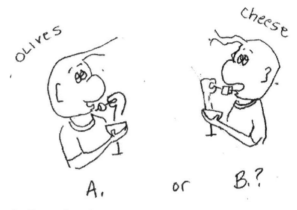

A. Introduction

We bring everything that you have learned to date to bear on this chapter. The chapter is not that long, but much of the reason for its brevity is that the foundation has been laid in the preceding chapters. Like the earlier chapters, this one covers only two of the many ways that relationships between variables can be examined when the variables represent sample data. The general idea behind this is to avoid overwhelming you with all of the details before you can form a general picture of how inferential statistics works and can actually use inferential statistics in an appropriate manner.

In this chapter, we will see how you can infer to a population, the relationships between nominal and ordinal variables you examine in samples. To do this, you will be using tools you have largely seen (and used, if you have been doing the assignments). The one tool you have not yet seen is the chi-squared ($\chi 2$) test, which is a form of hypothesis testing. However, you have learned how to set up your data in that you have built cross-tabulation tables and know the general framework of hypothesis testing. All you need to learn now is to do a χ2 test and interpret its result.

In terms of inferring to a population the relationships between ratio and interval variables you examine in samples, once again you will be using tools you have largely seen (and used). In fact, you have used all of the tools already. The main thing you will learn how to do is use the hypothesis tests you saw in Chapter 11 with a bivariate regression model's two coefficients, a and b. You may be thinking that if you can use a hypothesis test for the coefficients in a regression model, you could probably construct confidence intervals—and you are correct. So, in addition to seeing how hypothesis testing is used in regression, you also will see how confidence intervals can be used. In concluding the section on inferential statistics and regression, I will return to a topic mentioned in Chapter 3 and show how a "nominal level" variable can be used as an independent variable in a regression analysis.

B. Statistical Inference: Relationships Between Nominal and Ordinal Level Variables

The chi-squared (χ2) test may be the most common inferential test in sociology and related fields, since so much of social data is measured at the nominal or ordinal level and found in samples (Henkel, 1976; Hildebrand, et al., 1977; Mohr, 1990; Reynolds, 1977). It uses the hypothesis test structure to help you decide if the relationship you see between two nominal level variables in a sample is likely to exist in the population from which the sample was drawn. It also can be used between: (1) A nominal level variable and an ordinal variable; (2) a nominal level variable and "collapsed" versions of either interval or ratio level variables; (3) two ordinal level variables; and (4) between an ordinal level variable and "collapsed" versions of either interval or ratio level variables. In addition, there are many forms and uses of this test that go well beyond what I am describing (Greenwood and Nikulin, 1996).

The specific form of the χ2 test that we will use is "Pearson's χ2 Test." Karl Pearson (a name you have seen before) is credited with inventing this test and introducing it in 1900 (Stigler, 1999: 338). It can be used for two purposes: (1) Goodness of fit (to see if a distribution of observed values fits a theoretical distribution or some other standard in the form of a distribution; and (2) as a test of independence. Since we are looking at the relationship between two variables, we will use the "test of independence" approach, since two variables that are "independent" have no relationship. The idea of "independence" provides a clue on how the hypothesis test is structured for χ2.

The χ2 hypothesis test follows the general form of all hypothesis tests, as in advance of running the test, you first specify a null hypothesis (H_o), an alternative hypothesis (H_a), and an alpha (α) level. Once you have done this, you run the test, get the χ2 "statistic" that the test yields, which has a known probability distribution, from which it can be determined what the probability is (the p-value) is of getting the χ2 statistic if the null hypothesis is true. As the χ2 statistic becomes larger and larger, the probability of H_o being true becomes lower and lower. If the p-value is less than your alpha level (e.g., $\alpha = 0.05$), you reject H_o and by default go with H_a. You may have already surmised that H_o is always that the two variables are "independent" (no relationship), and H_a is always that there is a relationship (the two variables are not independent).

So, the general form of the χ2 hypothesis test of independence is

H_o: The two variables are independent
H_a: The two variables are not independent.
$\alpha = 0.05$ (or 0.01 or 0.001).

There is one additional step you have to take, which is to calculate the number of "degrees of freedom" (*df*) in your cross-tabulation table. You will need this to locate the appropriate value of χ2 and the probability corresponding to it that H_o is true. I will discuss this aspect of the χ2 test shortly, but "*df*" is a simple calculation. All you need to do is subtract 1 from both the number of rows and number of columns in your cross-tabulation table and multiply the result: $df = (r-1)*(c-1)$. As an example, if you have two rows and two columns in your cross-tabulation table, the number of degrees of freedom is 1, where $1 = (2-1)*(2-1)$. If you have three rows and two columns, $df = (3-1)*(2-1) = 2$. It is important to note that you do not include the column and row totals in the count of the cells.

The χ2 statistic is calculated in a straightforward manner, and its equation illustrates what it is doing.

$$\chi2 = \Sigma[(o_i - e_i)^2/e_i]$$

where

o_i is the observed value in a given cell (cell i) of a cross-tabulation table;

e_i is the "expected" value in a given cell (cell i) of a cross-tabulation table under the condition that the two variables are, in fact, independent (the value you would expect to see in a given cell (cell i) if the two variables had no relationship).

As an example, let's look at the cross-tabulation that was in Exhibit 12.1, which looked at the relationship between the presence of a VCR in a household and the sex of the Principal Income Earner (PIE) in the household. This table is reproduced below as Exhibit 13.1. Note that this is a table with four cells (we do not count the row totals or column totals, since these are not "cross-classifications"). A table with four cells is often called (for obvious) purposes a "2x2 cross-tabulation table," or more simply, a 2x2 table.

Exhibit 13.1. Cross-Tabulation of Sex of Principal Income Earner and VCR Presence

Learning Statistics
Cross-Tabulated Data

VCR BY SEX OF PRINCIPAL INCOME EARNER IN HOUSEHOLD*

PIE SEX

VCR	Male	Female	Total
Yes	112	20	132
	(.53)	(.30)	(.48)
No	98	46	144
	(.47)	(.70)	(.52)
Total	210	66	276
	(1.00)	(1.00)	(1.00)

* Percentages are expressed in terms of column totals.

As you may recall, our analysis of this cross-tabulation table suggested that PIE gender and VCR presence were related (not independent). Let's go through the $\chi 2$ hypothesis test and see what it yields. Here is what I set up to start the test.

H_o: PIE sex and VCR presence are independent
H_a: PIE sex and VCR presence are not independent
$\alpha = 0.05$
$df = (2-1)*(2-1) = 1$.

In preparing to do the calculation of the $\chi 2$ statistic, I know each value of "o_i" since I can see the "observed" values in each of the four cells representing the cross-tabulation of PIE sex and VCR: $o_1 = 112$; $o_2 = 20$; $o_3 = 98$; $o_4 = 46$. Where do the "e_i" values come from?" You already know that these values are supposed to represent what you would see in the four cells if, in fact PIE sex and VCR presence were independent. To do this, we use the row and column total along with the sample total. The row totals represent the distribution of VCRs in households ignoring PIE sex: The total for row 1 shows that 132 households (of the total 276 cases in our sample) report that a VCR is present; and the total for row 2 shows that 144 households (of the 276) do not report having a VCR. The column totals represent the distribution of PIEs by sex (ignoring VCRs): The total for column 1 shows that 210 households (of 276) report that the PIE is male; and the total for Column 2 shows that 66 households (of 276) report that the PIE is female.

The next step in finding the expected values for each of the four cells is to recall from the discussion of probability in Chapter 6 that if two "events" (i.e., variables) are "independent," then the joint probability of them occurring is found by multiplying the two probabilities together. We can use this in terms of our variables. If the presence of a VCR is "independent" of the sex of the PIE, we would expect to see the same distribution found in the column totals (132 households of 276 have a VCR present (0.48); and 144 households of 276 do not have a VCR present (0.52) in the columns under male PIE and female PIE. That is, if the two variables are independent, then we would expect that 100 (48%) of the 210 male PIE households would have a VCR, (where 100 = .48*210) and 110 (52%) would not (where 110 = 210 − 100 = 0.52*210). In regard to the 66 households with a female PIE, we would expect that 32 (48%) would have a VCR (where 32 = 0.48 * 66) if the two variables were independent and 34 (52%) would not (where 34 = 66 − 32 = 0.48*66). So, we now have "e_i" for each of the four cells: $e_1 = 100$; $e_2 = 32$; $e_3 = 110$; $e_4 = 34$. Now we can calculate $\chi 2$ as follows:

$$\chi 2 = \Sigma[(o_i − e_i)^2/e_i]$$
$$= [(112 − 100)^2/100] + [(20 − 32)^2/32] + [(98 − 110)^2/110] + [(46 − 34)^2/34]$$
$$= [(2)^2/100] + [(-12)^2/32] + [(-4)^2/110] + [(12)^2/34]$$
$$= [4/100] + [144/32] + [16/110] + [144/34]$$
$$= [0.04] + [4.50] + [0.15] + [4.24]$$
$$= 8.93$$

I can now look up the probability of getting $\chi 2 = 8.93$ in a cross-tabulation table with one degree of freedom ($df = 1$) in a "chi-squared probability table," which happens to be in the appendix. In so doing, I find that the probability of H_o being true is between 0.01 and 0.001, a range that is well below my alpha level of $\alpha = 0.05$. Thus, I reject H_o and by default go with H_a, which is that there is a relationship between PIE gender and VCR. That is, my decision is that they are not independent.

One item that needs to be covered is the idea of "degrees of freedom" (df) that are associated with the test. The degrees of freedom are needed, because the probability distribution of the $\chi 2$ statistic (such as the one found in the appendix) changes shape until the degrees of freedom become very large, at which point the probability distribution of the $\chi 2$ statistic starts to approximate a normal probability distribution. In terms of the $\chi 2$ test of independence used with a cross-tabulation table, the degrees of freedom can be interpreted as the number of cells that need to be filled in before the remaining cell values are automatically determined, relative to given row and column totals. Once a number is put into any of the cells, the other three cell numbers are automatically determined, such that the cells must sum to the row and column totals. For example, consider the "incomplete" version of the "PIE Sex x VCR Presence" cross-tabulation shown as Table 13.1.

Table 13.1. Incomplete Version of the PIE Sex by VCR Presence Cross-Tabulation Table

VCR Present	Male PIE	Female PIE	TOTAL
Yes	$Cell_{11}$	$Cell_{12}$	132
No	$Cell_{21}$	$Cell_{22}$	144
TOTAL	210	66	276

The row and column totals for $Cell_{11}$ are 132 and 210, respectively. Thus, I cannot put a number larger than 132 in this cell. However, once I do put a number between zero and 132 in it, the values of the other three cells are automatically determined. For example, if I put the number 132 in $Cell_{11}$ then the number in $Cell_{12}$ has to be zero, since the numbers must sum to 132. To continue, once I put the number 132 $Cell_{11}$, the number in $Cell_{21}$ has to be 78, since the total for column 1 is 210; finally, this all forces the number in $Cell_{22}$ to be 66, since the total of row 2 is 144 and the total of column 2 is 66. Thus, any 2x2 table has $(2-1)*(2-1) = 1$ *df*. For similar reasons, any 3x2 (or 2x3) table has $(3-1)*(2-1) = 2$ *df*.

There are some limitations to the χ2 test of independence. One is that if the expected value in any cell is less than 5, some major assumption violations occur such that the test should not be used.

OK, we now have a "statistically significant" finding that PIE sex and VCR presence are not independent. The next step is to see how "strong" the relationship is. For a 2x2 table, the measure I prefer is lambda (λ), since it is a "PRE" measure. Actually, you saw λ calculated for this same cross-tabulation table in Chapter 12, where we found it to be $0.1061 = (132 - 118)/132$. In other words, by knowing PIE sex, I can expect to reduce my misclassifications by 10.61% over the long run. This indicates a relationship, but a rather weak one.[1]

One reason I went through all of the steps needed to calculate χ2 is so you have an idea of its conceptual foundation. In addition, to use Excel's function for the χ2 test of independence, "CHITEST," you have to set up the actual values and the expected values in either a row or column. As an example of using "CHITEST," I collapsed values for monthly food expenditure into high, medium, and low (using 33rd and 66th percentiles) and cross-tabulated these collapsed values with "Presence of Garden." To do this, I had to use the "COUNTIF" function and some formatting to get the cross-tabulation, which is shown as Table 13.2.

Table 13.2 MONTHLY FAMILY FOOD EXPENDITURES				
PRESENCE OF GARDEN	LOW (UNDER $1,479)	MEDIUM (BETWEEN $1,479 AND $2,149)	HIGH ($2,149 AND OVER)	TOTAL
YES	14	4	2	20
NO	3	12	15	30
TOTAL	17	16	17	50

My hypothesis test is structured as follows:

H_0 : Food Expenditures and Presence of Garden are independent;
H_a: Food Expenditures and Presence of Garden are not independent;
α = 0.05;
$df = (3–1)*(2–1) = 2$.

I then calculated the "expected values" for each of the six cross-tabulated cells, which represent what we would expect to see if monthly family food expenditures and the presence of a garden were independent. The easy way to do this is to multiply the column total for a given cell by its row total and then divide this product by the overall total. For example, the expected value in $cell_{11}$ (where there are 14 observed families with low incomes and a garden) is 6.8 (where 6.8 = (20*17)/50). Table 13.3 shows the values expected in the six cross-tabulated cells if the two variables were independent (and given the distribution of gardens in the rightmost column and the distribution of income levels in the bottom row).

Table 13.3 EXPECTED MONTHLY FAMILY FOOD EXPENDITURES				
PRESENCE OF GARDEN	LOW (UNDER $1,479)	(BETWEEN $1,479 AND $2,149)	HIGH ($2,149 AND OVER)	TOTAL
YES	6.8	6.4	6.8	20
NO	10.2	9.6	10.2	30
TOTAL	17	16	17	50

With the observed and expected values in hand, I then copied and pasted the six observed values from Table 13.2 into cells L5:Q5 in my Excel worksheet and the six expected values from Table 13.3 in cells L6:Q6, making sure that the expected values correspond-ed to the observed values for each cell. I then entered "=CHITEST(L5:Q5,L6:Q6)" in cell N7 of my worksheet, which returned the value 0.001332 in cell N7. This value is the probability (calculated using the correct degrees of freedom ($df = 2 = (3-1)*(2-1)$) that H_o is true. Since 0.001 is far below my alpha level of $\alpha = 0.05$, I rejected H_o and by default go with H_a, which is that monthly family food expenditures and the presence of a garden are not independent, but related.

Now that the hypothesis test supports the idea that monthly family food expendi-tures are related to presence of a garden, I am ready to see how "strong" the relation-ship is. Knowing that the expenditures were essentially collapsed into thirds, with low expenditures representing 17 of 50, medium expenditure representing 16 of 50, and high expenditures representing 17 of 50, my "rule 1" for predicting where a given family would fall in this range would be to always say "low" or "high." Picking either one of these and using it to classify every family, I would expect to misclassify 33 of the 50 families.

However, if I know that there is a garden present, I would always say "low" family expenditures. In so doing, I would misclassify four of the families with medium expen-ditures and two with high expenditures for a total of six errors. For families without a garden, I would always select "high" expenditures, and thereby misclassify three of the families with low expenditures and 15 of the families with medium expenditures, for a total of 18 errors. Altogether, my "rule 2" for predicting monthly family food expenditures using the presence or absence of a garden would lead to 6 + 18 = 24 errors. Thus, my PRE score (which in this case is the λ measure) is 27.3% (where 27.3% = (33 −24/33)*100). By knowing if a garden is present or not, I can reduce my prediction errors by 27.3%. This is a weak-to-moderate relationship.

C. Statistical Inference: Relationships Between Interval and Ratio Variables

Because I covered the basics in Chapter 12, here I will look only at the basics of statisti-cal inference in conjunction with bivariate regression. Relevant in this regard are both confidence intervals and hypothesis tests. To do this, I will continue with the bivariate regression example I used in Chapter 12, in which monthly family food expenditures served as the dependent (Y) variable and family size as the independent variable(X). Exhibit 13.2 is a copy of Exhibit 12.8 from Chapter 12, which shows the Excel output of the results of this regression. In it, we will find all of the information we need for statistical inference using both confidence intervals and hypothesis tests. Let's start with confidence intervals.

Exhibit 13.2. Regression Function Results for Monthly Food Expenditures (Y) and Family Size (X)

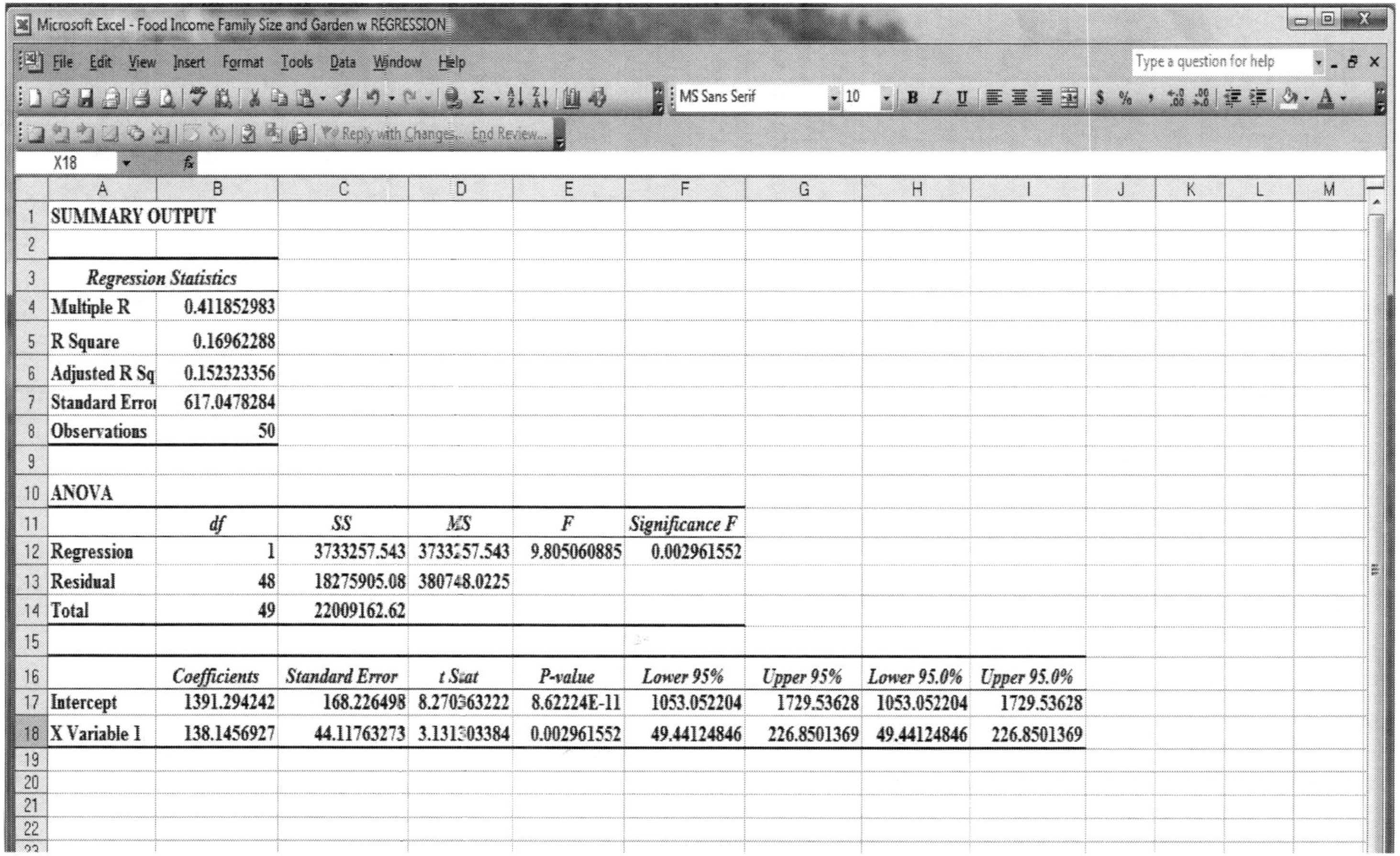

SUMMARY OUTPUT

Regression Statistics

Multiple R	0.411852983
R Square	0.16962288
Adjusted R Sq	0.152323356
Standard Error	617.0478284
Observations	50

ANOVA

	df	SS	MS	F	Significance F
Regression	1	3733257.543	3733257.543	9.805060885	0.002961552
Residual	48	18275905.08	380748.0225		
Total	49	22009162.62			

	Coefficients	Standard Error	t Stat	P-value	Lower 95%	Upper 95%	Lower 95.0%	Upper 95.0%
Intercept	1391.294242	168.226498	8.270363222	8.62224E-11	1053.052204	1729.53628	1053.052204	1729.53628
X Variable 1	138.1456927	44.11763273	3.131303384	0.002961552	49.44124846	226.8501369	49.4412846	226.8501369

As you should recall from Chapter 11, the standard error is the key to inferring from a (random) sample to a population in regard to arithmetic means, and this holds true for the components of a regression model. You can see the term "standard error" in two places of the output shown in Exhibit 13.2. The first is in cell A7, which is in the box directly beneath the heading "Regression Statistics." Next to cell A7 in cell B7 is the number 617.047824 (let's round this to two significant digits and express it in terms of dollars, viz., $617.05). This represents the "standard error of the estimate" (s.e.e.), which, in turn, represents the statistical uncertainty associated with estimates of Y generated by the regression model. However, let's hold off discussing this standard error until we discussed the other place we see the term, which is in cell C16.

Immediately beneath cell C16 (in cell C17) is the number 168.226498, which we can express in dollars and round to two significant digits, viz., $168.23. This is the standard error associated with our intercept term, which is in cell B17 (a =1391.294242, viz., $1,391.29). Immediately below the standard error of the intercept term in cell C18 is the number 44.11763273, which we can express in dollars and round to two significant digits, viz., $44.12. This is the standard error associated with our regression's "slope coefficient," which is in cell B18 (b = 138.456927, viz., $138.46). This standard error is really the key in terms of whether or not the regression model is statistically significant, so let's look at it before we look at the standard error of the intercept term (a).

Why is the standard error of b so critical? Because it is a test of the "slope" of the regression line. If there is no slope, then there is no relationship between X and Y. That is, unless Y increases or decreases on average as X increases or decreases, then there is no slope to the regression line. That is, the regression line will be "horizontal" (and, in fact, it will be a horizontal line starting at the mean value of Y if there is no association between X and Y). If a confidence interval around b encompasses zero, this will indicate that there is no slope to the regression line—i.e., there is no relationship between X and Y. So, let's put a 95% confidence interval (approximately) around b by multiplying the standard error of b by 2 and adding and subtracting this product from b. Since the standard error is $44.12 and b = $136.46, we have an approximate 95% confidence interval from $48.22 (where $48.22 = $138.46 – 2*$44.12) to $226.70 (where $226.70 = $138.46 + 2*$44.12). The 95% confidence interval tells us that in the population from which our 50-family sample was drawn, we are 95% certain that the "true" value of the slope coefficient (β) is between $48.22 and $226.70. This range is wide, and indicates that there is a fair amount of statistical uncertainty around where the population's slope coefficient is located, but importantly, it does not encompass zero (which would have indicated that we do not have a statistically significant regression model).

So far, it looks like there is a relationship between monthly food expenditures and family size in the population from which our sample was drawn. Let's now turn to the statistical significance of the intercept term. Here, we found that a = $1,391.29, with a standard error of $168.23. Thus, the 95% confidence interval for the "true" population intercept is from $1,054.83 (where $1.54.83 = $1.391.29 – 2*$168.23) to $1,727.75 (where $1,727.75 = $1,391.29 + 2*168.23). Now that it looks like we have a "statistically significant" regression model based on the 95% confidence intervals, let's return to the standard error of estimate and its 95% confidence interval.

Recall that the sampling distribution associated with a mean is the theoretical "universe" of all possible means generated by a given sample size. In a regression, the estimated values of a regression are, in essence, estimates of "conditional means." The means in a regression are conditional on a given value of X. These "means" all fall on the "regression line," and their respective sampling distributions are all the same. As is the case with a sampling distribution of an ordinary arithmetic mean where the mean of the sampling distribution is the mean of the population, the means of the sampling distributions associated with the regression line represent the mean of the values of Y given a value of X. It is, in fact, this "conditional mean" that the regression is trying to estimate rather than individual values of Y, but in practice, this distinction is often overlooked and we all act as if the regression is trying to estimate individual values of Y.

So, given this, how do we interpret the s.e.e. of $617.05? By multiplying it by two and adding and subtracting this product from an estimate of Y at a given value of X, we have (approximately) a 95% confidence for the "conditional" mean of Y at a given value of X. For example, when we have a family size of three, the regression model generates an estimated "mean" for monthly family food expenditures of $1,805.74 for a family of three (where $1,805.74 = $1.391.29 + $138.15*3). If we add and subtract 2*$617.05 to $1,805.74, we have a 95% confidence interval for the mean monthly family food expenditures of a family of three persons: We are 95% certain that the mean for a family of three in the population from which the sample was drawn is from $511.64 (where $511.64 = $1,805.74 – 2*$617.05) to $3,039.84 (where $3,039.84 = $1,805.74 + 2*617.05).

We can use this same confidence interval for the "conditional means of family food expenditures" for any family from one to nine persons (the range of family size in our sample). As the width of the 95% confidence interval for the mean food expenditures of a family of size three indicates, there is a lot of statistical uncertainty in our regression (due to a lot of variation in both the dependent and independent variables and the small sample size (n=50)).

In summary, our 95% confidence intervals suggest that in fact there is a relationship (linear) between monthly food expenditures and family size in the population from which our 50-family sample was drawn, but that there is a great deal of statistical uncertainty associated with it. This is useful information from the confidence interval side of the "statistical inference coin." Now, let's look at the other side of the coin—hypothesis testing.

As was the case for the confidence intervals we just constructed, we can, in fact, do hypothesis tests on a and b and any given estimate of the mean of Y given a value of X, using respectively, s.e. (a), s.e. (b), and s.e.e. with the test on b being the key one. I will go through the test for b since it is key one (if $\beta = 0$ in the population, there is no relationship between X and Y). Once you see it, the duplication of this test will be easy for a or any given estimate of the mean of Y given a value of X. As you can see, we are looking at the "T-Test" in which the statistic in question is compared to a "standard," a topic covered in regard to comparing a mean against a standard in Chapter 11.

The hypothesis test for b follows the same form as that for the hypothesis test of a mean. We first specify H_o, then any one of three choices for H_a, followed by an alpha level. We then run the test and based on the p-value it yields, and decide either to reject or not reject H_o. If we reject H_o, the p-value provides us with the probability of making a Type I error (rejecting a true null hypothesis).

So, before we ran the regression shown in Exhibit 13.1, we would have set up the hypothesis test. The null hypothesis is $H_o: \beta = 0$. Of the three possibilities for the alternative hypothesis, the one I chose (for obvious reasons) is $H_a: \beta > 0$. Following convention, I chose $\alpha = 0.05$ as my alpha level. Having done this in advance, I can now look at the output shown in Exhibit 13.1. The two key terms are "T-stat" and "p-value." The former is in cell C16 and the latter is found in cell D16. By looking two rows under the former in cell C18, I see the "T-statistic" for my hypothesis test, which is (rounded) 3.13; in the adjacent cell to the right (D18), I see the p-value associated with a T-statistic of 3.13, which is (rounded) 0.003. The p-value tells me that the probability of getting $b = \$138.15$, if in fact in the population the slope coefficient was zero is only 0.003. Thus, it is very, very unlikely that I would have this slope coefficient in this sample if it was drawn from a population in which the slope coefficient was zero. Moreover, my p-value of 0.003 is far below my alpha level of $a = 0.05$. Thus, I reject H_o and by default go with H_a, which is that in the population $\beta > 0$. I have a statistically significant regression model. By looking at r^2 I now can see how strong the (linear) relationship is between X and Y. Since $r^2 = .1696$ is far from 1.00, which would indicate a "perfect" (linear) relationship between X and Y, it looks like there is a weak relationship between food expenditures and family size in the population from which our 50-family sample was drawn.

There is some other information related to statistical inference in the output shown in Exhibit 13.2, namely "ANOVA" and "F-test." These are useful for regression models that have more than one independent variable (i.e., multiple regression), but for the bivariate regression the information they provide is redundant to the inferential information we just examined.

Before ending this chapter, let's return to the "dummy variable" regression discussed in Chapter 12, where we used regression analysis to look at the relationship between the presence of a garden and monthly family food expenditures. Recall from Exhibit 12.14 and its immediate discussion that $\hat{y}_i = \$2,169.15 - \$818.75^*x_i$, which shows that on average, families without gardens spend \$2,169.15 monthly on food, and those families with gardens reduce this expenditure, on average, by \$818.74. As was discussed, the intercept of \$2,169.15 is, in fact, the mean monthly expenditures for the 30 families without gardens. By algebraically adding the regression coefficient of -\$818.75 to the intercept, we obtain \$1,350.40 (where \$1,350.40 = \$2,169.15 - \$818.75), which is the mean monthly food expenditures for the 20 families with gardens. The question that we did not answer in the preceding chapter was whether or not our model was "statistically significant." The answer is that it is. In Exhibit 12.14, we see that the p-value associated with the hypothesis test for the intercept is far smaller than 0.05 at 0.000000000000001. The p-value associated with the hypothesis test for the regression coefficient is 0.0000033276, which also is far less than 0.05. From these two tests (both of which compare a sample mean with a standard, which in this case turns out to be zero), we see that the model is statistically significant. Moreover, the regression coefficient of $818.75 is not a trivial number, especially since the independent variable of "presence of a garden" has a moderately strong relationship with expenditures (r^2 = 0.3655). That is, the presence of a garden "explains" about 37% of the variation in monthly food expenditures.

ASSIGNMENT FOR CHAPTER 13

1. Use the cross-tabulation table you created in the first part of the assignment for Chapter 12 (where you collapsed monthly food expenditures into two categories, high and low, using the median as the dividing point and then cross-tabulating your collapsed categories with the presence of a garden). Now treat the data in the table as a random sample. Perform a χ^2 test to see if it seems likely that there is a relationship, and if there is, calculate lambda (λ) to see how strong it is. Write a two- to three-page essay on your work, and include in it the cross-tabulation table and the results of your χ^2 test and λ analysis. Save your Excel file with this work (e.g., swanson.assign-13part2.xls) and the MS-Word file (e.g., swanson.assign13part2.docx).
2. Open any or all of the MS-Word files you have created in earlier assignments and the Excel file you created for Assignment 12. Continue to pretend you are a research analyst working for a food retailer, and that your management wants to know the relationship between how much families spend monthly on food and other variables. For purposes of this assignment, treat the 50-family data set as random, and write something in MS-Word about the impact of income (X) on food expenditures (Y). Include in your three- to five-page essay any relevant elements of the work you did for the assignment in Chapter 12 and the results of your statistical tests on the regression between X and Y. Whatever new work is not in your previous Excel file, save it (e.g., swanson.assign13part2.xls) and save your updated MS-Word file (e.g., swanson.assign13part2.docx).

Appendix. The (Approximate) Probability Distribution of the χ^2 Statistic*

Degrees of Freedom (*df*)	Probability (*p*)										
N/A	0.95	0.90	0.80	0.70	0.50	0.30	0.20	0.10	0.05	0.01	0.001
1	0.004	0.02	0.06	0.15	0.46	1.07	1.64	2.71	3.84	6.64	10.83
2	0.10	0.21	0.45	0.71	1.39	2.41	3.22	4.60	5.99	9.21	13.82
3	0.35	0.58	1.01	1.42	2.37	3.66	4.64	6.25	7.82	11.34	16.27
4	0.71	1.06	1.65	2.20	3.36	4.88	5.99	7.78	9.49	13.28	18.47
5	1.14	1.61	2.34	3.00	4.35	6.06	7.29	9.24	11.07	15.09	20.52
6	1.63	2.20	3.07	3.83	5.35	7.23	8.56	10.64	12.59	16.81	22.46
7	2.17	2.83	3.82	4.67	6.35	8.38	9.80	12.02	14.07	18.48	24.32
8	2.73	3.49	4.59	5.53	7.34	9.52	11.03	13.36	15.51	20.09	26.12
9	3.32	4.17	5.38	6.39	8.34	10.66	12.24	14.68	16.92	21.67	27.88
10	3.94	4.86	6.18	7.27	9.34	11.78	13.44	15.99	18.31	23.21	29.59
	Not significant (P>.05)								Significant (P < .05)		

*Taken from Fisher and Yates (1963).

Endnote

1. There are many, many measures of strength that can be used with cross-tabulation tables, including different forms of lambda (the one I showed you is the "asymmetric lambda," which means its value can change if you try to predict X from Y instead of Y from X). Several of the other measures are based on χ^2, including Phi, the Coefficient of Contingency, and Cramer's V (Reynolds, 1977). However, none of these is a "PRE" measure, which leads to some difficulties in trying to interpret the meaning of "strength of relationship" when they are used. The PRE measures include the "asymmetric" lambda (which you have seen in action) and the "symmetric lambda," as well as measures designed more for ordinal rather than nominal level variables, such as Goodman and Kruskal's gamma, Kendall's Tau-b and Tau-c, and Somers's D (Hildebrand, Laing, and Rosenthal, 1977).

References

Fisher, R., and F. Yates (1963). *Statistical Tables for Biological, Agricultural and Medical Research*, *6th ed.*, Table IV. Edinburgh, Scotland: Oliver & Boyd, Ltd.

Greenwood, P., and M. Nikulin (1996). *A Guide to Chi-Squared Testing*. New York: Wiley-Interscience.

Henkel, R. (1976). *Tests of Significance*. Quantitative Applications in the Social Sciences No. 4. Newbury Park, CA: Sage Publications.

Hildebrand, D., J. Laing, and H. Rosenthal (1977). *Analysis of Ordinal Data*. Quantitative Applications in the Social Sciences No. 8. Newbury Park, CA: Sage Publications.

Mohr, L. (1990). *Understanding Significance Testing*. Quantitative Applications in the Social Sciences No. 73. Newbury Park, CA: Sage Publications.

Reynolds, H. (1977). *Analysis of Nominal Data*. Quantitative Applications in the Social Sciences No. 7. Newbury Park, CA: Sage Publications.

Stigler, S. (1999). Statistics on the Table: *The History of Statistical Concepts and Methods*. Cambridge: Harvard University Press.

14. What Is Statistics?— Revisited

Well, look who learned how to drive!

Before you start this chapter, I have one final instructional video I recommend on YouTube. You can use it as a diagnostic test to give you an idea of how much (or how little) you have learned from this book. You can find it at (http://www.youtube.com/watch?v=JS9GmU5hr5w&feature=related).

Given that you "passed" the test in the preceding YouTube video, you should know that "statistics" has two distinct meanings—descriptive and inferential—and that this book has focused on the latter.

You also should now know that inferential statistics refers to the use of a process to make decisions about numbers when we do not have access to all of the information. You should know how to use the special procedures that make up this process.

Can you recall the four types of "error" that occur in both population and sample data sets? The first is measurement error, the second, non-response error, the third is coverage error, and the fourth is coding or transcription error. Inferential statistics is affected by each of these types of error, but unlike Dillman's (2000) "Tailored Design Method," it is not designed to deal directly with any of them. Instead, inferential statistics is designed to deal with a special type of "error" that is unique to sample data sets—"sampling error." This refers to the fact that a sample is likely to be different from the population it was drawn. This may happen, even though there was no measurement error, non-response error, coverage error, or coding/transcription errors in our sample. It was simply the luck of the draw in terms of the sample we got.

We accept the presence of sampling error when we use a sample to gain information about a population of interest. We do this because it is cost effective to acquire information from a sample of a given population rather than attempt to survey (or census) the entire population. With sampling we save not only money, but time (and as we know, time is money, right?). Moreover, by using the process of inferential statistics, we also will have an idea of the size of our sample error simply from the information we get in our sample (its size and the variation within it). We get this bonus because of the simple but elegant foundation underlying inferential statistics.

You should now know that there are two general ways in which statistical inference operates: (1) Estimation (confidence intervals); and (2) hypothesis tests; and that these two methods represent two sides of the same (inferential) coin. The first is used to gain information about a single fact of interest based on the information in our sample. The second is used to make comparisons based on the information in our sample. Both estimation and hypothesis testing are based on the same foundation, which is why I described them as being two sides of the same (inferential) coin. This foundation is really simple, but like many things that are "simple," it also is elegant.

Inference is grounded in uncertainty. That is, we may have the percent of votes for our candidate in our sample, but because it is not the entire set of voters, we are "uncertain" what the actual percent is in the population. As a consequence, we are trying to make decisions in the face of sample error. This uncertainty is determined by two factors: (1) How much variation there is in the population of interest, as reflected in the sample we took from it; and (2) the size of the sample we took. Thus, statistical uncertainty is elegantly expressed as being a function of the size of the sample and how much "variation" exists in the population (which should be revealed in our sample): Uncertainty = f (sample size and variation).

In terms of sample size, if our sample was the same size as the total population, there is no uncertainty and we know, for example, the percent of votes for our candidate. This gets back to the point that if we have the entire population of interest, we do not need statistical inference.

The other element that contributes to uncertainty is variation. What is variation? In terms of an election between two candidates, there would be no variation if one of them received all of the votes. If this was the case, then we could predict the election outcome from one exiting voter. As would be the case if our sample of exiting voters was the same size as all of the voters, there would be no uncertainty in our sample. However, if the election was very close—say 50.2% of the votes were for our candidate and 49.8% were for candidate X, you can see that the sample we draw would have a difficult time telling which candidate is the winner unless the sample was of ALL of the voters.

What you should know by now is that uncertainty increases as the sample size gets smaller and as variation increases; it decreases as sample size gets larger and as variation decreases. In the case where either the sample is the same size of the population or there is no variation in the population, then there is no uncertainty in inferring from the sample to the population. You also should know that the standard error is the elegant measure that summarizes uncertainty and that is the key link between the sample you took and the mathematical and statistical theory that allows us to make inferences from our sample to the population from which it was drawn.

So, now you know the answer to the question, "What is statistics?" Namely, that cost and time constraints encourage the use of scientific sampling, through which the special procedures that make up statistical inference allow us to make decisions in the face of the uncertainty inherent in sampling. You also know that inferential statistics cannot be separated from good judgment and experience. You cannot effectively use statistical inference without understanding how to balance statistical significance and "substantive significance" (i.e., an "important difference").

If you can adequately answer the two questions found in the assignment for this chapter, then you are ready to leave the parking lot and start driving on the side streets. After you finish your work on the two questions, compare what you have to my suggested responses to get an idea of how ready you are to leave the parking lot.

ASSIGNMENT FOR CHAPTER 14

Question 1. This past week, the Riverside County Planning Department collected data on commuting distance in the form of a random sample of 81 people who reside in Riverside County and drive alone to work. The sample is representative of the population of Riverside County residents who drive alone to work. As a traffic analyst for Riverside County, your task is to use the following information from this random sample, in combination with your knowledge of inferential statistics to construct an approximate 95% confidence interval for the average commuting distance for the <u>entire population</u> of Riverside County residents who drive alone to work. Your memo will be used in conjunction with a report that the county will have to submit to the California Clean Air Authority regarding where the county stands in terms of meeting the 2009 goal of having an average distance of 25 miles for drivers who commute alone to work. You will need to put your results and recommendations in the form of a memo to the Director of Planning, Arturo Seppanen, who likes to have concise, informative memos.

Sample mean: 40.0 miles
Sample standard deviation: 45.0 miles

Suggested Response to Question 1

To: Mr. Arturo Seppanen, Director of Planning
From: D. Swanson, Traffic Analyst
Subject: Average Commute Distance for Residents Driving Alone to Work

In regard to the task you gave me concerning the average distance for commuters driving alone to work, I find that data from a recent survey indicate that we can be approximately 95% certain that the average commute distance for all county residents who drive alone to work is between 30 and 50 miles. This finding suggests that that it will be very difficult for Riverside County to meet the 25-mile goal set by the California Clean Air Authority (CCAA) for commuters driving alone to work in 2009. I recommend pleading fiscal exigency and seeking an exception to the requirement. My conclusion and recommendation are based on the following.

The sample of Riverside County commuters who drive alone to work is small (n = 81), but it was selected using scientific sampling principles and was, given its size, very cost effective. Because it is a "random" sample, we can use the standard tool from statistical inference to estimate what the "true" average distance is for all Riverside County commuters who drive alone to work. To do this, I used three pieces of information from the sample: (1) Its mean (40.0 miles); (2) its standard deviation (45.0 miles); and (3) the size of the sample (81). By dividing the standard deviation by the square root of the size of the sample, we get a measure called the "standard error." With this in hand, we can now estimate with a specified level of confidence what the "true" average distance is. As suggested, I used a "95% confidence interval (C.I.)" This means I multiply the standard error ($45/\sqrt{81}$ = 45/9 = 5) by 2 (an approximation that will work well for this purpose) and add and subtract the result from the sample mean of 40 miles. The result of this process is 40 – 5*2 and 40 + 5*2, which yields a 95% C.I. of 30 to 50 miles.

Thus, we can say we are 95% certain that the average distance to work for all Riverside County residents who drive alone is between 30 and 50 miles. Because the "lower bound" of this interval is greater than 25 (the target set by CCAA), we can be 95% certain that Riverside County does not meet this target currently. Moreover, given the current fiscal situation affecting the county, it is unlikely that there are funds to develop programs to meet the target. For the same reason, it is unlikely that the county can find grants and other sources of external revenue that can be used to develop programs designed to meet the target. I recommend pleading fiscal exigency to CCAA and seeking an exception to the requirement.

Question 2. Archaeologists who excavate burial sites are interested in getting "age at death" information because it helps them estimate the size and composition of the population they are studying. Archaeologists working with ancient Mayan burial sites in Belize have been able to date the age of a number of juvenile skeletons via dental information, a long and tedious process.

One of them, Dr. Indira Jones, believes that the length of the femur bone (which connects the hip to the knee) can provide a good estimate of age at death for juveniles. If this hypothesis works, it can save a lot of time in getting age-at-death data. To test the possibility of using femur length, Dr. Jones has assembled a random sample of juvenile skeletons from several Mayan burial sites in Belize. For each of the juvenile skeletons, she has used dental information to get a good estimate of age at death and also has a measurement of the femur length. Dr. Jones knows that you have a good background in statistics that includes regression analysis. She has asked you to see if a regression model can be constructed from her random sample of 77 juvenile skeletons that will provide a good estimate of age at death from femur length.

Dr. Jones's data are found in Table 14.1. Femur length is given in centimeters and age at death is given as the nearest whole year. Even though some of the 77 cases are missing burial site identification numbers, you should use them in your analysis. Your task is to generally analyze the data, to construct a regression model, and write a report to Dr. Jones that summarizes your findings. You will need to provide a recommendation to Dr. Jones on whether or not she should use the regression model, justify your recommendation, and provide caveats, if appropriate.

Table 14.1. Juvenile Mayan Burial Sites with Age at Death and Femur Length*

BURIAL NUMBER	AGE	FEMUR LENGTH
459	0	70
443	0	75
546	0	75
.	0	76
470	0	80
103	0	82
449	1	81
435	1	97
160	1	101
.	1	105
433	1	112
432	1	122
251	2	112
538	2	115

	2	123
.	2	123
291	2	125
266	3	120
388	3	122
386	3	142
346	3	142
458	3	145
170	3	147
521	3	147
505	3	150
485	3	153
431	3	157
.	3	158
457	3	162
430	3	163
445	3	178
506	4	175
195	4	175
451	4	188
329	5	175
501	5	177
25	5	185
411	5	193
162	5	202
478	6	180
139	6	180
41	6	193
434	6	195
475	6	200
181	6	225
.	6	226
487	6	227
517	6	255
382	7	192
397	7	215
.	7	219
398	7	223
392	7	224
125	7	225
548	7	248
127	7	260
416	8	257
530	9	241

30	9	247
339	9	250
212	9	265
359	9	268
68	9	270
143	10	284
401	10	284
509	10	285
281	10	290
396	10	296
464	10	305
408	11	273
482	11	305
494	11	313
276	11	315
477	12	293
.	12	310
381	12	312
265	12	313
79	12	320

*These data are from Danforth, Wrobel, Armstrong, and Swanson (2009).

Suggested Response to Question 2

To: Dr. Indira Jones
From: David Swanson, Graduate Research Assistant
Re: Estimating Age at Death for Juveniles from Femur Length

Using the 77 cases in your random sample, I have been able to construct a very good regression model for estimating age at death for juvenile skeletons from femur length in your Mayan excavations. I recommend that you use the model when you want a quick estimate of age at death and in cases where dental data are nonexistent. If time permits, I recommend that you continue to use dental data to obtain a more precise estimate of age at death. I also recommend that you not use the model when femur length is substantially less than 70 cm or more than 320 cm. The details underlying my recommendation are as follows.

The regression model is
Estimated Age at Death = -3.9 + .05*Femur Length (in centimeters)
$r^2 = 0.952$

Because the data are from a random sample, we need to use statistical inference to determine if there actually is an association between femur length and age at death. I did this in the context of a regression equation, because both femur length (the independent variable) and age at death (the dependent variable) are measured at the ratio level.

The key term in the regression equation to test is the slope coefficient, "b." The T-Test (H_o: b = 0) results led me to reject H_o, with p <.00001. Thus, I believe that for each cm increase in femur length, age at death increases by 0.05 year. Not surprisingly, the intercept term also is statistically significant (H_o: a = 0), with p <.00001. Thus, we are very sure that there is an association between age at death and femur length, and our best estimate of the precise nature of this relationship is to use the regression model constructed from the sample data.

The statistically significant model shown above, a = -3.9 and b = 0.05, explains 95% of the variation in estimated age at death. That is, if we use the model to predict age at death instead of mean age at death (where mean age at death = 5.57 years and the standard deviation of age at death = 3.63), we reduce our error by 95%.

We also can construct confidence intervals around the estimated ages at death resulting from the model. To do this, we use the standard error of estimate (s.e.e.), which is 0.793. If we want to be approximately 95% certain of the true age at death resulting from our model, we can multiply the s.e.e. by 2 and then add and subtract this product from the estimated age at death. For example, when femur length = 300, the estimated age at death = 11.10 = -3.9+.05*300. The 95% confidence interval is then approximately 11.10 -2*.793 and 11.10 + 2*.793, which is equal to 9.51 years and 12.69 years. If we round to whole years, we are 95% certain that the age at death of a juvenile skeleton with a femur length of 300 cm is between 10 and 13 years. As you can see, this is not a bad estimate, but there is a range of three years. Hence, my recommendation to use the model when dental data are lacking or a less accurate estimate of age at death will suffice than that obtained by using the more tedious process involving dental data.

The minimum femur length in the random sample (n = 77) is 70 cm and the maximum is 320 cm. This means that the regression will suffer a decline in accuracy if used to estimate age at death in juvenile skeletons in which the femur length is substantially less than 70 cm or substantially greater than 320 cm. If it is possible to measure other factors such as gender and social class that may be associated with age at death and femur length for Mayan juveniles, the model's accuracy may be improved.

The data and the details of my analysis are found in the attached Excel file. Please let me know if you have any questions about this analysis.

References

Dillman, D. (2000). *Mail and Internet Surveys: The Tailored Design Method.* New York: John Wiley & Sons.

Danforth, M., G. Wrobel, C. Armstrong, and D. Swanson (2009). "A Model Growth Curve for Juvenile Age Estimation Using Diaphyseal Long Bone Lengths Among Ancient Maya Populations." *Latin American Antiquity* 20 (1): 3–14.

Glossary of Selected Statistical Terms

ADJUSTED R-SQUARED. A regression goodness-of-fit statistic that is "corrected" for the degrees of freedom. It is interpreted as the fraction of variation in the dependent variable that is explained by the regression model (independent variables and constant).

AGGREGATION. The process of assembling individual elements into summary form for purposes of presentation or analysis. For example, to assemble census records for individuals in a given area into a summary for the area as a whole.

AGGREGATION BIAS. A type of distortion that can result by attributing relationships found among summaries to the individual elements from which the summaries were obtained.

ALPHA (α). The probability of committing a Type I error. A Type I error occurs when a researcher rejects a true null hypothesis. Alpha is also called the "level of significance." (See also BETA, HYPOTHESIS TEST, P-VALUE METHOD, POWER, TYPE I ERROR, and TYPE II ERROR.)

ALTERNATIVE HYPOTHESIS. The hypothesis that complements the null hypothesis; usually it is the hypothesis that the researcher is interested in proving. The alternative hypothesis is generally denoted as H_a. (See also HYPOTHESIS TEST.)

ANALYSIS OF VARIANCE. A statistical technique that uses the F-test to determine whether there is a significant difference in the means of two or more independent groups.

ARITHMETIC MEAN. (See MEAN.)

AUTOCORRELATION. A problem that arises in regression analysis when the data occur over time and the error terms are correlated; also called serial correlation.

BAYES RULE. An extension of the conditional law of probabilities discovered by Thomas Bayes that can be used to revise probabilities. (See also BAYESIAN.)

BAYESIAN. This refers to a way of doing statistics that is based on ideas developed by Thomas Bayes. It is a specific view of probability that, while not in total opposition to the "frequentist" view, is sufficiently different that this way bears Bayes's own name. Some Bayesian techniques incorporate extensions of logic and others incorporate personal or subjective probability (see also FREQUENTIST and SUBJECTIVE PROBABILITY.)

BERNOULLI TRIAL. A Bernoulli trial is an experiment whose outcome is random and can be either of two possible outcomes, such as "yes" or "no" or "heads" or "tails." (See also BINOMIAL DISTRIBUTION.)

BETA (β). The probability of committing a Type II error. A Type II error occurs when a researcher fails to reject a false null hypothesis. (See also ALPHA, HYPOTHESIS TEST, P-VALUE, POWER, TYPE I ERROR, and TYPE II ERROR.)

BIAS. The deviation of an estimate or set of estimates from the correct value(s) in one direction (i.e., above or below the correct value(s)).

BIMODAL. Data sets that have two modes. (See also MODE.)

BINOMIAL DISTRIBUTION. A discrete distribution which gives the probability of observing X successes in a fixed number (n) of independent Bernoulli trials. (See also BERNOULLI TRIAL.)

BOUNDS. The error portion of the confidence interval that is added and/or subtracted from the point estimate to form the confidence interval.

CASE. This is a set of information regarding the unit of study. If the unit of study is the family, then each case would be a family for which a set of information, such as annual income, monthly food expenditures, and size. If the unit of study is the number of migrants coming into and leaving U.S. counties, the unit of study would be the county. (See also UNIT OF ANALYSIS, VALUE, and VARIABLE.)

CENSUS. The count of a given population (or other phenomenon of interest) and recording its characteristics, done at a specific point and usually at regular intervals by a governmental entity for the geographic area or subareas under its domain. (See also SAMPLE.)

CENTRAL LIMIT THEOREM. A theorem that states that regardless of the distribution of a population, the sample means and sample proportions will be normally distributed as long as the sample sizes are large. This is a very important component of the theory that supports statistical inference. (See also EXPECTED VALUE, INFERENTIAL STATISTICS, and the LAW OF LARGE NUMBERS.)

CENTRAL TENDENCY. A term used to refer to finding the "average" value in a set of data, acknowledging that there are several ways that this can be done, to include the mean, the median, and the mode, in addition to the geometric mean and the harmonic mean. (See also MEAN, MEDIAN, and MODE.)

CHEBYSHEV'S INEQUALITY. A theorem stating that at least $1 - 1/k$ values will fall within +/- k standard deviations of the mean, regardless of the shape of the distribution.

CHI-SQUARED ($\chi 2$) DISTRIBUTION. A continuous distribution determined by the sum of the squares of k independent, normally distributed random variables.

CHI-SQUARED ($\chi 2$) GOODNESS-OF-FIT TEST. A statistical test used to analyze probabilities of multinomial distribution trials along a single dimension; it compares expected frequencies of categories from a population's distribution to the observed, or actual, frequencies from a sample distribution. (See HYPOTHESIS TEST and INFERENTIAL STATISTICS.)

CHI-SQUARED ($\chi 2$) TEST OF INDEPENDENCE. A statistical test used to analyze the frequencies of two variables with multiple categories (variables at the nominal or ordinal level of measurement) to determine if the two variables are independent. That is, if there is or is not a relationship between the two variables. (See GOODMAN AND KRUSKAL'S LAMBDA (λ), HYPOTHESIS TEST, and INFERENTIAL STATISTICS.)

CLUSTER SAMPLING. A type of random sampling in which the population is divided into non-overlapping areas or clusters and elements are randomly sampled from the areas or clusters. (See also SAMPLE and RANDOM SAMPLE.)

COEFFICIENT OF DETERMINATION. A "Proportionate Reduction in Error" measure that shows the proportion of variability of the dependent variable accounted for or explained by the independent variable in a regression model. (See also PROPORTIONATE REDUCTION IN ERROR and R-SQUARED.)

COEFFICIENT OF SKEWNESS. A measure of the degree of skewness that exists in a distribution of numbers; compares the mean and the median in light of the magnitude of the standard deviation.

COEFFICIENT OF VARIATION. The ratio of the standard deviation to the mean, usually expressed as a percentage.

CONFIDENCE INTERVAL. This is the range placed around an estimate in a sample so that we can infer what the range is likely to be in the population from which the sample was drawn. For example, if we have the average monthly expenditure on food in a sample of 50 families, we would use the standard error in conjunction with a desired "level of confidence" to provide the likely range for average monthly expenditure on food by the population of families from which the sample was drawn. (See also ESTIMATE, INFERENTIAL STATISTICS, and STANDARD ERROR.)

CORRELATION. A measure of the degree of relatedness of two or more variables.

COVARIANCE. The variance of two variables, X and Y, together.

COVERAGE ERROR. In principle, this refers to the difference between the "true population" and the number reported in a set of data such as a census, survey, or set of administrative records. In practice, it is the difference between an *estimate* of the true number and the number reported in a set of data such as a census, survey, or set of administrative records. (See also CODING/TRANSCRIPTION ERROR, MEASUREMENT ERROR, NON-RESPONSE ERROR, SAMPLING ERROR, and TOTAL ERROR.)

CRITICAL VALUE. The value that divides the non-rejection region from the rejection region.

CURRENT POPULATION SURVEY (CPS). In the United States, a sample survey conducted monthly by the Census Bureau designed to represent the civilian noninstitutional population. The survey obtains a wide range of socioeconomic demographic data.

CURVE. A mathematical function, usually continuous and otherwise "well behaved" that can be used as a model. The primary example is the normal curve, but there are many others. (See also NORMAL DISTRIBUTION.)

CURVE-FITTING. The process of finding a mathematical function that serves as a model for a given demographic process.

DATA. Data is the plural form of "datum," which is a single fact or observation. Thus, a set of data is a set of facts or observations. These facts or observations can be in the form of numbers, words, or other symbols. (See DATA SET.)

DATA AGGREGATION. Compounding primary data into an aggregate to express data in summary form. National income is an example of aggregate data.

DATA SET. This the general term applied to a collection of data. It may be a sample or an entire population. The data may be in terms of numbers, words, other symbols, or all three. (See DATA, POPULATION, and SAMPLE.)

DATUM. The singular from of data. (See DATA.)

DEDUCTIVE REASONING. This is a type of reasoning where the conclusions follow from a set of premises (or hypothesis). It is generally very formal. One type of deductive reasoning is the syllogism, which has the following form:

> Major Premise: All Alfa Romeo automobiles are fast.
> Minor Premise: This is an Alfa Romeo automobile.
> Conclusion: This automobile is fast.

If the minor premise was changed to "This automobile is fast," could you conclude that the automobile was an Alfa Romeo?

DEGREES OF FREEDOM. A mathematical adjustment made to the size of the sample; used along with alpha to locate values in statistical tables.

DEPENDENT VARIABLE. In looking at the relationship between two variables, this is the variable that is being predicted. (See also INDEPENDENT VARIABLE, PROPORTIONATE REDUCTION IN ERROR, and REGRESSION.)

DESCRIPTIVE STATISTICS. Statistics that have been gathered on a group to describe or reach conclusions about that same group. (See INFERENTIAL STATISTICS and STATISTICS.)

DISCRETE DISTRIBUTIONS. Distributions constructed from discrete random variables.

DISPERSION. This refers to how "spread out" a set of data is. (See RANGE.)

DISTRIBUTION. This is the range of values that a given variable has in a data set. (See DATA SET, VALUE, VARIABLE, STANDARD DEVIATION, and VARIANCE.)

DUMMY CODING. Another name for a qualitative or indicator variable measure at the nominal level that has two values (e.g., yes or no); usually coded as 0 or 1, and represents whether or not a given item or person possesses a certain characteristic. This is useful because this variable now can be treated as being at the ratio level of measurement, although with limitations. For example, the "arithmetic average" of the set of nominal level variable that is dummy coded is the proportion of cases that have the attribute in question. In the sample of 50 families used throughout this book, the variable "Presence of Garden" is dummy coded, such that having a garden is 1 and not having a garden is 0. The arithmetic average of this variable is 0.40, which can be multiplied by 100 and interpreted as "40% of the families in the sample have a garden." (See also LEVEL OF MEASUREMENT and NOMINAL LEVEL OF MEASUREMENT.)

ENUMERATION. The act of counting the members of a population in a census. (See also CENSUS and SAMPLE.)

ERROR. In the field of data analysis and statistics, this term can be used to refer to one of the four types of error that can potentially affect every data set (measurement, non-response, coverage, and coding/transcription) and the fifth type—sampling error—that affects only data sets generated from random sampling. (See also CODING/TRANSCRIPTION ERROR, COVERAGE ERROR, MEASUREMENT ERROR, NON-RESPONSE ERROR, and SAMPLING ERROR.) It also is used to refer to differences within a data set between all of the values of a given variable and their arithmetic mean and to the process of squaring these differences and summing them up in the mathematics underlying regression and Analysis of Variance. (See also REGRESSION, SUM OF SQUARES, SUM OF SQUARES ERRORS, STANDARD DEVIATION, and VARIANCE.)

ESTIMATE. In the sense of statistical inference, this is what we get from a random sample. For example, we may have the average monthly expenditure on food for 50 families that were in a random sample. We can use the information in the sample to make an "estimate" of what the average monthly expenditure on food is for the entire "population" of families from which the sample was drawn. (See also CONFIDENCE INTERVAL, HYPOTHESIS TEST, and INFERENTIAL STATISTICS.)

EVENT. A change in condition or status (e.g., single to married) or the realization of a value (e.g., rolling a seven with a pair of dice).

EXHAUSTIVE EVENTS. A set of events is jointly or collectively exhaustive if at least one of the events occurs: For example, when rolling a six-sided die, the outcomes 1, 2, 3, 4, 5, and 6 are exhaustive, because they encompass the entire range of possible outcomes. (See also MUTUALLY EXCLUSIVE EVENTS.)

EXPECTED VALUE. The long-run average of occurrences; sometimes referred to as the mean value. (See also INFERENTIAL STATISTICS and LAW OF LARGE NUMBERS.)

EXPERIMENTAL RESEARCH. In this type of research design, the researcher can control the research design to look at the effects of a given variable on a variable of interest. For example, it is possible to see how motivation affects the running time of laboratory rats by controlling the reward (e.g., amount of food) they get for successfully completing a simple maze. The research hypothesis might be that motivation (as operationalized by the amount of food at the end of the maze) affects run time, with the experimental group of rats getting a larger set amount of food than the rats in the control group. (See NONEXPERIMENTAL RESEARCH.)

EXPONENTIAL DISTRIBUTION. A continuous distribution closely related to the Poisson distribution that describes the times between random occurrences.

EXTRAPOLATION. The process of determining (estimating or projecting) values that go beyond the last known data point in a series (e.g., the most recent census or estimate). It is typically accomplished by using a mathematical formula, a graphic procedure, or a combination of the two. (See also INTERPOLATION.)

F DISTRIBUTION. A distribution based on the ratio of two random variances; used in testing two variances and in analysis of variance. (See also HYPOTHESIS TEST.)

F VALUE. The ratio of two sample variances, used to reach statistical conclusions regarding the null hypothesis; in ANOVA, the ratio of the treatment variance to the error variance. (See also ALPHA, HYPOTHESIS TEST.)

FREQUENCY DISTRIBUTION. A summary of data presented in the form of class intervals and frequencies.

FREQUENTIST. This refers to a way of doing statistics that is based on an interpretation of probability that defines an event's probability as the limit of its relative frequency in a large number of trials. This is the perspective underlying the concepts discussed in this book. (See also BAYESIAN and SUBJECTIVE PROBABILITY.)

GOODMAN AND KRUSKAL'S LAMBDA (λ). This is a measure of strength of relationship between nominal-level variables. It measures the extent to which prediction of a given (dependent) variable can be improved by knowledge of another variable (i.e., an independent variable). It is a Proportionate Reduction in Error (PRE) measure, because it shows how much prediction error is decreased by using the additional information found in the independent variable. (See also DEPENDENT VARIABLE,

INDEPENDENT VARIABLE, PROPORTIONATE REDUCTION IN ERROR [PRE], and REGRESSION.)

HETEROSKEDASTICITY. The condition that occurs when the error variances produced by a regression model are not constant. (See also HOMOSKEDASTICITY.)

HOMOSKEDASTICITY. The condition that occurs when the error variances produced by a regression model are constant. (See also HETEROSKEDASTICITY.)

HYPOTHESIS TEST. This is a standard tool in statistical inference used to make decisions involving comparisons. For example, if we have two samples, one from city A and the other from city B and we are going to site a retail store in the city that has the highest mean household income, we would use a hypothesis test to assist in making the decision about which city has the higher mean household income. (See also ALTERNATIVE HYPOTHESIS, ALPHA, BETA, ESTIMATE, INFERENTIAL STATISTICS, NULL HYPOTHESIS, ONE-TAILED TEST, P-VALUE METHOD, POWER, T-TEST, TWO-TAILED TEST, TYPE I ERROR, TYPE II ERROR, and Z-TEST.)

IMPORTANT DIFFERENCE. (See SUBSTANTIVE SIGNIFICANCE.)

IMPUTATION. In a sample survey or census, a general term used to describe the assignment of values to cases for which one or more variables have missing values due to "non-response." Four common methods are (1) Deductive imputation, which is based on other information available from the case in question; (2) hot-deck imputation, which is based on information from "closest-matching" cases; (3) mean-value imputation, which uses means of variables as the source of assignment; and (4) regression-based imputation, in which models are constructed using cases with no missing values, and a dependent variable is the one whose missing values will be imputed and the independent variables are those that yield acceptable regression equations. (See also NON-RESPONSE.)

INDEPENDENT EVENTS. Two events are independent if the occurrence of one event makes it neither more nor less probable that the other event occurs.

INDEPENDENT VARIABLE. In looking at the relationship between two variables, this is the predictor variable. (See also DEPENDENT VARIABLE, PROPORTIONATE REDUCTION IN ERROR, and REGRESSION.)

INDUCTIVE REASONING. This is a type of reasoning that makes generalizations from limited data. For example, if every Alfa Romeo automobile you ever saw was red, then you might conclude that all Alfa Romeo automobiles are red. Inferential statistics uses a form of inductive reasoning to use a premise (hypothesis) in conjunction with a sample to make an inference about the population from which the sample was drawn. (See also DEDUCTIVE REASONING and INFERENTIAL STATISTICS.)

INFERENTIAL STATISTICS. Statistics that have been gathered from a sample and used to reach conclusions about the population from which the sample was taken. (See also CENTRAL LIMIT THEOREM, DESCRIPTIVE STATISTICS, ESTIMATE, EXPECTED VALUE, HYPOTHESIS TEST, INDUCTIVE REASONING, LAW OF LARGE NUMBERS, NORMAL DISTRIBUTION, SAMPLING DISTRIBUTION, SAMPLING ERROR, and STATISTICS.)

INTERPOLATION. The calculation of intermediate values for a given series of numbers. It is typically accomplished by using a mathematical formula, a graphic procedure, or a combination of the two. It typically imparts or even imposes a regularity to data and can, therefore, be used for smoothing, whether or not the imposed regularity is realistic. (See also EXTRAPOLATION and SMOOTHING.)

INTERQUARTILE RANGE. The range of values between the first and the third quartile.

INTERVAL ESTIMATE. A range of values within which it is estimated with some confidence where the population parameter lies. (See CONFIDENCE INTERVAL and ESTIMATE.)

INTERVAL LEVEL OF MEASUREMENT. This refers to the type of measure where the distance between attributes has meaning, which means we can do meaningful addition and subtraction. For example, the difference in temperature (in Fahrenheit) between 30 and 40 is the same as the distance from 70 to 80: 10 degrees. This means that we have a fixed distance between the points—like using a ruler where the distance between two degrees Fahrenheit and four degrees Fahrenheit is the same as the distance between seven and nine degrees Fahrenheit. Note, however, that ratios don't make any sense—80 degrees is not twice as hot as 40 degrees. The ratio makes no sense because there is no "true" zero on the Fahrenheit scale in that all molecular action ceases so that there is a complete absence of heat. This means that numbers measured at the interval level cannot be multiplied or divided in a meaningful way. (See also LEVEL OF MEASUREMENT and RATIO LEVEL OF MEASUREMENT.)

KURTOSIS. The degree of peakedness of a distribution. (See also SKEWNESS.)

LAMBDA (λ). (See GOODMAN AND KRUSKAL'S LAMBDA.)

LAW OF LARGE NUMBERS. This is a theorem that describes the result of performing the trials (e.g., rolling the dice) a large number of times. According to the theorem, the average of the results obtained from a large number of trials should be close to the expected value, and will tend to become closer as more trials are performed. (See also CENTRAL LIMIT THEOREM and EXPECTED VALUE.)

LEAST SQUARES. The process by which a regression model is developed based on calculus techniques that attempt to produce a minimum sum of the squared error values. (See also SUM OF SQUARES and SUM OF SQUARES ERROR.)

LEVEL OF MEASUREMENT. This refers to a system of classifying numbers in terms of what operations can legitimately be done with them. There are several ways the classification can be done. This book uses the fourfold classification system proposed by S.S. Stevens (1946), which classifies numbers as being: (1) Nominal; (2) ordinal; (3) interval; and (4) ratio. There are other systems, such as the twofold classification of: (1) Discrete; and (2) continuous. The fourfold system developed by Stevens is useful in that it points the way to specific measures to be used with numbers at given levels of measurement. For example, it is not meaningful to find the arithmetic average for a nominal level variable, except only in the special case where a "nominal level" variable with two values is dummy coded as 1 and 0. In some situations, the arithmetic average for an ordinal level variable is meaningful, while in others it is not. It is always meaningful to have an arithmetic average for a variable at either the interval or ratio level of measurement. (See also INTERVAL LEVEL OF MEASUREMENT, DUMMY CODING, NOMINAL LEVEL OF MEASUREMENT, ORDINAL LEVEL OF MEASUREMENT, and RATIO LEVEL OF MEASUREMENT.)

LEVEL OF SIGNIFICANCE. The probability of committing a Type I error; also know as alpha. (See also HYPOTHESIS TEST, TYPE I ERROR, and TYPE II ERROR.)

MATCHED GROUPS. A group constructed on a case-by-case basis through matching of sets of records according to a limited number of characteristics.

MATCHED PAIRS. Data or measurements gathered from pairs of items or persons that are matched on some characteristic or from a before-and-after design and then separated into different samples; also called paired data or related measures.

MATCHED PAIRS TEST. A T-test to test the differences in two related or matched samples; sometimes called the T-Test for related measures or the correlated T-Test.

MEAN. This refers to the arithmetic mean of a set of data, where the mean is the sum of the values of the distribution divided by the total number of cases. (See AVERAGE, MEDIAN, and MODE.)

MEAN ABSOLUTE DEVIATION. The average of the absolute values of the deviations around the mean for a set of numbers. (See also STANDARD DEVIAITON and VARIANCE.)

MEASUREMENT ERROR. The result of poor wording in a survey or in a form designed to capture data or presenting the questions or data collection entries in such a way that inaccurate or uninterpretable answers are obtained.

MEDIAN. The middle value in an ordered array of numbers. (See MEAN and MODE.)

METRIC DATA. Interval and ratio level data; also called quantitative data. (See LEVEL OF MEASUREMENT.)

MODE. The value that occurs most often in a set of data. (See also BIMODAL, MEAN, and MEDIAN.)

MODEL. A generalized representation of a process, set of relationships, or patterns. The Normal Curve serves as a mathematical model as does a regression equation. (See also CURVE and NORMAL DISTRIBUTION.)

MULTIPLE REGRESSION. Regression analysis with one dependent variable and two or more independent variables, or at least one nonlinear independent, variable.

MUTUALLY EXCLUSIVE EVENTS. Two events are mutually exclusive if they cannot occur at the same time. An example is tossing a coin once, which can result in either heads or tails, but not both. (See also EXHAUSTIVE EVENTS.)

NOMINAL LEVEL OF MEASUREMENT. Here, the values just "name" the attribute uniquely and they do not imply any ordering of the cases. For example, the variable "Religion" is inherently nominal. Suppose we decide in a study that it is useful to have three values for this variable: Christian; Muslim; and All Other. Thus, we have three values (mutually exclusive and exhaustive). We could code these values as "C," "M," and "A," respectively; we can also code them as "1," "2," and "3," respectively. In the latter case, the numbers are really not numbers in the sense that we can add and subtract them. It makes no sense to say a "Christian (1)" is the result of subtracting "Muslim (2)" from "All Other (3)." Thus, numbers assigned to serve as values for nominal level variables such as "Religion" cannot be added, subtracted, multiplied, or divided in a meaningful way. (See also DUMMY VARIABLE and LEVEL OF MEASUREMENT.)

NONEXPERIMENTAL RESEARCH. In this type of research design, it is difficult—if not impossible—for the researcher to achieve the level of control possible in an experimental research design, since the data are gathered from random samples of the population of interest. What can occur is "quasi-control" via the manipulation of variables and data subsets after the data have been gathered. For example, it is not possible to assign families certain levels of income in order to see the effects of income on food expenditures, but it is possible to use regression analysis and inferential statistics with sample data to look at the effect of income on food expenditures. (See also EXPERIMENTAL RESEARCH.)

NONLINEAR REGRESSION. Regression models in which the models are nonlinear, such as polynomial models, logarithmic models, and exponential models.

NONMETRIC DATA. Nominal and ordinal level data; also called qualitative data.

NONPROBABLITY SAMPLING. (See NONRANDOM SAMPLING.)

NONRANDOM ERROR. All errors not due to the effects of random sample selection (i.e., random error). It can occur both in a sample survey and in a population census. Examples include non-response, incorrect answers by a valid respondent, answers given by a non-valid respondent, as well as coding and other processing errors. Statistical inference can only be used to estimate random error, not nonrandom error. (See also NET CENSUS UNDERCOUNT ERROR, NON-RESPONSE, POPULATION, RANDOM ERROR, SAMPLE, and TOTAL ERROR.)

NONRANDOM SAMPLING. Sampling in which not every unit of the population has the same or a known probability of being selected into the sample. (See also RANDOM SAMPLING.)

NON-REJECTION REGION. Any portion of a distribution that is not in the rejection region. If the observed statistic falls in this region, the decision is a failure to reject the null hypothesis. (See also ALPHA, BETA, and HYPOTHESIS TEST.)

NON-RESPONDENT. In a sample survey or census, a respondent who refuses to be interviewed, or is otherwise unable to take part. (See also NON-RESPONSE.)

NON-RESPONSE. Missing data on a form used in a survey or census due to a number of reasons, including the refusal of a respondent to answer, the inability to locate a potential respondent, the inability of a respondent (or informant) to answer questions, or the omission of answers due to a clerical or some other form of error. Total non-response refers to a case (i.e., an observation) in which all variables have missing values, and item non-response refers to a case in which fewer than all variables have one or more missing values. Imputation is often used to estimate values for cases in which they are missing. (See also ERROR, IMPUTATION, CODING/TRANSCRIPTION

ERROR, COVERAGE ERROR, MEASUREMENT ERROR, NONRANDOM ERROR, NON-RESPONDENT, and SAMPLING ERROR.)

NON-RESPONSE ERROR. (See NON-RESPONSE.)

NORMAL DISTRIBUTION. A widely known and much-used continuous distribution. Because of its widespread use as a model for a sampling distribution, it has been called the fundamental distribution in inferential statistics. (See also CURVE and SAMPLING DISTRIBUTION.).

NULL HYPOTHESIS. The hypothesis that assumes the status quo—that the old theory, method, or standard is still true; the complement of the alternative hypothesis. (See also ALTERNATIVE HYPOTHESIS, HYPOTHESIS TEST, and STATISTICAL SIGNIFICANCE.)

OBSERVATION. (See CASE.)

OBSERVED SIGNIFICANCE LEVEL. Another name for the p-value method of testing hypotheses. (See ALPHA, HYPOTHESIS TEST, P-VALUE METHOD, STATISTICAL SIGNIFICANCE.)

ONE-TAILED TEST. A statistical test wherein the researcher is interested only in testing one side of the distribution. (See also HYPOTHESIS TEST and TWO-TAILED TEST.)

ORDINAL LEVEL OF MEASUREMENT. This refers to the fact that attributes can be rank ordered, but that the distances between attributes are not fixed. For example, suppose we had a questionnaire in which we asked people if they thought statistics was a great subject to study and had the following five response categories: (1) Strongly disagree; (2) Somewhat disagree; (3) Neither disagree nor agree; (4) Somewhat agree; and (5) Strongly agree. We can see that "Strongly agree," coded as "5," indicates more agreement than does a response coded as "4" ("Somewhat agree"), and so on. However, the "distance" between the categories is not fixed. That is, we are not able to say if the "distance" from "Strongly disagree" (coded as "1") to "Somewhat disagree" (coded as "2") is the same as the distance from "Strongly agree" (coded as "5") to "Somewhat agree" (coded as "4"). All we can say is that codes 1 through 5 preserve the order of agreement. The central issue is that the distances between the numbers are not fixed. It is as if we are using a rubber band for a ruler. Numbers coded at the ordinal level occupy an interesting "gray area" between nominal level variables on the one hand (for which there is no meaningful addition, subtraction, multiplication, and division), and on the other, interval level variables (for which there is meaningful addition and subtraction and ratio level variables, for which there is meaningful addition, subtraction, multiplication, and division). In some situations, one can treat variables inherently at the ordinal level as being interval, and in other situations, one cannot. The situations largely depend on the coding assigned to the attributes of ordinal level variables. (See also DUMMY VARIABLE and LEVEL OF MEASUREMENT.)

OUTLIERS. Data points that lie apart from the rest of the points.

P-VALUE. The probability returned by a hypothesis test that the null hypothesis is true. (See also ALPHA, BETA, HYPOTHESIS TEST, and STATISTICAL SIGNIFICANCE.)

P-VALUE METHOD. A method of testing hypotheses in which there is no preset level of alpha. The probability of getting a test statistic at least as extreme as the observed test statistic is computed under the assumption that the null hypothesis is true. This probability is called the p-value, and it is the smallest value of alpha for which the null hypothesis can be rejected. (See also ALPHA, HYPOTHESIS TEST, and P-VALUE.)

PAIRED DATA. Data gathered from pairs of items or persons that are matched on some characteristic or from a before-and-after design and then separated into different samples; also called matched pairs data or related measures.

PARAMETER. A descriptive measure of the population.

PARAMETRIC STATISTICS. A class of statistical techniques that contain assumptions about the population and that are used only with interval and ratio level data.

PERCENT. (See PROPORTION.)

PERCENTILES. Measures of central tendency that divide a group of data into 100 parts.

POINT ESTIMATE. An estimate of a population parameter constructed from a statistic taken from a sample. (See also CONFIDENCE INTERVAL, ESTIMATE, and INTERVAL ESTIMATE.)

POPULATION. In the statistical sense, it is a collection of persons, objects, or items of interest. It generally refers to the set of ALL persons, objects, or items of interest. There is not statistical uncertainty in regard to measures taken over all members of a population. However, as is the case with a census, gathering the information can be costly and time consuming. It is from a "population" that a sample is taken with the idea of obtaining information about the population, knowing that statistical uncertainty has now been introduced by using sampling and statistical inference in return for reduced costs and time. (See also CENSUS, INFERENTIAL STATISTICS, and SAMPLE.)

POST-STRATIFICATION. This is a method used to make a sample more representative of the population from which it is drawn. For example, a sample of adults may consist of 65% females, but you know (usually from census data) that approximately 51% of the adult population is composed of females. To the extent that females tend to give different answers than men, the results of your sample will then be biased, because females are overrepresented. To make the sample more representative, each female and male would receive "weights" designed to provide more representative results for the sample as a whole.

In applying post-stratification to our example, each of the adult females would receive a weight of ".78" (where .78 = .51/.65) and each adult male would receive a weight of 1.40 (where 1.40 = .49/(1 − .65). If in the original survey we had 1,000 respondents (650 adult females and 350 adult males) and 35% of the females answered yes to a given question while 70% of the males did so, we would have a biased estimate of the percent answering yes, since the females tend to answer yes less often than males and they are overrepresented in the sample. Specifically, we would believe that 47.3% of the population would say "yes" to this question (where 47.3 = 100*(473/1,000), where 473 ≈ ((.35*.65*1,000) + (.70*.35*1,000)). However, this is "biased downward" by the overrepresentation of adult females in the sample relative to their share of the adult population.

By using the post-stratification weights, we would get a picture not biased by the overrepresentation of adult females—namely, that about 52% of the population would say yes (where 52.0 = 100*(520/1,000), where 520 ≈ ((.35*.78*.65*1,000) + (.70*1.40*.35*1,000)). If this sample involved polling voters before an election, you can see that there is a "substantive significance" between the biased estimate of 47.3% and the unbiased estimate of 52% that resulted from using post-stratification. (See also STRATIFIED RANDOM SAMPLING, SUBSTANTIVE SIGNIFICANCE, and WEIGHTED AVERAGE.)

POWER. The probability of rejecting a false null hypothesis. (See also ALPHA, BETA, and HYPOTHESIS TEST.)

PROBABILITY. A ratio in which the numerator consists of those in a population experiencing an event of interest (e.g., death) over a specified period of time, while the denominator consists of the at-risk population. (See also AT-RISK POPULATION, PROPORTION, RATE, and RATIO.)

PROBABILITY DENSITY FUNCTION. This describes the probability of a random variable to occur at a given point. It is usually used with theoretical sampling distributions and refers to "Continuous Random Variables" (see Exhibit 6.3 in Chapter 6).

PROBABILITY DISTRIBUTION. This is a function that describes the probability of a random variable taking certain values. (See also RANDOM VARIABLE.)

PROPORTION. A ratio used to describe the status of a population with respect to some characteristic (e.g., married), where the numerator is part of the denominator. When multiplied by 100, a proportion is known as a "percent." (See also PROBABILITY, RATE, and RATIO.)

PROPORTIONATE REDUCTION IN ERROR (PRE). The PRE framework is a way of looking at the possibility of a relationship between two (or more) variables that first looks at how one accurately one can "predict" the values of a given variable from information found in the data for the variable itself (Rule 1) . After finding the accuracy of this way of predicting, it then considers if the relationship between the given variable and some other variable improves the accuracy of the prediction (Rule 2). The basic PRE framework is that you subtract the number of errors made using Rule 2 (e.g., PIE sex) from the number of errors made using Rule 1, and then divide this difference by the number of errors made under Rule 1:

$$PRE = \frac{(\text{Prediction Errors Using Rule 1}) - (\text{Prediction Errors Using Rule 2})}{(\text{Prediction Errors Using Rule 1})}$$

A PRE measure is always between zero and 1.00. If the measure is zero, it says that the additional information associated with using Rule 2 provides no improvement in accuracy over and above using Rule 1. If a PRE measure is 1.00, it says that the additional information associated with Rule 2 provides a 100% reduction in error. In other words, by using Rule 2, we can predict values of the variable in question perfectly. (See also GOODMAN AND KRUSKAL'S LAMBDA (λ), MEAN, REGRESSION, and R-SQUARED.)

QUARTILES. Measures of central tendency that divide a group of data into four subgroups or parts.

RANDOM ERROR. (See SAMPLING ERROR.)

RANDOM SAMPLING. Sampling in which every unit of the population has a known probability (in a pure random sample the known probability is that each member has the same probability of being selected) of being selected for the sample. (See also NONRANDOM SAMPLING.)

RANDOM VARIABLE. A variable that contains the outcomes of a chance experiment. (See also PROBABILITY DISTRIBUTION.)

RANGE. The difference between the largest and the smallest values in a set of numbers.

RATE. Technically, this type of ratio is the same as a probability. However, the term is often applied to the type of ratio known as a proportion, as in the case of "vacancy rate," which is the ratio of unoccupied housing units to all housing units. It is also applied to other types of ratios in which the denominators are not precisely the "at-risk populations," as is the case of the crude birth rate. (See also AT-RISK POPULATION, PROBABILITY, PROPORTION, and RATIO.)

RATIO. A single number that expresses the relative size of two other numbers—i.e., a quotient, which is the result of dividing one number by another. (See also PROBABILITY, PROPORTION, and RATE.)

RATIO LEVEL OF MEASUREMENT. This refers to numbers at the interval level of measurement for which a "true zero" exists. This means that in addition to adding and subtracting numbers, we also can divide and multiply them in a meaningful way. For example, in the Fahrenheit system for measuring temperature, zero is not the absence of heat. Thus, while we can say that the distance between 60 and 45 degrees is the same as the distance from 15 to 30 degrees, we cannot say that 60 degrees is twice as hot as 30 degrees. Hence, it is at the interval level of measurement because the distance between the points is fixed. However, in the Kelvin system for measuring temperature, there is an absolute zero at which molecular action ceases. So, we can say that 20 degrees Kelvin is twice as hot as 10 degrees Kelvin, since not only are the distances fixed (it is the same distance from 1 degree Kelvin to 2 degrees Kelvin as it is from 15 degrees Kelvin to 16 degrees Kelvin), but there also is a true zero, which means that the Kelvin scale is at the ratio level of measurement. (See also LEVEL OF MEASUREMENT.)

R-SQUARED (R^2). The coefficient of multiple determination; a value that ranges from 0 to 1 and represents the proportion of the dependent variable in a multiple regression model that is accounted for by the independent variables. (See also PROPORTIONATE REDUCTION IN ERROR [PRE] and REGRESSION.)

REGRESSION. The process of constructing a mathematical model or function that can be used to predict or determine one variable by any other variable. (See also GOODMAN AND KRUSKAL'S LAMBDA (λ), PROPORTIONATE REDUCTION IN ERROR [PRE], and R-SQUARED.)

REJECTION REGION. If a computed statistic lies in this portion of a distribution, the null hypothesis will be rejected. (See also ALPHA, BETA, HYPOTHESIS TEST, TYPE I ERROR, and TYPE II ERROR.)

RELATIVE FREQUENCY. The idea that the probability of an event can be approximated by the proportion of times that the event occurs. For example, in tosses of a single die, the relative frequency of the number "1" is 1/6.

RESIDUAL. The difference between the actual Y value and the Y value predicted by the regression model; the error of the regression model in predicting each value of the dependent variable. (See also REGRESSION.)

RESIDUAL ANALYSIS. An analysis of residuals. (See also RESIDUAL.)

ROBUST. Describes a statistical technique that is relatively insensitive to minor violations in one or more of its underlying assumptions.

SAMPLE. A subset of a population (in the statistical sense) for which data are typically collected in a "survey," which is a way of providing respondents with questions to be answered (e.g., through personal interviews, telephone interviews, mail-out/mail-back questionnaires). Samples may also be selected from administrative and other records such that interviews are not needed because data are taken directly from the records themselves (e.g., from Medicare files). Samples may be defined in a number of ways, but if statistical inference is to be used, a sample's elements should have a known probability of selection, or at least a reasonable approximation thereof, so that "random error" can be estimated. (See also CENSUS, NONRANDOM ERROR, POPULATION, and RANDOM ERROR.)

SAMPLE PROPORTION. The quotient of the frequency at which a given characteristic occurs in a sample and the number of items in the sample.

SAMPLE SIZE ESTIMATION. An estimate of the size of sample necessary to fulfill the requirements of a particular level of confidence and to be within a specified amount of error.

SAMPLE SPACE. A complete roster or listing of all elementary events for an experiment.

SAMPLING DISTRIBUTION. This is a theoretical model used in inferential statistics. The most common model is "normal distribution." (See also NORMAL DISTRIBUTION, SAMPLING ERROR, and STANDARD ERROR.)

SAMPLING ERROR. The difference between a statistic of interest (e.g., mean age) found in a sample unaffected by nonrandom error and its corresponding parameter (e.g., mean age) found in the population from which the sample was drawn. Sampling error can only occur in a sample, never in a population. It is often referred to as sample error or random error. (See also CODING/TRANSCRIPTION ERROR, COVERAGE ERROR, IMPUTATION, MEASUREMENT ERROR, NONRANDOM ERROR, POPULATION, SAMPLE, SAMPLING ERROR, and TOTAL ERROR.)

SERIAL CORRELATION. A problem that arises in regression analysis when the error terms of a regression model are correlated due to time-series data; also called autocorrelation. (See AUTOCORRELATION.)

SIGNIFICANCE. (See STATISTICAL SIGNIFICANCE.)

SIMPLE RANDOM SAMPLING. The most elementary of the random sampling techniques; involves numbering each item in the population and using a list or roster of random numbers to select items for the sample. Each member has the same probability of being selected. (See also NONRANDOM SAMPLING and RANDOM SAMPLING.)

SKEWNESS. The lack of symmetry of a distribution of values. (See also COEFFICIENT OF SKEWNESS and KURTOSIS.)

STANDARD ERROR. This is a key item that links an empirical sample to a theoretical model in order to do statistical inference. In general, a standard error is the ratio of the standard deviation of a sample to the square root of the sample size. This ratio encompasses the two determinants of statistical uncertainty—variation and sample size. In conjunction with a desired level of confidence, it is used to find the likely range in the population from which a sample was drawn. For example, if the average monthly expenditure on food is \$1841.65 in a sample of 50 families and the standard deviation is \$670.20, the standard error is of the mean is \$94.78 = (\$670.20(/[(50)^{0.5}]$. We can construct a 95% confidence interval for what is the average monthly expenditure on food in the population from which our sample of 50 families was taken, which is approximately \$1,652.09 and \$2,031.21 (\$1,841.65 – 2*\$94.78 = \$1,652.09 and \$1,841.65 + 2*\$94.78 = \$2,031.21). Thus, we can say that we are about 95% certain that the average monthly expenditure on food for all families in our population is between \$1,652.09 and \$2.031.21. (See also CONFIDENCE INTERVAL, ESTIMATE, SAMPLING DISTRIBUTION, and SAMPLING ERROR.)

STANDARD ERROR OF THE ESTIMATE. The standard deviation of the error in a regression model. (See also REGRESSION.)

STANDARD ERROR OF THE MEAN. The standard deviation of the distribution of sample means. (See also STANDARD ERROR and INFERENTIAL STATISTICS.)

STANDARD ERROR OF THE PROPORTION. The standard deviation of the distribution of sample proportions.

STANDARDIZATION. In the statistical sense, where the mean of a set of observations is subtracted from a given observation and the result divided by the standard deviation of the set of observations.

STANDARDIZED NORMAL DISTRIBUTION. Z distribution; a distribution of Z scores produced for values from a normal distribution with a mean of 0 and a standard deviation of 1.

STANDARDIZED RATE. A rate that has been subjected to standardization. (See also STANDARDIZATION.)

STATISTIC. A descriptive measure of a sample.

STATISTICAL SIGNIFICANCE. This indicates only that the null hypothesis is rejected; it does not mean that the difference is important in a substantive sense. Similarly, "statistically not significant" only indicates that the null hypothesis was not rejected. It does not indicate that there is no important difference in a substantive sense. (See also ALPHA, HYPOTHESIS TEST, P-VALUE, STANDARD ERROR, and SUBSTANTIVE SIGNIFICANCE.)

STATISTICS. A science dealing with the collection, analysis, interpretation, and presentation of numerical data. There are two major aspects of statistics—descriptive and inferential. (See DESCRIPTIVE STATISTICS and INFERENTIAL STATISTICS.)

STRATIFIED RANDOM SAMPLING. A type of random sampling in which the population is divided into various non-overlapping strata and then items are randomly selected into the sample from each stratum. (See also POST-STRATIFICATION, RANDOM SAMPLING, and WEIGHTED AVERAGE.)

SUBJECTIVE PROBABILITY. A probability assigned based on the intuition or reasoning of the person determining the probability. (See also FREQUENTIST.)

SUBSTANTIVE SIGNIFICANCE. This indicates that there is something of importance. For example, if you took a sample of 10,000 single-person households in San Jose, California, and found that the average monthly expenditure on wine was $139.75 while a sample of 10,000 single-person households in San Francisco showed that it was $140, the difference is not of substantive significance. Moreover, given that the standard deviations were small, with sample sizes this large, it is likely that a T-Test would return a p-value that would lead you to reject the null hypothesis that the means were equal in the two populations from which the two samples were drawn. However, the finding of "statistical significance" would lead to a big-time "so what?" for a marketing company or public health organization interested in wine consumption in the two cities, given the nearness of the two means. In contrast, differences on the order of $100 or more would likely get the attention of both the marketing company and the public health organization. That is, if the average monthly expenditure on wine in San Jose was

$139.75 while in San Francisco it was $240, the difference would likely be something of "substantive significance." (See also STATISTICAL SIGNIFICANCE.)

SUM OF SQUARES ERROR. The sum of the residuals squared for a regression model. (See also ERROR.)

SUM OF SQUARES. The sum of the squared deviations about the mean of a set of values. Conceptually, this is similar to the sum of squares error in a regression model.

SURVEY. (See SAMPLE.)

T-DISTRIBUTION (also known as Student's T Distribution). A distribution that describes the sample data in small samples when the standard deviation is unknown and the population is normally distributed.

T-STATISTIC. The computed value of T used to reach statistical conclusions regarding the null hypothesis in small-sample analysis. (See also T-TEST.)

T-TEST. A statistical test in which the test statistic follows the "T-Distribution." (See also HYPOTHESIS TEST, T-DISTRIBUTION, and Z-TEST.)

TOTAL ERROR. In a sample, the theoretical sum of random error and nonrandom error, which in practice can at best only be roughly approximated because of the difficulty of estimating nonrandom error. This also is known as Total Sample Error. In a census, total error is comprised solely of nonrandom errors. (See also IMPUTATION, CODING/TRANSCRIPTION ERROR, COVERAGE ERROR, MEASUREMENT ERROR, NONRANDOM ERROR, RANDOM ERROR, and SAMPLING ERROR.)

TRUE POPULATION. In theory, the population that would be counted if there were no errors in a census. In practice, it is a value representing the theoretical actual number for the population at a given date, which cannot be precisely measured, but which can be roughly approximated by adjusting a census for net census undercount error. (See also CENSUS and NET CENSUS UNDERCOUNT ERROR.)

TWO-TAILED TEST. A statistical test wherein the researcher is interested in testing both sides of the distribution. (See also HYPOTHESIS TEST and ONE-TAILED TEST.)

TYPE I ERROR. An error committed by rejecting a true null hypothesis. (See also HYPOTHESIS TEST and TYPE II ERROR.)

TYPE II ERROR. An error committed by failing to reject a false null hypothesis. (See also HYPOTHESIS TEST and TYPE I ERROR.)

UNIFORM DISTRIBUTION. A relatively simple continuous distribution in which the same height is obtained over a range of values; also called the rectangular distribution.

UNIT OF ANALYSIS. This refers to what is being studied. In a social survey, the unit of analysis may be an individual, a family, a household, or a county population, among many other possibilities. (See also CASE.)

VALUE. This is what is assigned to represent an attribute, where the attribute is what is observed for a case in regard to a given variable in a data set. For example, a given family in a sample of families (the data set) may spend $1,250 per month where the variable is monthly family food expenditure, and the value for this family (case) is $1.250. (See also CASE, LEVEL OF MEASUREMENT, UNIT OF ANALYSIS, and VARIABLE.)

VARIABLE. This is something of interest that in principle can have different values. For example, monthly family expenditures on food is a variable because the amount spent can vary by family. (See also CASE, LEVEL OF MEASUREMENT, VALUE, and UNIT OF ANALYSIS.)

VARIANCE. The average of the squared deviations about the arithmetic mean for a set of numbers.

VENN DIAGRAM. Venn diagrams represent a visual means of showing all possible logical relations between a finite collection of sets. They were developed by John Venn (1888).

WEIGHTED AVERAGE. Usually an arithmetic mean of an array of specific rates or ratios, with variable weights applied to them representing the relative distribution of the populations on which the rates or ratios are based. More generally, a summary measure of a set of numbers (absolute numbers or ratios), computed as the cumulative product of the numbers and a set of weights representing their relative importance in the population. An unweighted average is one in which each number in the set has the same weight (e.g., 1 or 1/n, where n is the total set of numbers). (See also MEAN and POST-STRATIFICATION.)

Z-DISTRIBUTION. A distribution of Z scores; a normal distribution with a mean of 0 and a standard deviation of 1. (See also Z SCORE and Z-TEST.)

Z SCORE. The number of standard deviations a value (X) is above or below the mean of a set of numbers when the data are normally distributed.

Z-TEST. A hypothesis test for which the distribution of the test statistic can be approximated by the normal distribution. (See also HYPOTHESIS TEST, NORMAL DISTRIBUTION, T-TEST.)

REFERENCES

Stevens, S. S. (1946). "On the Theory of Scales of Measurement." *Science* 103 (2684): 677–80.

Venn, J. (1888). *The Logic of Chance: An Essay on the Foundations and Province of the Theory of Probability with Especial Reference to Its Logical Bearings and Its Application to Moral and Social Science, and to Statistics, 3rd ed. Rewritten and Enlarged.* London, England: MacMillan.